THE VICTORIAN SOCIETY BOOK OF

# — THE —
# VICTORIAN
# HOUSE

The·Red·House·Nº 3 Bayswater·Hill.⁕ John·J·Stevenson·Architect.

THE VICTORIAN SOCIETY BOOK OF

# — THE —
# VICTORIAN HOUSE

## Kit Wedd

*For Steven*

First published in 2002 by Aurum Press Limited,
7 Greenland Street, London NW1 0ND, www.aurumpress.co.uk
This paperback edition first published 2007

A catalogue record of this book is available from the British Library.

ISBN 10: 184513 294 7
ISBN 13: 9781 84513 294 1

1 3 5 7 9 10 8 6 4 2
2007 2009 2011 2010 2008

Designed by Robert Updegraff
Printed in Singapore by CS Graphics

HALFTITLE: *The Red House in Bayswater Hill, London (1871–3), designed for himself
by the architect J.J. Stevenson. This manner of dressing a standard terraced house in
red brick and Queen Anne details influenced many suburban developments by
speculative builders.*

FRONTISPIECE: *A terrace of the late 1880s in Hackney, East London. Details such as
stucco mouldings, contrasting brickwork, stained glass windows and decorative
wrought iron finials were used to lend character to this and countless similar
speculatively-built terraces in Victorian suburbs.*

# CONTENTS

# Preface

The Victorian period encompasses six decades, during which population growth, changing work patterns, improved communications and growing prosperity provided the impetus for the development of the inner suburbs of most British towns and cities. It was a period of great technological innovation, during which new building and decorating materials and methods were enthusiastically exploited. Architects and designers plundered the styles of the past and delved into their own imaginations to come up with original and innovative designs. The new technologies of steam, gas, mains water and sewerage, and eventually electricity, provided previously unimaginable levels of comfort and convenience.

It is not possible to do justice to the full range of Victorian housing in one volume, so this book concentrates on middle-class housing. The term 'middle class' embraces a wide social stratum: the educated artisan, the humble clerk, doctors, solicitors, military men, tenant farmers and industrialists could all lay claim to it, and it applies equally to a vast range of houses, from schoolteacher's cottage to modest mansion. The book also deals with the kind of housing, such as railway workers' cottages and gate-keepers' lodges, that were originally intended as working-class housing but which, by a process of greater social mobility and rising property values, have undergone gentrification and been colonized by middle-class residents.

Although some explanations of technical matters have been included in order to illuminate the narrative, this book is not a DIY manual (there are already several detailed house repair manuals on the market: see Further Reading, p.259). It should, however, give you the knowledge and vocabulary you need to decide what needs doing and whether you can tackle it yourself, and enable you talk to architects, surveyors and contractors in their own language and with confidence. Conservation principles, good housekeeping and regular maintenance are stressed, in the hope that understanding your house and looking after it so that problems do not develop in the first place will be the key to handing it on in good shape to subsequent owners.

I have received a great deal of help during the preparation of this book, and I owe thanks in particular to Patrick Baty, the late Chris Brooks, Ian Dungavell, John Fidler, William Filmer-Sankey, Tony and Kathy Herbert, Chris Miele, Ian Parry, Beata Reynolds, Brian Ridout, Jacqueline and Jerry Rokotnitz, Treve Rosoman and Richard Seedhouse and to my family, particularly Steve Parissien and Julia Parissien. The Architectural Heritage Fund helped to finance the original *Care for Victorian Houses* booklets, on which much of this book is based, and The Jonathan Vickers Trust has given generous support to the Victorian Society education and publications programme, of which this book forms a part.

Kit Wedd

OPPOSITE: *A middle-class villa in Nottingham designed in an eclectic style by T.C. Hine, 'the father of the Midlands architects' in the 1850s.*

# PART I
## *The House*

# AN AGE OF BUILDING

B Y 1901, THE YEAR OF QUEEN VICTORIA'S DEATH, it was widely felt that British domestic architecture had reached a level of efficiency and attractiveness that could hardly be improved upon. The German cultural attaché in London, Hermann Muthesius, was so impressed by the 'sound and unostentatious but finely developed taste' he detected in English domestic architecture since 1860 that he was moved to compile a survey of recently built houses, published as *Das englische Haus* in 1904, in the avowed hope that it would help German architects to improve the design of housing in his own country.

The evolution of the English house to this pitch of perfection was a process begun long before Victoria came to the throne: many of the characteristics that distinguish early Victorian houses and building practices were introduced in the Georgian period and refined during the Regency. Nor did her death mark the end of a style of housing that had proved immensely serviceable. Few early twentieth-century country middle-class suburban houses were truly innovative; most continued to be built according to nineteenth-century patterns, updated only in their superficial decorative detail, until World War I.

Anybody attempting to describe houses of the period 1837–1901 should therefore be wary of applying these dates as arbitrary cut-off points. Equally to be avoided is to generalize broadly about Victorian taste and attitudes to domestic architecture, as if these were consistently maintained across more than six decades. It is more helpful, perhaps, to see Victorian houses as the result of a continuous process of adaptation of pre-existing building types to suit precisely the temper of the times and the needs of their occupants.

## Population growth, industrialization and urbanization

The main reason for the astonishing increase in the number of houses built in Britain during Victoria's reign was the incease in population, which doubled between 1841 and 1901. Self-evidently, all these people needed houses to live in; furthermore, individual households also became smaller and more numerous. The old extended family sharing the communal life of the rural village in an almost feudal dependence on their landlord was fragmented into smaller, single-family units with new standards of privacy and independence.

Large-scale urban and suburban development first took place in the eighteenth century with the rise of steam power and mass production methods, but it happened on a

ABOVE: *A house by E.J. May in Bedford Park, West London, exhibits the combination of red brick, white-painted joinery and terracotta decoration that is the hallmark of the Queen Anne revival style.*

OPPOSITE: *The imposing stucco frontage of Warwick Square, Pimlico, built by Thomas Cubitt in 1843. High-quality terraced housing continued to be built in this dignified, classical style until the 1870s.*

11

much larger scale and at a much greater speed in the Victorian period, as modern manufacturing methods were applied to building materials such as brick, glass and cement, and steam power facilitated the conversion of natural resources such as slate, timber and stone. These better, cheaper building materials were also more easily carried to where they were needed. The spread of the railways in the 1840s and 1850s made it possible to carry items all over the country more quickly and at less cost than by canal and sea routes. By 1867 there were 13,500 miles of railway in the United Kingdom. St Pancras Station in London and the Midland Grand Hotel that stands in front of it, designed by George Gilbert Scott and built in 1868–74, are practical advertisements for the ease with which heavy materials could now be carried long distances: they incorporate Ancaster, Mansfield and Ketton stone, grey and red granite, cast iron from Coventry and bricks from Nottinghamshire, all carried on the Midland Railway straight to its own terminus.

## Public health

As towns grew larger and more crowded, public health became a more important issue. The Health of Towns Act 1848 was the first to specify the provision of 'proper water closets' in new housing (although this was often interpreted as access to a shared closet, not necessarily one per house), and was followed by further legislation in 1858 and 1875, the latter making local authorities responsible for providing mains sewers and collecting refuse. In addition, thousands of local byelaws regulated the building of new developments. These were often concerned with the public face of the development, specifying in minute detail the width and lighting of streets and emphasizing the importance of the building line. Byelaws also made developers responsible for providing adequate water supplies and drainage to individual houses.

The problems of water supply and sewage disposal were inextricably linked, as raw sewage was often dumped in the same rivers that provided drinking water: in just one year (1848–9) cholera claimed the lives of 53,293 people in England and Wales. The engineer James Simpson had devised a method of purifying water by filtering it through sand in 1829, but it was not until the 1850s that the private companies supplying water to London were obliged to filter their supplies. In 1854 Dr John Snow's demonstration of the link between cholera and polluted water lent weight to official efforts to improve public sanitation. As the demand for water increased, the question of whether water supplies should be controlled by private companies or taken into public ownership became an important political issue. Manchester's water supply was under local authority control as early as 1847 and others were incorporated into their respective municipal authorities in due course, although London had to wait until 1904.

Early water pipes were made of lead or wood, which were prone to decay and damage and could not cope with the quantity and pressure of water necessary to supply densely populated areas. Cast-iron pipes were used in London by 1827, and were widespread by the 1840s. In 1846 Henry Doulton found a more durable solution and began making impervious, glazed earthenware pipes at his pottery in Lambeth. Throughout the nineteenth century, while the network of mains water supplies gradually spread to cover the entire kingdom, the old systems continued to operate alongside the new. In 1865 Mrs Beeton described how to collect rainwater for household use by letting the rain wash the roof for ten minutes before closing the tap on the water butt and allowing the rest to accumulate. A larger supply could be obtained by fitting the butt with an overflow pipe that discharged into a storage tank. Such methods remained the norm in rural areas where mains water provision was patchy; when that failed, water was obtained from the communal well.

## Sewage

The other half of the sanitation equation, sewage disposal, was solved in an equally piecemeal fashion. Small communities used sewage as agricultural fertilizer, while ports and coastal towns had it carried out to sea. In densely populated inland towns and cities, however, the task of sewage disposal became overwhelming. Any river, canal, ditch or gutter became a dumping-ground for human waste, and in many inner-city alleys and courtyards the filth was simply allowed to pile up, creating an intolerable stink.

In the summer of 1858 the sewage-laden Thames smelt so bad that it was impossible for Parliament to sit at Westminster. The 'Great Stink' helped persuade Parliament to provide £3 million to the Metropolitan Board of Works to undertake Sir Joseph Bazalgette's plan to provide a comprehensive network of underground sewers for the whole of London. Within ten years 1,400 miles of brick sewers had been completed, and other major cities were vying with each other to build similarly impressive systems. No other civic improvement did more to drag the Victorian city into the modern age.

## Suburban commuters

The picture of overall urbanization is complicated by the middle-class movement out of the cities, which happened as fast as the growing suburbs could accommodate it. Rich and poor no longer lived side by side; beyond a few fashionable streets in the best part of town, the residential districts of the inner cities became the preserve of the very poor, the only tenants who would accept the decayed condition of formerly elegant Georgian houses. The evils of overcrowding, pollution and a perceived increase in crime and

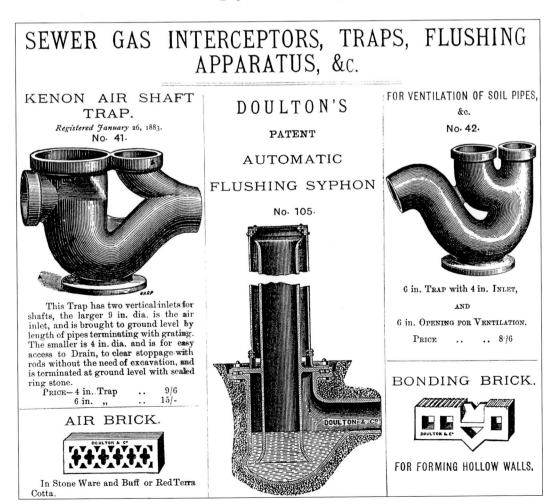

*Glazed earthenware fittings for sewage systems, from a catalogue of the 1880s, issued by Doulton & Co. of Lambeth.*

immorality in the inner cities made the suburb an attractive alternative for a wide swathe of the population, from professional men to the new, lower middle class of clerks and respectable artisans. A certain level of education and the ability to maintain outward respectability were the defining characteristics of this broad middle class. The question of house ownership was irrelevant: most people – even the aristocratic occupants of London mansions – rented, and there was no stigma attached to being a tenant.

The social differentiation between urban and suburban environments was also a symptom of the increasing separation between home and workplace. Since the early nineteenth century commuters had been able to travel between the early suburbs of Islington or Hampstead and central London on regular stagecoach services. Commuting became even easier after George Shillibeer started his regular omnibus service, from Paddington to the Bank of England, in 1829, and the London Omnibus Company was established in 1856. The second great phase of railway development, in the 1850s, carried suburban lines out of all the major London termini. Though there was less incentive to build suburban railways in many provincial cities because of the shorter journey to work, every large conurbation eventually acquired 'railway suburbs'. The Tramways Act, which regulated the installation of horse-drawn tram systems, was passed in 1870. By 1890 the technical difficulties of electrification had been solved and by 1900 several towns, including Leeds, Wolverhampton, Lincoln and London, had electric trams powered by overhead trolleys.

## Speculative builders

The suburbs were built by speculative builders, following the eighteenth-century model of development. As a rule, the pressure of urban expansion would eventually cause land at the edge of a growing town to become more valuable as a building plot than as agricultural or park land. When this happened, the landlord would divide up the site into leasehold parcels and offer them for sale to speculative builders. Mostly small tradesmen, ambitious joiners or bricklayers, they would borrow the capital to buy a building lease and pay for the necessary materials and labour. They had to complete and lease or let the houses quickly in order to repay the loan and have a small profit to put towards their next project. Thus

*A team of builders stands outside a nearly completed set of houses in Clapton Passage, Hackney, east London (1882).*

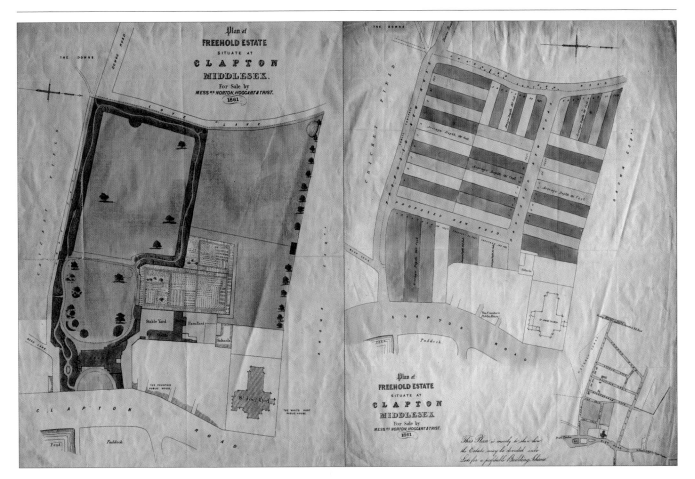

many suburbs were built a handful of houses at a time, and it is often possible to detect subtle breaks in streets or terraces that indicate where one phase of building ended and another began as new funds were raised. In the 1860s it cost about £4,000 to build a town mansion at the very top end of the speculative market. In 1900 a cottage could still be built for as little as £100, while a two-storey house in London cost about £150 to complete.

Building in this way was risky. The profit margin was narrow, the market unpredictable and bankruptcy common. This uncertainty deepened the natural conservatism of landowners and builders, causing most to stick to familiar and well-tried formats such as the classic London townhouse, and adopt new architectural fashions only when they had proved their staying power. It was reassuring to be able to follow printed instructions, and architects and builders increasingly relied on the use of pattern books and practical treatises on building. These had been expensive and correspondingly few in number in the eighteenth century, but demand from a newly literate building trade led to an increase in the number of titles available at moderate prices in the early nineteenth century.

The rudiments having been acquired, builders had to address the question of architectural style. The most influential design guide was John Claudius Loudon's *Encyclopaedia of Cottage, Farm and Villa Architecture and Furniture*, a comprehensive, up-to-date summary of small house architecture first published in 1833. It remained an essential work of reference for decades. Many of the designs it contained were adaptations of the kind of picturesque villa that John Nash, the Prince Regent's favourite architect, had developed for Regent's Park in North London in the 1820s. Thanks to Loudon, these designs were still being used, with minimal adaptation, in the 1850s.

Although most speculators were local builders constructing a handful of houses at a time on a knife-edge of profitability, there were some spectacular success stories.

*These maps show the sale particulars of an estate in Clapton, London, from 1861. The plan on the left shows the mansion (on Lower Clapton Road) and its grounds before development, while the plan on the right indicates how the land could be divided up into building plots.*

Thomas Cubitt, the son of a Norfolk carpenter, founded a building firm that eventually employed over a thousand men, and was responsible for building most of Belgravia and Pimlico. He also built Osborne, the royal family's country house on the Isle of Wight, collaborating with Prince Albert on the design.

William Willett had a more modestly successful career. Starting out as a supplier of marble chimneypieces, he expanded into building homes to a conspicuously high standard of design and finish for the upper middle class. Throughout the 1870s Willett constructed houses in London and Hove, usually to his own designs, but from 1884 he started to employ in-house architects, first Harry B. Measures, and then A.F. Faulkner, who designed in the fashionable Queen Anne style.

Some developers let it be known that they were employing well-known or up-and-coming architects, in the hope that this would lend extra cachet to their developments. Bedford Park in West London was created in the 1870s as a garden suburb specifically intended for the artistic middle classes. The entrepreneur behind the scheme, Jonathan Carr, commissioned a number of distinctive house designs from E.W. Godwin, Richard Norman Shaw and E.J. May, calculating that these 'names' would strike a chord with design-conscious potential purchasers.

Most suburban houses were built without the benefit of professional architectural advice, and were consequently despised by architects, who were becoming increasingly concerned about the status of their profession, and resented speculative builders muscling in on their territory, stealing ideas from architect-designed housing in order to reproduce them in watered-down versions for the mass market. Alfred Lang, the author of *Hints on Houses* (1853), distinguished between two kinds of suburban villa: the first was designed by an architect, the second 'built by the speculative builder, who will build as he pleases; he conforms to no rule, and does not study the comfort of the occupants, and cares for little else than "to cover the ground and sell"'.

A specialist architectural press grew up, promoting the interests of the profession and encouraging progressive and artistic design of all types of housing. New designs were published in great detail and thus became available to every level of the building trade, speeding up the process by which fashions filtered down from the custom-built commissioned house to the speculatively-built suburban terrace. *The Builder* was founded in 1842 and after a shaky start thrived under the editorship of George Godwin. For over forty years Godwin brought 'for the first time within the reach of art workmen and students, an illustrated weekly record of professional news... [*The Builder*] published views of churches and manor houses, with details drawn to a larger scale. These woodcuts, rudely as they at first were executed, became very serviceable for reference and information.' These illustrations, along with those published by Maurice B. Adams in the *Building News*, were an inexhaustible fund of design ideas for the architect, developer and builder alike.

## Twentieth-century attitudes to the Victorian house

Suburbs have always suffered from critical abuse, but the sheer scale of Victorian suburbanization ensured that it attracted the most venom. Both suburbs and Victorian architecture as a whole were excoriated for most of the twentieth century. In particular, their eclectic, colourful and exuberant aspects were unfavourably compared with the classical restraint of Georgian, or the 'rational' designs of Modernist architects' buildings.

A small group of pioneering enthusiasts, including Nikolaus Pevsner and John Betjeman, founded the Victorian Society in 1958 in an effort to save important nineteenth-century buildings and monuments under threat of demolition. In its early days

'Before' and 'after' photographs of the hall in a typical Victorian house as remodelled by the architect Wells Coates in 1932. From Duncan Miller's Interior Decorating (first published in 1937 and reissued after World War II) which suggested that 'heavy cornices should be removed altogether, dado rails taken down and doors made flush ... ugly balusters can be covered with plywood'.

the Society concentrated its limited resources on significant public buildings in London. It failed to prevent the demolition of the Euston Arch (Philip Hardwick, 1834–8) and the Corn Exchange (J.B. Bunning, 1846–9), but won an important battle to save the Foreign and Commonwealth Office (George Gilbert Scott, 1861–75). A gradual softening of public and official attitudes towards Victorian architecture, partly the result of the Society's ceaseless campaigning, led to an increase in casework, and to official recognition of the role of the Society in assessing planning applications concerning nineteenth- and early twentieth-century buildings. By the 1980s the Society was dealing with an increasing number of enquiries about conservation areas, minor buildings and even requests for information on how to restore and decorate 'ordinary' family houses.

Their very ordinariness is the greatest enemy of Victorian houses. They are everywhere in such quantity that familiarity has bred contempt, and they are brutally treated. The modern mania for light and space has led to 'knocking-through' of ground floors, loss of individual rooms and the addition of oversized extensions and loft conversions. A misguided belief in the miracle of 'maintenance-free' materials has led to the wholesale replacement of perfectly serviceable original windows and doors, and the consequent destruction of irreplaceable, high-quality building materials. Well-meant but inappropriate 'improvements' – double glazing, painted brickwork, aggressive repointing – have eroded the uniformity of most nineteenth-century terraces. Untouched ensembles are becoming increasingly rare. In location after location, hardly any Victorian house (and certainly no terrace, apart from those lucky enough to be protected by listed building or conservation area status) has been left unspoilt. Yet by any standard these houses are now antiques, certainly old enough to be accorded the same kind of respect as that awarded without hesitation to Georgian houses. In the chapters that follow, the reasons why the Victorian house developed as it did will be explained, in the hope that better understanding will engender that respect.

# THE VICTORIAN HOUSE

A VICTORIAN HOUSE can be a 'back-to-back' in a Yorkshire mill town, a model farm in Hampshire, a Kensington townhouse or a millionaire's mansion in the Scottish Highlands – or one of dozens of other kinds. Different types of housing were established for all classes and sectors of society, and subtle variations in size, plan, materials and finish indicated what sort of occupant each house was intended for. Architects and builders tailored their output to specific markets: the terraced cottage for the artisan, the suburban villa for the professional man and his family, the quirkily original house for the successful artist, or the lavish country house for the industrial magnate.

Grand country houses are outside the scope of this book, except in so far as they affected the design of smaller houses. They helped to make new architectural fashions acceptable, and their rigid separation of members of the household – whether male and female, child and adult or employer and servant – provided a model of how to allocate domestic space that was followed in smaller houses as closely, and as far down the social scale, as possible. As the centrepiece of an estate, a country house also had a direct impact on local housing. Wealthy landowners were keen to house their tenant farmers and agricultural workers in high-quality buildings that not only reflected well on the estate, but also helped to maintain the value and appearance of the land.

In 1838 the Duke of Devonshire began to develop the hamlet of Edensor on the Chatsworth estate in Derbyshire. His architect, John Robertson, created a model village of stone houses, much like those illustrated in Loudon's *Encyclopaedia*. That useful volume opened with 250 pages of designs and suggestions for 'Cottage Dwellings in Various Styles', obviously intended for this market (the cottage as defined by Loudon was a 'small, genteel residence', definitely not a labourer's hovel). It was the most influential of an architectural sub-literature which included Francis Goodwin's *Rural Architecture: Designs for Rustic, Peasants' and Ornamental Cottages, Lodges and Villas, in Various Styles of Architecture* (2nd edn, 1835) and P.F. Robinson's *Rural Architecture, or, A Series of Designs for Ornamental Cottages* (1836). Robinson's designs came with plans, scale drawings of all the elevations, a sheet of details and a budget. The clincher was a fine perspective view of each building in a landscape peopled with attractively-costumed rustics. Armed with these seductive images, the jobbing architect could sell his services to

ABOVE: *P.F. Robinson's* Designs for Gate Lodges and Park Entrances *showed how early Victorian architects borrowed and reworked medieval precedents. This detail is from a design 'acknowledged to be in the style of Wolterton Hall, Norfolk, as illustrated in Pugin's "Examples"'.*

OPPOSITE: *The front entrance of 'Sunnycroft', a late nineteenth-century middle-class villa at the centre of a mini-estate that included pigsties, a kitchen garden and orchards.*

the landowner in need of a dairy, lodge or almshouse in any style. The success of *Rural Architecture* led to two further volumes, both published in 1837.

This picturesque approach to rural housing was succeeded by a more serious study of the specific requirements of agriculture in the 1840s. These were boom years in farming, and in the period 1850–70 the scientific approach to farm architecture was seen in numerous model farms; Prince Albert proved himself a worthy president of the Royal Agricultural Society when he built Shaw Farm at Windsor, to designs by the specialist farm architect George Dean, in 1853. The new breed of tenant farmers expected to be well housed: in his history of model farms, Roy Bigden has pointed out that the tenants attracted to improved farms were well educated, professional men who saw themselves as the equals of urban commercial managers, 'so the ideal house for the forward-looking Victorian tenant-farmer was in most respects distinguishable from the large suburban villa only by the extra offices – such as dairy, brew-house or apple store – that agriculture demanded'.

Many well-built cottages for labourers and their families bear witness to the enlightened paternalism of some aristocratic landlords concerned for the welfare of 'their' peasantry. Even those who regarded their farm workers as 'living engines' saw the sense in housing them at least as well as the livestock. Ardington and Lockinge on Lord Wantage's estate in Oxfordshire, and Walton in Warwickshire, built in the 1890s to house the workers on the Walton Hall estate, constitute entire villages, with their own schools, teachers' houses and churches. The most charming, eccentric and individual estate houses were the gatekeepers' lodges, built where the private estate met the public highway and often designed to give a foretaste of the architectural splendour

*The model village of Westonbirt, Gloucestershire, built in the mid-nineteenth century to designs by C.F. Beverston.*

to be met with at the other end of the drive. But despite the provision of estate housing, rural accommodation remained in short supply throughout the nineteenth century, and casual labourers who were not entitled to tied cottages often lived in appalling conditions.

*The monotony of late nineteenth-century housing for industrial workers: Easington, Co. Durham.*

## Industrial estate housing

Living conditions for most of the urban poor, especially those living in the old town centres, were not much better, unless a particularly enlightened employer intervened to provide the industrial equivalent of rural estate housing. The Yorkshire wool baron Titus Salt built a complete factory town on the banks of the River Aire between Shipley and Bingley in West Yorkshire, from 1853 to 1870. Although modest in scale and austere in design, the terraced houses of Saltaire were a significant improvement on the jerry-built back-to-backs that had begun to sprawl around mills outside Leeds, Bradford, Nottingham, Sheffield, Liverpool, Manchester and Birmingham, and which (despite efforts to legislate them out of existence) were still being built in the 1890s in some areas. Towards the end of the century, settlements such as Port Sunlight on Merseyside (begun in 1888) showed how the garden suburb could be adapted for cottage-style workers' housing, under the control of a single employer-landlord.

House plans, especially those of working-class houses, were the object of relentless scrutiny and improvement throughout the nineteenth century. Even the Prince Consort turned his hand to the design of model housing. As President of the Society for Improving the Conditions of the Labouring Classes, he sponsored the erection of a set of model 'cottages' designed by the Society's architect, Henry Roberts, at the Great Exhibition of 1851. The four cottages were arranged in paired sets around a central open staircase – a device widely used in working-class flats over the next fifty years. They were eventually dismantled and re-erected in Kennington Park, South London, where they still stand.

Numerous organizations and charities, such as the Peabody and Guinness Trusts, became involved in housing the urban working classes. They raised dozens of solidly-made blocks of flats, sparing hardly a penny for non-essential features. The result, according to one writer, was 'severely plain, not to say dreary-looking structures which remind one rather of Pentonville than the cosy home of the well-to-do artisan'. The most sustained and architecturally successful campaign was waged by the Greater London Council, starting with their Boundary Estate flats in Bethnal Green, of 1893–9.

# Speculative building

## Middle-class housing: Villas

Houses commissioned by individual clients or organizations for a particular site and with a narrowly-defined kind of occupant, if not an individual tenant, in mind are greatly outnumbered by speculatively-built houses. These, the houses that compose the inner suburbs of every town and city in the United Kingdom, are what most people think of when asked to picture a typical Victorian house: modest detached, semi-detached or terraced houses, built for middle-class occupants in their hundreds of thousands between 1840 and 1900.

The house to which every prosperous professional aspired was a villa on the edge of town. The idea of the villa had originally been imported into England from Italy in the eighteenth century by classical architects who admired the country houses of the great sixteenth-century architect Palladio. The name was adopted for houses in picturesque developments in the 1820s. By 1860 the definition of a villa had stretched to include houses in Gothic and eclectic styles, which no longer had to be the centrepieces of supporting agricultural estates; any large detached house with a good-sized garden qualified. In 1855, according to E.L. Tarbuck, author of *The Builder's Practical Director*, such a 'convenient family residence' could be built for £1,500.

*OPPOSITE: Early philanthropic housing ventures in the inner cities were utilitarian and built to last. These Peabody Trust flats in Islington, built in 1865 to designs by the Trust's architect, Henry Darbishire, are now Listed Buildings. The original tenants of the two- and three-room flats had to share kitchens and toilets with their neighbours.*

*A pair of model houses for working-class families designed by Henry Roberts, incorporating suggestions by Prince Albert, and built for the Great Exhibition of 1851; they were later re-erected, with some alterations, in Kennington Park, South London, where they still stand.*

### Semi-detached houses

The enormous status gap between the detached house in its own grounds and the terrace of identical houses facing the street was bridged by paired houses, in designs that confessed their semi-detachedness in varying degrees. Two houses under a single pediment might pass at first glance as a single dwelling, and if the front doors were placed on the side elevations, the illusion was strengthened. Where there was not enough space to provide side approaches, the front doors were placed in a central bay set back from the main façade, so that an oblique view showed a rhythm of projecting and receding blocks that mimicked separate houses. On smaller budgets it became harder to maintain these distinctions: separate paths between the houses were amalgamated into a shared path, and finally the gap between the pairs was reduced to the merest slit, allowing the free passage of air only – but still permitting that all-important 'semi-detached' designation.

### Terraced houses

The most economical use of land was to build terraced housing. And build it the Victorians did, in breathtaking variety and quantity. The speculative builders of the eighteenth century had developed a classic townhouse plan – two rooms deep, and one room plus a corridor and stairwell wide – which was used, albeit with increasing freedom, throughout the Victorian period. 'Compactness, as regards site at least, is a primary question,' acknowledged one authority, 'and hence the Basement-Offices, the First-floor Drawing-rooms, and the long ascents of stair to story after story of Bed-rooms, two or three on a floor.' More rooms were gained by going up into extra storeys or by adding a narrow back extension for sculleries, bathrooms and WCs entered off the staircase at half-landings. The Phillimore Estate in Kensington, developed between 1868 and 1874 by the builder Joseph Gordon Davies, consists entirely of houses of this type, with their associated mews. Although the proportions of these houses have changed, their basic plan is identical to that of the houses built by the Bedford Estate in Bloomsbury in the 1770s and 1780s.

The plan gradually evolved to reflect changing tastes and needs. In early Victorian houses, kitchens and associated service rooms were in the basement. A desire for better hygiene, and the need to provide better working conditions in order to retain servants, meant that the basements provided as a matter of course in the 1840s had all but disappeared from progressive housing forty years later. This was reflected in the tendency during the mid-nineteenth century for house plans to grow deeper and wider, with kitchens accommodated in rear extensions. Overall there was a tendency for houses at all levels to become bigger: four rooms was the minimum in the poorest house in 1900, whereas the equivalent house in 1800 would have had only one room.

In terraced housing the façade was exceptionally important as an indicator of social status. If the best semis strove to look like detached houses, the best terraces tried to pass as semis. Recessed or projecting entrance bays sometimes did the trick, and a curved street was a gift to the developer, as it enabled the building line to be staggered every one or two houses. Since all terraced houses shared the same basic plan, subtle differences of decoration became all the more significant. The difference between a pillared porch and a pilastered doorcase, or between plain quarries and hand-painted roundels in a glazed door panel, trivial in themselves, signified changes in rental value that proclaimed the tenants' incomes and aspirations. One of the most popular ways of ornamenting the façade was to add a bay window to one or more storeys. In the 1840s bow and bay windows were associated with seaside towns such as Brighton, Worthing and Scarborough, where they were used to maximize sea views. By the mid-1860s, however, the canted bay window was ubiquitous.

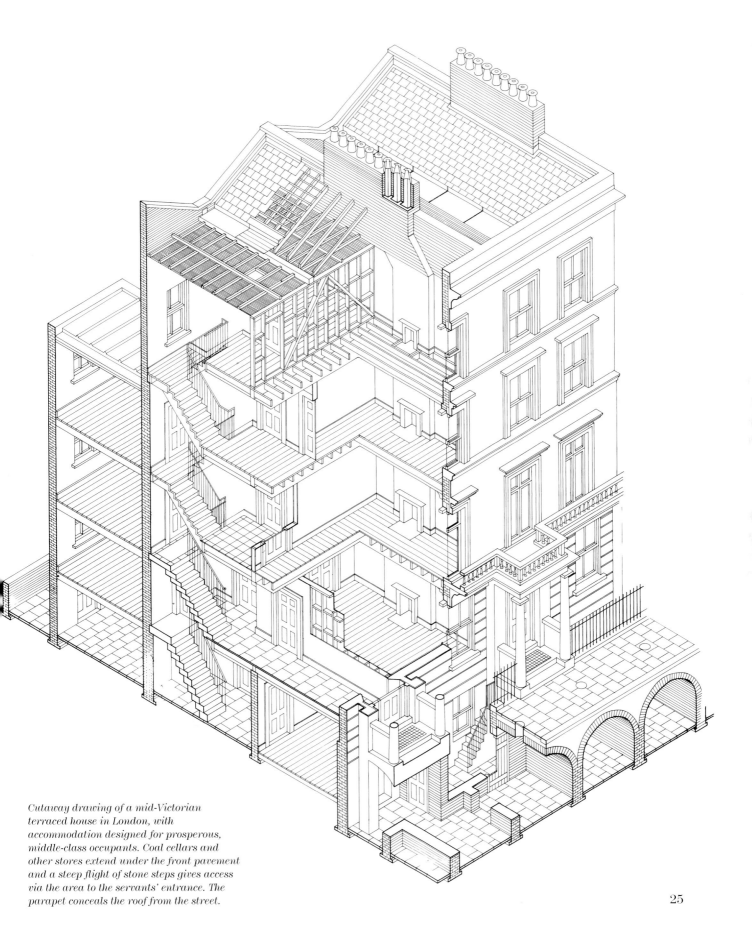

*Cutaway drawing of a mid-Victorian terraced house in London, with accommodation designed for prosperous, middle-class occupants. Coal cellars and other stores extend under the front pavement and a steep flight of stone steps gives access via the area to the servants' entrance. The parapet conceals the roof from the street.*

25

# Architectural style

In the 1830s and 1840s the classical style established in the eighteenth century and so elegantly developed in Newcastle, Cheltenham and elsewhere continued to prevail. It was based on a smooth, well-proportioned façade of ashlar or stucco, with symmetrically arranged sash windows and a doorcase with classical detailing. A cornice at eaves level was surmounted by a parapet concealing a low-pitched slate roof. This well-established, conservative style was associated with the inner suburbs – or rather, with suburbs that became 'inner' as more fashionable houses were built beyond them and further out from town centres. It was a dignified style of housing that never disappeared entirely, but after about 1850 its classical austerity became submerged under increasingly exuberant mouldings, balustrades, balconies, porches and other decorative features.

The picturesque, and Gothic tendencies that early Victorian builders inherited from Nash and his contemporaries also found expression in stucco fantasies, but were soon superseded by a more earnest and analytical approach to the question of style. The change was led by the young architect Augustus Welby Northmore Pugin. In 1836, at the age of 24, Pugin published *Contrasts*, a polemic urging architects to reject 'pagan' classical forms and rediscover the true ancient architecture of England, the evidence for which was all around in surviving medieval – mainly ecclesiastical – buildings. In the *True Principles of Gothic Architecture* (1841), Pugin stated the two great principles of the Gothic Revival: 'there should be no features about a building which are not necessary for convenience, construction or propriety', and 'all ornament should consist of enrichment of the essential construction of a building'. In practice, the strict geometry of classical plans would be abandoned in favour of an organic plan that reflected the most convenient disposition of the rooms. The façade would be allowed to express the internal arrangement of the house, regardless of classical proportions and balance. Stucco and

*Contrasting styles.*
RIGHT: *the classical regularity of a stucco façade under a parapet on a house built in the 1840s.*
OPPOSITE: *coloured brick and carved stone details in a Gothic house of about 1870 in North Oxford.*

smooth finishes would be replaced by exposed brick, stone and timber, and factory-produced decoration by hand-made items lovingly produced by dedicated craftsmen.

Interpreted by a skilled architect such as George Edmund Street, Pugin's ideas produced subtle and powerful effects, but many early Gothic Revival houses looked stark and clumsy in comparison with what had gone before. A kinder version of Pugin's uncompromising medievalism was wanted before the style could become truly popular. In any case, it was impossible for speculative builders to abandon old formulas so practical, economical and ingrained, thus there was no radical reappraisal of the plan and materials of the suburban house, where the main impact of the Gothic Revival was on the decoration

27

*Eclectic villa with rustic detailing and lean-to conservatory in The Park, Nottingham, a mid-nineteenth-century picturesque estate designed by T.C. Hine.*

of the façade. The writings of the art critic John Ruskin, especially *The Stones of Venice* (1851–3), were key texts for the High Victorian Gothic of the 1850s. In his *History of the Gothic Revival in England* (1872), Charles Locke Eastlake noted how, thanks to Ruskin, 'discs of marble, billet-mouldings, and other details of Italian Gothic, crept into many a London street-front. Then bands of coloured brick (chiefly red and yellow) were introduced, and the voussoirs of arches were treated after the same fashion. In the suburbs this mode of decoration rose rapidly into favour for cockney villas and public taverns, and laid the foundation of that peculiar order of Victorian Architecture which has since been distinguished by the familiar but not altogether inappropriate name of the Streaky Bacon Style.' By the mid-1870s Gothic capitals and stained glass were becoming conventional in the design of middle-market housing.

For Pugin, Ruskin and later William Morris, the dignity of the craftsman-builder and the touch of the human hand were essential to the true Gothic. Morris built his first home, Red House in Bexleyheath, to designs by Philip Webb in 1858. Morris and his friends, unable to find the fittings they wanted, made the stained glass, tiles and furniture themselves. Inevitably, industry found ways to mass-produce such items, and it was the resulting suburban Gothic of stained glass, encaustic tiles, terracotta mouldings and cast stone 'carvings' that led Ruskin to complain, 'I have had indirect influence on every cheap villa builder between [Denmark Hill, South London, where Ruskin lived] and Bromley ... And one of my principal notions for leaving my present house is that it is surrounded everywhere by the Frankenstein's Monsters of, indirectly, my own making.'

For most architects working in the mid-nineteenth century, the 'Battle of the Styles' (between classical and Gothic) and the harrumphings of disillusioned Goths were irrelevant. Styles were chosen according to the whim of the client or the nature of the commission. Francis Goodwin, for example, believed that the 'Old English' style was the most appropriate for farmhouses. In *The Gentleman's House* (1864), Robert Kerr identified the 'Rural-Italian' style of architecture as the most appropriate for a modern villa, but he and his contemporaries were equally happy to build in Elizabethan, Gothic, French Renaissance or 'Cottage' style. In the aptly named Park Estate in Nottingham, a development of several villas in secluded gardens, the local architect Thomas Hine demonstrated his proficiency in a range of styles. The first houses on the estate were 'the stucco or sham stonework type' typical of the 1840s, but these were succeeded over the next thirty years by Italianate, Gothic and frankly eclectic houses.

The Queen Anne revival promoted by architects like Richard Norman Shaw, J.J. Stevenson and William Eden Nesfield in the 1870s and 1880s was the result of a new interest in English domestic architecture of the late seventeenth and eighteenth centuries. Its materials – plain brick walls relieved by white paintwork – were modest, but the detail of the decoration in the best houses was exquisite, with fine cut-and-rubbed brickwork, deeply undercut timber mouldings, and complex patterns in the window joinery. The style lent itself to sweetly pretty decoration, which was perfect for the suburbs once eclecticism finally ran out of steam. Once again, in speculative housing it was the superficial elements of the façade that were updated, with carved brick 'aprons' under the windows, terracotta panels of sunflowers and the upper sashes of the windows subdivided into multiple panes.

The Gothic Revival's insistence on 'truthful' construction and appreciation of natural materials were shared by the Arts and Crafts architects of the next generation, who turned for inspiration not to medieval churches but to the traditions of vernacular architecture. They rediscovered lime plaster, thatch and oak framing, rejected the use of machine-made decoration, and prized homeliness, originality and local materials. Edwin Lutyens began his career in the 1890s with some sensitive recreations of old Surrey houses in brick and tile; E.S. Prior's use of local materials and organic forms in the same decade seem to prefigure today's 'green' housing; and the white-painted roughcast of C.F.A. Voysey's houses provided inspiration for countless early twentieth-century suburbs.

Victorian houses might have been built in a bewildering variety of styles, but one thing they had in common was that all were extraordinarily well built. The designer and critic Charles Eastlake predicted gloomily in 1868, 'to speak plainly, it will be a miracle if half the houses which are now being raised in and about London do not ... tumble down long before their allotted time'. His apprehension was not justified. The fact that so many of these houses in all parts of the country are still standing well beyond their 'allotted time' and continue to provide comfortable, practical and attractive housing for the owners who cherish them bears witness to the enduring values of comfort, convenience and aesthetic appeal that they embody.

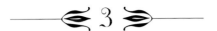

# LIVING IN THE VICTORIAN HOUSE

## ORIENTATION AND PLAN

Despite the huge technological advances of the nineteenth century, domestic comfort continued to depend greatly on natural heat, light and ventilation, and so the orientation of houses remained important. As late as 1897, H.H. Statham, author of *Modern Architecture*, could do no more than reiterate ideas that had predominated for centuries: kitchens should look north. and the dining room north or east, to avoid 'the intrusion of the southern sun at lunch or the western sun at dinner, when people are seated round the table and cannot shift their places'. In acknowledgement of the relatively new importance given to children's rooms, Statham added that nurseries should always look south facing the sun.

While architectural theorists devoted a great deal of attention to site and orientation, only the architect lucky enough to be commissioned to build a new house on a virgin site could follow their advice. Most builders had to use predetermined plots on restricted sites in areas where there was demand for their houses. They followed familiar plans evolved to suit the current practical and social requirements. In terraced housing, adjoining halls not only provided an opportunity to create an imposing entrance under a shared pediment, but also insulated the principal rooms from noise in the neighbouring house. Regardless of the nature of the household, space was rationed according to the sex, age and status of the occupants: the 'masculine' dining room, library and study, the 'feminine' drawing room, and the low-status rooms allocated to children and servants.

The most basic division was between the service areas and the rest of the house. As Robert Kerr explained, 'the family constitute one community: the servants another ... each class is entitled to shut its door upon the other and be alone'. Service areas included spaces now regarded as redundant, such as lamp rooms, sculleries, pantries, larders and coal cellars.

OPPOSITE: *an imposing marble chimneypiece surrounds a cast iron tiled grate in the front room of a terraced house of the late 1880s. Original features such as these are now highly prized.*

ABOVE: *the coal to feed these fires was delivered via a coal-hole in the pavement, many of which had very decorative cast iron covers.*

## Services

### Heating and lighting

The open fire had an almost mythical status in the English home. Coal fires were the principal source of domestic heat throughout the nineteenth century, and required staggering quantities of fuel. The amount of coal consumed in London alone went up from 2.3 million tons in 1835 to over 10.2 million tons in 1861. In most urban housing, where space was scarce, the coal was stored in a separate cellar under the pavement. A chute connected the cellar to a circular hole in the pavement or front step, covered with a self-locking plate of cast iron. The coalman emptied the sacks of coal down the chute and closed the plate before proceeding on his rounds. Some of the plates were very decorative and are worth preserving *in situ*, even if their practical function has been superseded by central heating. Houses without cellars had a coal bin in the back yard, or used the cupboard under the stairs as a 'coal hole'.

Open fires produced unimaginable amounts of dirt inside and outside the house. The battle against the greasy film of soot left on every interior surface was waged by an army of female domestics. Meanwhile, the effect on the external atmosphere – and on public health – was catastrophic: the Great Fog of January 1880 killed 700 Londoners.

Gas supplies were available in new suburbs from about 1860. According to the 1868 edition of *Haydn's Dictionary*, 'the gas-pipes in and round London extend upwards of 2000 miles, and are daily increasing'. Gas was used for lighting but rarely for cooking and heating before the end of the century. The heat produced by gas lights was seen as a necessary evil, if not a positive health hazard. R.W. Edis recommended fresh air inlets in the corners of the ceiling, 'arranged to form part of the decorative treatment of the room' and connected to vents on the exterior of the house. Fine silk stretched over the internal openings of the vents prevented dust from the outside being blown into the room.

Electricity was pioneered by wealthy individuals at their country houses, most famously by Lord Armstrong at Cragside in Northumberland. The first public supply was installed at Godalming in Surrey in 1881, but it was at least another twenty years before supplies were standardized and widespread. The introduction of these new technologies did not wipe out the old: the simultaneous use of candles, oil lamps and gaslight was common before the universal provision of electricity.

*The stairs and back hall of 18 Stafford Terrace, Kensington, the home of the* Punch *cartoonist Edward Linley Sambourne. The house, with its fashionable decoration of the 1870s and 1880s, has been carefully preserved and is open to the public.*

*Hip baths, hot water
cans and ewer-and-
basin sets were essential
for maintaining
personal hygiene before
the advent of plumbed-in
bathrooms.*

## Sanitation

The most notable advance in house design was the provision of internal bathrooms and
WCs, leading to unprecedented improvements in personal and domestic hygiene. At the
beginning of the period hot water had to be heated at the kitchen fire and carried, losing
heat all the way, to wherever it was needed. After use, the dirty water had to be disposed
of equally laboriously. By the end of Victoria's life a hygiene revolution had taken place:
most towns had public supplies of clean water and sewage disposal systems, and most
new houses were provided with bathrooms, running water and plumbed-in water closets.

Despite these advances, large sections of the working-class population at the beginning of the twentieth century were still having to share privies, wash in cold water at the
scullery sink and take baths in portable tubs. Those at the opposite end of the social
scale were also slow to adopt bathrooms, although in their case it was through choice.
Some wealthy families were enthusiastic about indoor plumbing, but there was a great
deal of aristocratic resistance to bathrooms, and to plumbed-in fittings generally. As
long as there was a ready supply of cheap labour to fetch and carry water for them, the
upper classes had little incentive to install expensive equipment for the same purpose.

Thus the development of the modern bathroom was largely a middle-class phenom-
enon. The effort of keeping a family clean in a house with neither a bathroom nor an
army of servants was a powerful motive to acquire indoor plumbing.

The owners of this late Victorian semi-detached house were lucky enough to inherit original fittings and decoration, including relief-patterned dado paper, grained woodwork, door furniture and even the stair rods. Note the hierarchy of decoration: the inside of the bathroom door (just visible at the top of the stairs) lacks the mouldings that enhance the sitting-room door, and the geometric floor tiles stop at the boundary between the 'polite' part of the house and the service quarters.

*Door knockers from a late Victorian builders' merchant's catalogue. In 1897 the example shown at the top was available in japanned (i.e. enamelled) iron at 12 shillings (60p) per dozen, or in polished brass at 5 shillings and 5 pence (28p) each.*

### Communications

Communications between individual members of the household and with the outside world were transformed during the Victorian period. Servants could be summoned using a system of bells worked by wires and pulleys, but in well-run households the servants' lives were not dominated by the constant jangling of bells, as regular routine and fixed timetables reduced the need for individual messages. Bell systems were installed and attended to by plumbers or chimney sweeps accustomed to dealing with hidden pipes and flues. The handles and wires were tightened and oiled during the annual spring clean. Speaking tubes on the same principle as those used on board ship were introduced in the 1840s. The mouthpiece of such a system survives on the top landing of 18 Stafford Terrace, a terraced house built in the 1860s in Kensington, West London, where it was used to summon help from four floors below.

The penny post, introduced in 1840, revolutionized external communications. Its most visible effect on the house was the mutilation of the front door to make a letter slit. Even swifter communications were made possible by the telegraph, brought to England in 1838, and direct personal contact was possible from 1880, when Bell and Edison established the United Telephone Company in London. Private telephones were still a luxury in the 1890s, and frequently installed in special cubbyholes or booths in acknowledgement of their novelty and special status.

Despite all these improvements, the Victorian house could not function without a great deal of manual labour. An aristocratic household in a London mansion might house as many as sixteen domestic servants, and every lower-middle-class clerk could hope to employ one live-in servant. The conditions in which servants were housed varied greatly. Although the houses he described were for the gentry, the architect Robert Kerr still thought it necessary to point out that 'every one of the servants' rooms ought to have a fireplace, for use in case of illness if no more'.

The undoubted drudgery involved in running the Victorian house was acknowledged in the many labour-saving precautions taken by the occupants. Cleaning carpets with a dustpan and brush was such hard work that the use of druggets, crumb cloths and even sheets of newspaper to keep floors clean was widely accepted. Rooms were shut up when not in use – the chimney was swept, the furniture draped with dustsheets, ornaments were put away and the blinds and shutters closed to exclude sunlight.

## The hierarchy of decoration

The importance of the entrance to the house was signalled on the exterior by an elaborate front door framed with pillars or a pediment. The entrance hall, however small and narrow, was always given the most dignified architectural treatment the builder could afford, with deep skirting boards and ornamental plasterwork on the ceiling. The vestigial boundary between the 'front' and the 'staircase' halls was marked with a bracketed arch. The hall gave access to the principal rooms, and also to the service areas, which had to be decently separated. Kerr was scathing about 'the ordinary class of suburban "Speculation Villas" [in which] a Kitchen doorway in the Vestibule or Staircase exposes to view the dresser or the cooking-range, and fills the house with unwelcome odours'.

The principal reception rooms were on the upper ground floor if the house was built over a basement, on the first floor in mid-century houses of conservative design, and on the ground floor in most houses built after 1870. Architectural finishes and interior decoration were devised according to the status of individual rooms, with elaborate plasterwork and detailed joinery reserved for the reception rooms. Family bedrooms were more simply decorated, while servants' quarters and domestic offices received the bare minimum of functional finishes. Most households aspired to reserve one room 'for best', like the suburban villa parlour of the 1890s remembered by Flora Thompson: 'There was not a book or a flower in the room and not so much as a cushion awry to show that it was lived in. As a matter of fact, it was not. It was more a museum or a temple or a furniture showroom than a living-room.' This apparently absurd waste of space was psychologically important as a vital indicator of respectability.

As far as interior decoration was concerned, 'the present age is distinguished from all others in having no style of its own' declared H.W. and A. Arrowsmith in *The House Decorator and Painter's Guide* (1840). The Arrowsmiths, who counted Queen Victoria among their clients, turned this apparent failing into a virtue that gave scope for the use of various historical revival styles. They recommended 'Tudor style' decoration for the dining room, 'arabesque' for the sitting room, and 'the gorgeous French styles' for the drawing room. It was not enough simply to rummage through this decorator's dressing-up box of styles, however; the problem was to choose the *right* wallcoverings, carpets, curtains and upholstery from the many patterns on offer. As early as 1844, the *Journal of Design* identified a 'morbid craving for novelty', complaining that 'it is not sufficient that each manufacturer produces a few patterns of the best sort every season, they must be generated by the score and by the hundreds'. The implication was clear: mass-production and popularity were incompatible with good design.

Writers and designers wrestled with the problem of design reform throughout the 1840s and 1850s. While Pugin, Morris and the designer Owen Jones addressed rather specialized readerships and Ruskin theorized to the educated middle classes, it was left to others to give practical substance to the debate and carry it to a wider audience. Eastlake was heavily influenced by William Morris, whose medievalist fantasies he translated into brisk common sense in a series of magazine articles, later collected in *Hints on Household Taste* (1868). Edis carried on where Eastlake left off, publishing complete schemes of decoration in *Decoration and Furniture of Town Houses* (1881).

*Decorative plaster corbels in designs derived from Classical architecture were used to decorate the join between wall and arch in a front hall.*

The Gothic taste promoted by these writers was based on honesty, simplicity and fitness for purpose. Furniture was made of solid wood in robust styles that revealed their constructional pegs and joints. Pattern was stylized and two-dimensional, with no illusionistic shading, and colours were subdued. Market forces were against the reformers, however, as the public would insist on pursuing their own debased preference for imitative materials such as ormulu and papier-mâché, veneers, illusionistic architectural wallpaper and floral-patterned carpets. More than one working designer bowed to the inevitable; in the 1890s Alexander Millar felt compelled to address an essay on 'carpet designing' to 'an imaginary young designer, who, while he desires to do good, artistic work, is also alive to the fact that he cannot always force his own ideas upon a half-educated public'.

The thirty years between 1860 and 1890 were the high point of eclecticism, when, according to the textile historians Mary Schoeser and Celia Rufey, 'most rooms were at best a *mélange* and at worst a chaotic hodgepodge of different styles'. The most exuberant phase of exploiting the new materials and manufacturing techniques coincided with the growth of a house-owning middle class, who for the first time had responsibility for decorating their own environment and money to spend on it. Retailers, whether old-established furniture shops or new department stores, were eager to take their money. In London, Shoolbred's the drapers had been established as early as 1814 and in premises on Tottenham Court Road since 1817. Heal's and Maples opened in the

The Awakening
Conscience *by William
Holman Hunt, 1853
(detail). Unreformed
mid-Victorian taste,
with its fondness for
'dishonest' gilt or
veneered furniture, and
Berlin woolwork
(a particularly
repetitive, unoriginal
kind of needlework), is
here imbued with a
moral message.*

early 1840s, but the 1860s were the boom years for home furnishings retailers: Morris & Co, Derry & Toms, William Whiteley, John Lewis and Bentalls of Kingston were all established in that decade, and were soon followed by Liberty, which opened as 'East India House' in Regent Street in 1875.

Alongside the pleasures of conspicuous consumption, there came a new unease about taste. More than any other activity, home decoration betrayed one's class, aspirations, education, even one's moral character. Fear of exposure was exploited in high art and low: when Holman Hunt painted the boudoir of a fallen woman in *The Awakening Conscience* (1853), he filled it with gilt mouldings and veneered furniture to underline the empty vanity of the concubine's life; when the popular novelist Rosa N. Carey described a morning-room 'fitted up more for comfort and use than for outward show', she was using her character's preference for faded but genuine antique furnishings to symbolize moral vigour. Happily, advice on how to negotiate the minefield was plentiful. Such helpful titles as *The Art of Decoration* (1881) by Mrs Haweis, and Mrs Panton's *From Kitchen to Garret* (1888) show that aspirational literature about interiors is nothing new. Mrs Panton wrote for a notional reader with an income of £1,000 a year, but most of the people who consulted her books were less well-off.

The dominant influence in fashionable interior decoration in the last quarter of the nineteenth century was the Aesthetic movement, promoted by figures like Oscar Wilde and James McNeill Whistler. Originally a reaction against overblown eclecticism, and heavily influenced by the simplicity and purity of Japanese design, it was seized upon as a novelty by retailers, who produced their own, debased versions of Aesthetic furniture and wallcoverings. George du Maurier's cartoons for *Punch* satirized both the preciousness of the thoroughgoing aesthete and the ineptitude of the amateur. In the wrong hands, as contemporary writers enjoyed pointing out, so-called 'artistic' decoration could be anything but: 'the fireplace was draped with art serge and muslin to represent a spider's web, with a huge imitation spider involved in it. Bulrushes stood in a big jar, wooden stools had red satin ribbon tied round them, and a mirror on the wall had water-lilies painted on it.'

It should be remembered that most house owners were not deeply committed to sophisticated interior decorating styles. For every aspiring aesthete agonizing over the best way to arrange bulrushes and peacock's feathers, there were a dozen housewives content to arrange their drawing rooms or parlours much as they had always done, with a conventional mix of inherited and new furniture, family portraits and maiden aunts' watercolours, sentimental keepsakes and perhaps one or two more fashionable items.

Victorian interiors are often rather dismissively described as 'cluttered', implying that no thought went into the acquisition and arrangement of furnishings, which were simply allowed to accumulate. The modern eye, trained to appreciate the beauty of clean lines, functional design and neutral colours, often recoils at the exuberantly-patterned

*Poor Relations by*
*George Goodwin*
*Kilburne (1875) depicts*
*the drawing-room of a*
*prosperous middle-class*
*household. The vase on*
*the mantelpiece and the*
*fireside armchair are*
*the only conspicuously*
*up-to-date items in a*
*room in which the*
*decoration appears to*
*have evolved so as to*
*epitomize comfortable,*
*cultured domesticity.*

*Contrasting styles of interior decoration from* Academy Architecture, 1898. RIGHT: *the owner of this drawing room willingly submitted to the overarching vision of the designer, George Walton.* BELOW: *a less homogeneous design by the architects H.B.W. Steel and Balfour is overwhelmed by a miscellany of furniture, fabrics and accessories.*

*In the 1870s George du
Maurier's cartoons for
Punch made relentless
fun of the Aesthetic
mania for spindly,
ebonized furniture and
peacock feathers.*

wallpaper and furnishing fabrics the Victorians loved. But things that now appear garish or vulgar to our eyes may in fact have provided a very necessary splash of colour or glitter in a fog-bound house lit by gas or candles. As to the quantity of objects, careful study of photographs, watercolours and contemporary accounts of interiors suggests that Victorian householders did indeed devote great thought to the arrangement of their rooms to suit their tastes and purposes. We can sympathize with their preoccupations, even if we do not want to copy their style of decoration.

## Using the Victorian house today
### *General principles*
There are ways to achieve modern standards of comfort, hygiene, insulation and security in a Victorian house without sacrificing its essential character. Each of the subsequent chapters in this book ends with suggestions to help you in different areas of the house. There are also some good general principles that are worth bearing in mind:

- Take your time. On first moving into a Victorian house, do not rush into big decisions about alterations but take a few months to find out how the house works best for you.
- Respect the plan: original room divisions are not to be discarded lightly. Kitchens nowadays tend to be used both as social and functional rooms, but consider retaining the old larder or scullery in order to shut out unsightly and noisy domestic machines. An alternative to 'knocking through' two living rooms to make one big space is to install double doors, which will give you the best of both worlds: privacy and quiet when you need it, and room to expand on more sociable occasions.
- Respect the historic fabric: remove as little as possible of the original structure and materials, and repair existing fabric wherever possible. When you have to remove original elements, replace them on a like-for-like basis, matching the original materials and workmanship as closely as you can.

*Neighbourliness and sensitivity to design and materials are essential to the preservation of the historic streetscape. New walling in mismatched brick, flimsy mild steel railings and pretentious pineapple finials are blatantly at odds with the original timber fencing in this 1870s estate.*

• Distinguish between reversible and non-reversible alterations, and take the reversible approach wherever possible. Changing the colour of your front door with a new coat of paint is a reversible change (it can be repainted). Throwing away the front door and replacing it with a modern design in uPVC is borderline (it will be troublesome and expensive, but not impossible, to reinstate a panelled timber door). Spraying the front of the house with 'Tyrolean' render is non-reversible (it cannot be removed without irreparable damage to the brickwork).

• Accept the inevitable signs of age. Good maintenance and regular redecoration are essential to keep a house in good repair, but aggressive cleaning, obtrusive repointing, and painting every scrap of external joinery with brilliant white polyurethane gloss will not only fail to make the house 'look like new', but will strip it of much of its historic interest. The patina of benign neglect is preferable to the chastened look of an over-restored house.

• Be a good neighbour. This means respecting the uniformity of the external appearance of a terrace or street. By all means express your personality through decoration *inside* the house.

• In all restoration work, make sure there is a historical precedent for the work you are doing. Best avoided are twee additions such as carriage lamps, cast iron nameplates with decorative motifs picked out in bright enamel colours, wall-mounted mailboxes and 'bullseye' glass panes. Advertisements for 'Victorian style' items may carry attractive images, but their primary purpose is to sell products, not to provide historically accurate information.

• Beware of 'miracle' products and 'maintenance free' materials.

• Find out as much as you can before you start. 'Further Reading' (p.259) lists books to help you take your research further or deepen your understanding of Victorian domestic architecture. 'Places to Visit' (p.264) lists Victorian houses open to the public, museums containing Victorian domestic items, and some that display complete room settings. A stately home will not provide an accurate template for the decoration of a modest terrace house, but it will help you to 'get your eye in'.

• You can discover a great deal about your house, particularly when you redecorate, by looking for old layers of paint, wallpaper and carpet (traces of lost mouldings or fingerplates often show up as faint lines in the paint on doors; floorboards that are stained or painted at the edge of the room but not in the middle indicate that the room once contained a large central carpet, rather than a fitted floorcovering). Where original architectural details have been lost, you may find them preserved in a neighbouring house of similar age and style, and can ask your neighbours for permission to take measurements and photographs to help you replicate them in your house.

### Contractors

Word of mouth is often the best way to find good builders and other contractors. The conservation officer of the local authority may give advice on suppliers and tradesmen in your area. A few basic checks will help to weed out the 'cowboys': make sure that any quotes specify the work to be undertaken and the extent of any guarantees, that the contractor has the skills and staff to complete the work, that any claims to membership of trade associations or other professional organizations are genuine, and that the contractor has adequate and appropriate insurance. It is a good idea to obtain several quotes before choosing a contractor, and to agree a schedule of payments for a large job. At no stage should payments to the contractor exceed the value of the work that has been completed.

### Planning permission

If your house is a listed building or stands within a conservation area, you must contact the local planning department to check whether you need special planning consent for the work you want to do. You must have all the necessary permissions *before* you start the work.

Listing applies to the whole house, inside and out, to some fixtures and fittings, and to associated structures such as outhouses or boundary walls 'within the curtilage'. Listing protects the house as it was when it was added to the list, so you may need consent even though you intend to return the house to its original state. If, for example, you want to remove a 1930s tiled fireplace in order to install a Victorian grate in your listed house, you will need listed building consent. Controls over alterations to houses in conservation areas are not so stringent, but it is still important to check the legal position before you start.

### Safety and security

Whether you are undertaking major renovation work or a simple DIY job, safety is vital:

• Equip yourself properly for the job in hand, with protective clothing, goggles, a mask, gloves and sturdy footwear as appropriate.
• Make sure that you have the right tools and materials for the job before you start.
• Ensure that any scaffolding, trestles or ladders are properly installed, and never work at height when you are alone on site.
• Use naked flames and other sources of heat such as hot air guns with great caution. Build bonfires away from flammable materials, and never leave them to burn unattended.

- Use chemicals safely: read the manufacturer's advice and instructions. Never mix bleach (chlorine) with chemicals containing ammonia: when the two are combined they give off a toxic gas.
- Old houses sometimes contain lead-based paints, wallpaper printed with colours containing arsenic, and asbestos tiles. The risks involved in disturbing these are not negligible. If in doubt about how to handle such substances safely, seek expert advice from your local authority or the Health and Safety Executive (see Useful Addresses, p.266).
- Use accredited tradespeople to deal with gas, electricity and water supplies. Electricians should be registered with the Institute of Electrical Engineers (see Useful Addresses, p.266). Gas boilers must be fitted by CORGI registered engineers. Alterations to sewage pipes, sumps and overflows require local authority inspection.
- Be aware of the many hazards that arise during the course of work, such as gaps where floorboards have been lifted, or rusty nails sticking out of old timbers. Have a first aid kit on site.
- Keep children and pets away from building works.

If you are leaving the house empty, or providing special access such as scaffolding or the removal of the garden fence while the work is going on, check that this will not invalidate your household insurance.

Crime prevention officers will advise on all aspects of home security, but you need to be especially watchful while the house is under repair. Original architectural features are highly sought after, and this has created a market for stolen items. On the exterior of the house, garden ornaments, gates and even gatepost finials are attractive to thieves. Fireplaces, panelling, doors, stained glass panels and architectural ironmongery have been stolen from interiors. Building materials have disappeared from front gardens where they were left overnight in tidy stacks ready for use. When workmen and their vehicles are coming and going, it can be difficult to tell legitimate visitors from opportunist thieves. Be vigilant about security, especially if the house is left empty overnight. Ask neighbours to keep an eye out for any suspicious or out-of-hours activities. Finally, photograph everything so that if the worst does happen, you can reclaim your property or find appropriate substitutes.

# PART II
## Structure and Materials

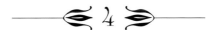

# BRICK AND TERRACOTTA

A T THE BEGINNING of the nineteenth century brick was often regarded as an inferior building material, to be avoided by those who could afford to build in stone. Brick masonry was frequently hidden behind a coat of stucco scored to imitate ashlar, as even fake stone was preferred to the 'garish' colours of new brick. This prejudice was not entirely unjustified: bricks were often of poor quality because they were hastily made on site, using the clay that had been dug out to make the foundations of the houses. With clays of variable quality, and using makeshift kilns or 'clamps' to fire the bricks, it was impossible to achieve a consistent and reliable product. Brick had also become associated with shoddy workmanship: naturally, bricklayers who knew that their work was to be covered over would take few pains with it, and many 'jerry-builders' owed their continuing livelihoods to all-concealing stucco.

By the end of the century this attitude had been completely reversed. Brick had attained a new respectability thanks to improvements in manufacturing technology, better distribution, and to the work of a handful of influential architects. Traditional methods of using coloured, cut, rubbed and moulded bricks had been revived, and it had become the predominant walling material for houses in all but the most remote parts of the country.

Brick making became mechanized in stages following the introduction in the 1830s of pug mills to grind the clay to the correct, uniform consistency, and machines for wire-cutting brick-sized pieces of extruded clay. But, as Roger Dixon and Stefan Muthesius have noted:

> The actual processes of brick manufacture in the period before 1850 owed very little to technological change, the great expansion in output from 841 million in 1815–19 to 1,794 million in 1845–9 being almost entirely due to more intensive use of traditional methods of manufacture. The brick making industry in the period was characterised by a large number of firms of small size, and even in 1870, by which time some growth in scale had occurred, there were still 1,770 works employing on average only 13 men each. 'Getting' the clay remained a matter of pick and shovel, and bricks were almost entirely hand-made by being pressed into moulds.

The repeal of the brick tax in 1850, coinciding with a renewed interest in the architectural possibilities of exposed brick, gave impetus to the industry and encouraged manufacturers to invest in new technology. The Oates machine of 1856 mimicked traditional brick making by pushing moist clay into moulds many times faster than a

47

man could. Mixing and moulding by machine made it possible to use a much wider range of clays, and the number of colours, as well as the variety of brick types on offer, increased greatly. There were also improvements to the firing process during the 1850s, such as the Hoffmann kiln, which reduced fuel consumption and provided evenly regulated heat. As canals and railways made it possible to transport bricks all over the country, it was no longer necessary for builders to make their own on site, and the industry became concentrated in areas where large deposits of suitable clays were combined with availability of fuel and good canal or rail links.

The decisive change in architectural fashion brought about by the Gothic Revival increased demand for brick. Gothic architects argued that the structure and materials of the building should be plainly visible. Decoration should spring from the materials used, not from superficial coatings. Stucco was a dishonest sham, while bare brick was nothing to be ashamed of – in fact, it was to be celebrated. Why use plaster and paint for decoration when coloured bricks would last longer, cost less and embody the great virtue of structural honesty? In the 1850s a few pioneering buildings such as William Butterfield's All Saints Church, Margaret Street, London, showed how vivid effects could be economically achieved using multi-coloured brickwork. This 'constructional polychromy' subsequently became so popular that it has been called a 'kind of trademark of Victorian architecture'. Another influential building was named after the colour of its plain brick walls: Red House, built for William Morris by the architect Philip Webb in 1859–60, helped to reconcile the artistic and intellectual middle classes to brick houses. The new generation of architects enjoyed the contrasts in texture achieved by combining different kinds of brick, or brick and stone, in one building. Bricks also had the great practical virtue of being able to resist the British climate. Polychrome brickwork was soon being used for all kinds of housing, from the large villas built for the university community in North Oxford, to humble railway and farm workers' cottages in all parts of the country. In speculative housing polychromatic effects were reserved for the front elevations, the rear of the houses being commonly built of plain brickwork.

Mass-produced bricks offered some tremendous advantages to builders. They were cheap and easy to use, and their size, colour, texture, strength and structural quality were uniform and predictable – all of which made it easier to plan developments in any part of the country, regardless of local building materials and traditions. Using bricks also made it easy to build to precise measurements, enabling builders to make the most economical use of materials. The expansion of cities, towns and villages was achieved by building uniform streets of brick houses, which, although they were often criticized for their monotony, provided cheap, practical and often very attractive accommodation for thousands of families.

By the last quarter of the nineteenth century an aesthetic reaction against brick had begun, but the material's cheapness ensured that it remained overwhelmingly the most common walling material. It was possible to build a red-brick house that avoided the commonplace associations of suburban uniformity by copying the kind of fine workmanship associated with the seventeenth and early eighteenth centuries, the 'golden age' of English domestic architecture. Queen Anne revival houses of the 1870s and 1880s relied heavily on the attractive contrast between plain brick walls and white-painted joinery. Polychromy was abandoned, but in its place came a new interest in the craft of the bricklayer. Decoration was now achieved with moulded, carved and rubbed bricks laid with joints of pure lime putty so fine as to be almost invisible.

Hundreds of small, local brickworks flourished, producing a tremendous variety of brick colours, textures, shapes and sizes. There are so many different bricks and regional variations in their use that it is not possible to describe here more than a handful of the principal varieties that may be found in Victorian houses. London is famous for its 'stock' brick, which gets its yellow colour from long, slow firing of local clays rich in iron and magnesium. Eastlake called this 'the meanest and most uninteresting of building materials', deploring the way in which, particularly in London, it

*Red House, Bexleyheath, named for the colour of its plain brick walls, was designed in 1858 by Philip Webb for his friend William Morris. This pioneering statement of Arts and Crafts ideals had a huge influence on subsequent house design.*

speedily acquired a dingy appearance. 'Flettons', another relatively soft kind of brick, derive their name from clay deposits discovered at Fletton in the East Midlands in the late nineteenth century. They are susceptible to frost damage and so their blotchy pink colour is not often exposed to view; instead they are used for internal walls and load-bearing walls that are to be rendered or faced with stone or better quality bricks. 'Rubbers' are made from fine-textured clay, which can be rubbed into precise shapes for fine work; many Victorian houses have panels carved with decorative designs, or window arches made with close-jointed voussoirs of these high-quality red bricks.

The dark, almost purple colour of 'Staffordshire blue' bricks (sometimes referred to as 'engineering bricks') is the result of firing clay with a high iron content in a high temperature kiln. These bricks are dense and immensely strong, and were sometimes used in the foundations of houses. They were also used as contrasting bands of colour within the wall and as copings on garden walls. The use of white bricks in East Anglia, especially Cambridgeshire, is due to the pale gault clay in the chalk belt of south-east England, which makes a hard, pale brick. The deep red bricks made from shale found near Accrington in Lancashire are sharp-edged, smooth-textured and very dense; one manufacturer sold 'Accrington reds' under the trade name 'Nori' ('iron' spelled backwards). The use of local clays gave rise to some distinctive regional variations, such as the use of silver-grey brick contrasted with cream-coloured brick quoins in Reading.

Brick clay could be moulded into different shapes and sizes for practical and decorative purposes. 'Bullnose' bricks had rounded arrises for corners, kerbs and copings; other moulded shapes were used for widow openings and mullions. Some bricks were stamped with patterns to make attractive courses or panels to enliven otherwise blank walls.

The manner of laying bricks in a wall is called the 'bond'. Different bonds were chosen for different uses, a Flemish bond (in which headers alternate with stretchers in each course) being the most common choice for elevations. English bond (alternate courses of headers and stretchers) was favoured by Gothic Revival architects. It is immensely strong but expensive, as it uses a large quantity of bricks. English garden wall bond, in which a course of headers is only used once for every three or five courses of stretchers, is a more economical variation. Bonds were also chosen according to regional preferences: English bonds were widely used in the north of England, and header bond (in which each course consists entirely of headers) was favoured in the north-west, especially around Manchester.

*Cream detailing contrasts with the characteristic silver-grey brickwork of Reading, Berkshire.*

*Lines of nailhead and rosette moulded bricks enliven a façade of plain red brick and stone dressings.*

Nine-inch (230mm) solid walls were the most common form of load-bearing wall, although cavity walls were advocated by some writers and are occasionally found in nineteenth-century houses. Cavity walls consist of an inner and an outer 'leaf' of brick separated by a void that can be anything between 2 and 6 inches (50–150mm) wide. The two leaves are tied together at intervals by wrought iron ties, by bricks laid across the void, or by the sills, jambs and soffits of the door and window openings. In the *Builder* of 1860 it was claimed that 'at least 80 per cent of the dwellings of the working classes erected [in Southampton] within the last ten years have their external walls hollow', but this figure, even if it was accurate, was not approached elsewhere.

The Victorian builder was as preoccupied with damp proofing as his present-day counterpart. A common form of damp proof course was two or three courses of slate set in cement mortar in the external wall below the level of the suspended ground floor. These often cracked as the building settled, and alternatives with more flexibility, such as asphalt or tar mixed with sand, were also tried. Thick lead sheet was effective but expensive; the cheaper zinc sheet decayed. One solution was to build two or three courses of engineering bricks into the wall at the correct level. Set in cement mortar, these were sufficiently hard to prevent water from travelling further up the wall.

Ordinary Portland Cement (OPC) was patented in the 1840s and in commercial production by the 1850s, but until about 1870 most houses were built using lime mortar, which might be mixed with ash to make a black mortar that pre-empted any change in colour caused by exposure to polluted air. The pointing applied by Victorian bricklayers was more reticent than the protruding 'weatherstruck' pointing generally used by modern builders, although tuck pointing was used in high-class work. Towards the end of the nineteenth century, cement-based mortars began to be more widely used, but lime was not totally superseded until well into the twentieth century.

## Terracotta

*The enduring fashion for decorative terracotta details was introduced in suburban houses in the 1870s. This moulded leaf forms part of a frieze on a London house of 1892.*

Architectural terracotta enjoyed a revival in domestic architecture in the late 1860s. Its appeal was both practical and decorative. It was fireproof, with a hard, impervious 'fire-skin' that resisted damp and pollution. In theory it was washable, especially in the glazed form known as faience, although in practice architectural terracotta was rarely cleaned and soon became as grimy as any other building materials. It came in a palette of natural clay colours ranging from pale cream and grey through blue and fiery red to chocolate brown (although most production was in buff yellow or bright red). Capable of being moulded into relief patterns, it was welcomed by Gothic architects as more genuine than stucco, cheaper than carved stone and an effective complement to polychromatic brickwork. It also had a long historical pedigree, having been used for mullions and dressings since the sixteenth century.

Terracotta was reintroduced on museums and schools of design, particularly the South Kensington Museum (now the Victoria and Albert Museum, by Fowkes and Sykes, 1862–3) and the Natural History Museum (Alfred Waterhouse, 1868). By this time Waterhouse was a devotee of terracotta, having already designed several houses with terracotta decoration in Reading (including one for himself) in the mid-1860s. He went on to design many public and commercial buildings using the material.

Waterhouse and other terracotta enthusiasts would have their designs made up to order by one of the many architectural ceramics companies that flourished in England and Wales in the second half of the nineteenth century. Fortunes were to be made, and famous terracotta companies, some of which are still making architectural ceramics, include the Hathern Station Brick and Terracotta Company (founded in 1874 and now trading as Hathernware), Doulton of Lambeth and Shaw's of Darwen. Like all good entrepreneurs, they diversified their product. Doulton produced the salt-glazed 'Doultonware', unglazed 'Siliconware' and, from about 1888, 'Carraraware', a stoneware with a matt white glaze resembling Italian marble.

The use of terracotta on high-profile buildings associated with all that was most advanced in art and design, and the close involvement of architects in the manufacturing process, made terracotta briefly fashionable for high-class housing developments. The architectural partnership of Ernest George and Harold Peto produced varied and exuberant terracotta houses in London throughout the 1870s. Meanwhile, good use of the material was made by provincial architects, notably John Douglas, who used it on houses of the late 1870s in Chester.

Most manufacturers issued catalogues of architectural ceramics, which could be ordered from stock. Structural elements such as doorcases and mullioned window frames, and decorative flourishes such as pierced ridge tiles, crestings and finials, could be made out of terracotta. In many small houses terracotta 'sunflower' tiles were used to enliven a window bay or the blank wall over the front door. However, it was difficult for speculative builders to incorporate catalogue items into their developments,

*Sheet of brick and terracotta 'specials' offered by the Hathern Station Brick Co. in 1885.*

as they had to be coursed in with brickwork and sizes were not standardized. Individual decorative elements such as finials and pier caps, which did not need to correspond to surrounding brickwork, were carried to all parts of the country.

## Repair and maintenance

Fine brickwork and the use of coloured and moulded bricks distinguish many Victorian houses but are not always treated with the respect they deserve. Brick walls may be covered with inappropriate render or stone cladding, painted or otherwise disfigured. Even misguided attempts to maintain or 'improve' brick walls by overzealous repointing or cleaning may do permanent damage.

The first question to ask when considering the maintenance or repair of brickwork should be, 'is the work really necessary?' Many expensive treatments are carried out on structurally sound walls: repointing is done to entire buildings that only needed careful attention to a small, badly-weathered patch on one wall, and large-scale cleaning operations are undertaken on buildings whose weathered colour was part of their charm. It is reasonable to expect old brick walls to look weathered, worn and perhaps rather dirty, and it is not necessary to regard these characteristics as problems.

Until about 1900 the foundations of most Victorian houses were constructed by digging trenches through the topsoil until firm rock was reached, and then building stepped 'footings' of brick, which would carry the weight of the building. These foundations are vulnerable to soil movement, either shrinkage (in drought conditions) or expansion (when there is frost after heavy rain), which can cause cracking and uneven settlement. Tree roots can also disrupt the foundations, not only by their physical presence, but also because of the large quantities of water they suck out of the soil. Underpinning, which involves propping the foundations and pouring in concrete to make a solid 'raft' to support the building, is one solution, but is a job for a structural engineer. If there is genuine cause for concern about the soundness of any brick masonry, it is best to consult an architect, structural engineer or surveyor who has experience of historic buildings and their conservation.

## Damp

Damp is one of the commonest problems to affect brickwork. However, there is no point in spending money and effort on treating the brickwork when the real problem lies elsewhere, so before commissioning work on the walls, check whether the water can be stopped at source. The roof covering, rainwater goods, internal plumbing and 'hidden' drains such as valley gutters should be kept in good repair. Thick planting, stacks of firewood, building materials or garden rubbish should not be allowed to build up at the base of walls, as these can trap water against the masonry. Raising the ground level outside the house or installing hard landscape surfaces up to the wall without adequate drainage to cope with water run-off can also cause problems. Airbricks must be kept clear so that underfloor spaces are properly ventilated.

Basements were usually lined with brick, which was given an exterior coating of asphalt before backfilling, to waterproof the side of the brickwork in contact with the surrounding earth or gravel. This damp proofing was often omitted in uninhabited cellars and pavement vaults, and they are consequently somewhat damp, especially where the surrounding soil contains a lot of moisture. It is therefore essential to ventilate cellars well to prevent dry rot. Cellars can be 'tanked' or 'dry-lined' to make them fit for conversion into living space.

Brick is a porous material that will regulate its own moisture content by absorbing and releasing water, as long as it is allowed to do so. Impermeable renders, hard cement pointing and 'weatherproof' coatings can all upset this natural balance by preventing evaporation and trapping moisture within the wall.

There are several ways to improve the condition of a damp wall. Inserting airbricks can help by ventilating the space under suspended floors or restoring air circulation within sealed-off chimneys, as can inserting or renewing a damp proof course. Heavy-duty polyethylene sheeting is the present-day substitute for the organic materials the Victorians used for damp proof courses. Chemical damp proof courses are a relatively recent development. These consist of a silicone solution drip-fed or injected into the wall via holes drilled at 150mm intervals; the solution is absorbed into the bricks and mortar and forms a barrier as it cures. There are also various electro-osmotic systems. Each method has its disciples and detractors, and may be more or less appropriate for different situations, so it is worth taking expert advice before proceeding.

## Replacement bricks

In some cases brickwork may have deteriorated to the point where it needs to be wholly or partly rebuilt. This may be because the bricks were of poor quality to begin with or have weathered badly (a problem affecting chimney stacks in particular), or because ground movement or settlement has caused cracks and bulges that are too serious to be stitched or tied together.

Single bricks can be carefully cut out of the wall and replaced with new bricks bedded in matching mortar. If a wall has to be dismantled and rebuilt, it may be possible to save the bricks, clean and re-use them. Old lime-based mortar (see below) is easy to scrape off. Damaged bricks can sometimes be turned so that the damaged side faces inwards, but it will often be necessary to buy a stock of new or second-hand bricks to match the old. Architectural salvage yards can be a useful source, although it can be difficult to find enough bricks of the right type from a single yard. New bricks are available to match many of the common Victorian varieties, and it may be possible to have 'specials' made to order. When matching bricks, it is important to look for more than just the right size and colour. Shape, texture and hardness are equally important. In one batch of bricks there may be

*Repointing with over-hard, cement-based mortar has caused these soft red bricks to crumble, as water that cannot escape through the mortar has forced its way through the less resistant clay body of the bricks.*

*The cottage on the right of this picture suffers the disastrous 'string vest' effect of bad repointing.*

many subtle variations of colour, so make sure that you have the opportunity to compare several samples of the new and the original bricks before agreeing to buy a large quantity.

### Mortars

Most Victorian houses were built with traditional lime-based mortars. Limestone is crushed and heated in a kiln to produce calcium oxide, known as 'quicklime' or 'unslaked lime'. When quicklime is added to water, a chemical reaction occurs, producing a soft, greasy mass of calcium hydroxide, known as 'slaked lime' or 'lime putty'. This is stored for at least three months before use, under a layer of water in an airtight container. The longer the putty is stored, the better; if it dries out at this stage it can be made workable again by 'knocking it up' (i.e. chopping and mixing it well) without the addition of any extra water. Slaked lime is the basis for many kinds of mortars, plasters and renders. In its pure form it is used for very fine joints in stone masonry and gauged brickwork, and for the finishing coat in plasterwork. Mixed with sand and other aggregates, it makes a basic mortar or render known as 'coarse stuff'. Slaked lime products stiffen and harden when they are exposed to carbon dioxide in the air, but this is a very slow process. It can take several years for a lime mortar in an external wall to harden completely, and the material will always remain responsive to changes in temperature and humidity, allowing the wall to absorb and release water – to 'breathe' – naturally and to move without cracking.

Ordinary Portland Cement (OPC) is not usually appropriate for older buildings because it is too strong, brittle and impermeable. It can trap water in the masonry and may also contain harmful salts. Good basic mortar mixes for repointing are:

- soft masonry in a sheltered position: lime putty/sand 1:3
- harder masonry in a sheltered position: OPC/lime/sand 1:3:12
- harder masonry in a more exposed position: OPC/lime/sand 1:2:9
- harder masonry in a very exposed position (e.g. chimneystacks and below DPCs): OPC/lime/sand 1:2:9

These are general guides only; each case should be assessed individually and with reference to detailed information on mortar mixes contained in the publications of the SPAB and English Heritage (see Further Reading, p.259).

### Repointing

Three things are essential for successful repointing: correct preparation of the joints, new mortar of the same colour and texture as the original, and matching the profile and finish of the original work as closely as possible.

To prepare the joint, the old mortar should be raked out by hand to a depth of at least 20mm. Never allow the use of power tools such as disc grinders to clean out the pointing on old brick walls. They damage the edges of the bricks, leaving the joints much wider than they should be and making it impossible to match the new pointing to the old. The raked-out joints should be wetted with clean water before the repointing commences to stop the dry bricks and mortar around the joint from drawing the water out of the new mortar and thus weakening the mix.

Lime mortars are sometimes described as 'weak', but this does not mean that they are not strong enough to hold the wall together – it refers to the porosity and flexibility of the mortar, which should be matched in any new work. Much damage has been done by repointing old brickwork with strong, cement-rich mortar. If the mortar mix is too strong, it will not allow moisture to evaporate, but will drive it out of the wall through the bricks, causing them to crack or flake away. It may be necessary to experiment with different mortar mixes until the correct recipe is established, and to allow a test area of pointing to dry out to check that colour and texture are right, before mixing up a large quantity.

Equally important to the success of the work is to match the style and shape of the original pointing. Victorian pointing was usually flush with the face of the bricks or slightly recessed so that the brick predominated. New pointing should be equally reticent. Where joints have widened, the faces of the bricks should not be smeared or buttered over with mortar to make a flush surface. Weather-struck or ribbon pointing should be avoided at all costs. Ask to see a sample area of repointing before giving the builder the go-ahead to complete the work, and carry out regular checks on work in progress to ensure the same high standard is being maintained and that the same people are doing the work throughout. Gauged brickwork repairs and complex techniques such as tuck pointing should only be undertaken by skilled specialists.

Brick requires no finishing coat. On no account should a brick wall be given a coat of paint in order to 'smarten it up'. Apart from destroying the historic appearance of the building and being difficult to remove, paint must be re-applied every five years or so in order to maintain its appearance, whereas bare brick requires no special attention. Waterproof sealants can change the appearance of brick, giving it a plasticky shine and making it impossible for water trapped within the masonry to evaporate naturally. Likewise, there is no aesthetic justification for covering decent brickwork with render or fake stone cladding. Like paint, these sham finishes can trap water in the masonry, and it may be impossible to remove them without doing irreparable damage.

### Cleaning

Victorian masonry may contain many different types of brick, or terracotta and stone, each with its own colour and texture and each responding in its own way to soiling and to cleaning treatments. The old mortar will be softer and more absorbent than the rest

*The preparation of brickwork joints for repointing should always be done by hand: power tools are too damaging to the edges of the bricks.*

of the wall, and may be damaged by cleaning that works well on brick and stone. Any cleaning treatment must not only remove the dirt, paint or staining as intended, but must do so without damaging the materials underneath. It is therefore essential to test-clean a small, unobtrusive area and to ensure that all the materials making up the wall are included in the trial before tackling the entire area.

When damp walls dry out, problems often occur because the moisture within the wall contains soluble salts. As the water evaporates, the salts are left behind on the surface of the brick, often appearing as a pale, powdery bloom or 'efflorescence'. Loose salts on the surface of the brick can be cleaned off with a soft brush or vacuum cleaner, and will eventually stop appearing – as long as the source of the moisture has been eliminated. It may be necessary to call in a specialist cleaning firm to deal with more serious salt deposits by applying poultices of clay, fuller's earth or other absorbent material. Both brushing and poulticing may need to be repeated several times until the wall has dried out and no more loose salts appear.

Loose dirt, like efflorescing salts, can be brushed off with a natural bristle brush (never use a wire brush, as it will scratch the surface of the bricks). Brushing down with water is another DIY option that cannot do much harm – as long as the wall is not saturated with water, the dirt once dissolved is thoroughly rinsed off, and the wall has the chance to dry out properly afterwards. Pressure washers delivering up to 3000 psi can be too aggressive for all but garden paths and garage driveways, but pressures in the range 300–600 psi are usually not harmful. Proprietary chemical solutions, gels, packs and poultices are also available, but should only be used under professional supervision; consult an independent building conservator for advice before proceeding. Large-scale cleaning operations should be carried out by professional masonry cleaning contractors, who should be able to demonstrate that they can provide adequate protection against spray, deal with any run-off and observe the appropriate health and safety requirements. Indiscriminate cleaning strips away the patina of old brick buildings, leaving an unattractive 'scrubbed' appearance. It can also leave the bricks more vulnerable to water penetration. It is better to leave the brickwork looking slightly dingy than to overclean. For more information on cleaning materials and techniques, see Chapter 5, Stone.

### Caring for terracotta

Terracotta is very vulnerable to damage from damp and salts. It can suffer over time if there are cracks or defects in the glaze, allowing water to penetrate the clay body causing spalling, cracking or salt efflorescence. Iron rods or cramps were often used to fix the ceramic blocks, and these will rust and expand if they become wet. The mortar joints between terracotta blocks are another source of problems, particularly as the impervious surface of terracotta (especially glazed types) increases rainfall run-off. *Practical Building Conservation 2: Brick, Terracotta and Earth* (see Further Reading, p.259) contains detailed information on repair materials and techniques.

The bright colour, smooth surface and apparent toughness of terracotta suggest that it should be easy to clean, but there have been several instances of irreparable damage being done to the material by inappropriate cleaning. The use of any kind of abrasive method (including carborundum discs, air abrasives and scrubbing with metal-bristle brushes), acids, or high-pressure water lances is very damaging to the glazes and the fireskin of terracotta blocks. At present, according to English Heritage, the only absolutely safe method of cleaning glazed or unglazed terracotta is with warm water, neutral pH liquid soap and a plastic pot scourer, but this is unlikely to removed all soiling. If in doubt, leave well alone.

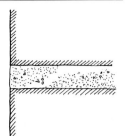

*Section through original flush-pointed brickwork bed joint.*

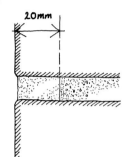

20mm

*Section through carefully repointed brickwork bed joint, after raking out to a minimum depth of 20mm.*

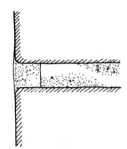

*Badly repointed brickwork: the mortar has been smeared over the rounded edges of the weathered bricks to create a flush surface.*

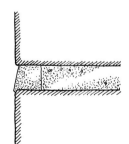

*Badly repointed brickwork: 'weatherstruck' pointing stands proud of the brick surface and casts a shadow that emphasizes the pointing at the expense of the brick.*

# 5

# STONE

T HE COMPLEX GEOLOGY of the United Kingdom is rich in good workable stones, a wealth fully exploited by Victorian architects and masons. The dignity and status that only stone, 'the aristocrat of building materials', can confer certainly constituted a large part of its appeal to the nineteenth-century house builder.

Before the mid-nineteenth century, stone was so difficult to extract and transport – carriage often costing more than the stone itself – that it was not usually carried very far from the quarry. Strong local traditions grew up of building with particular stones in the areas where they were found: granite in Scotland and Cornwall, sandstone in Yorkshire, flint in East Anglia, limestone in the Cotswolds and so on, and these regional loyalties were remarkably persistent.

In the nineteenth century, however, new technology applied to quarrying, stone-cutting and transport made it easier than ever to build with stone in all parts of the kingdom. By the turn of the century all the activities of the stonemason's yard, apart from carving, were mechanized. Many standard items such as sills, mouldings and copings were available dressed and ready for use direct from the quarry. Buying in this way was much cheaper and encouraged suburban builders to incorporate large amounts of stone into their speculative housing.

The brickmaking industry benefited from similar technological improvements in the same period, to the extent that brick supplanted stone as the most common masonry walling material throughout the country. Nevertheless, demand for stone actually increased after 1860. Its high status ensured that it continued to be used for country houses, and large quantities were required to provide decorative details that would lend something of the same cachet to houses lower down the social scale. Stefan Muthesius has observed that 'dressed stone decoration became universal, even for small houses', and some stone was also required in every house for those parts of the basic structure that could not be made in brick or any other material.

Loudon specified slate, a metamorphic rock found in the West Country, the Lake District and, most famously, Wales, for skirting and roofing. Because it splits easily, it was used for flat elements such as paving, steps, sills, shelves, hearths and chimney-pieces. A layer of slate was often incorporated into the wall about 1 foot (300mm) above ground level to provide a damp-proof course. Slate used in this way is often found to have cracked, and other measures have to be taken, if necessary, to deal with damp. The principal use of slate in Victorian houses was for roofing, and further information on this is given in Chapter 7, Roofs.

ABOVE: *detailed carved stone decoration on the window bay of a house in Tyndall's Park, a Bristol suburb of the 1860s.*

OPPOSITE: *squared rubble blocks in random courses contrast with smoothly-dressed window surrounds and porch on this house of about 1860.*

*Humble, local materials and traditional techniques were often used with great skill by Victorian builders. This cottage in Sheringham, Norfolk, is built of pebble flint with brickwork. Chips of flint are 'galletted' (bedded in the mortar) to emphasize the contrasting brick courses.*

The other principal British building stones are varieties of limestone, granite and sandstone. The two main ways of using them in masonry walling are ashlar and rubble. 'Ashlar' is the term used for closely-jointed, squared-off blocks of stone with a smooth surface finish. It may not be solid all the way through the wall, often consisting of thin sheets of stone applied to a core of brick or rubble, which give the appearance of solid stone at a fraction of the cost. Ashlar is often used contrasted with other textures, for example above a rusticated basement, or in quoins and window and door surrounds in a brick wall. This type of stonework is associated with the flat planes, accurate geometry and symmetry of classical architecture, and was much used by Victorian architects for Italianate villas and formal town houses.

Rubble work uses stone in its natural, unworked state. The harder building stones are often used in this way to save the effort of cutting and dressing them. Rubble can be used entirely randomly, although it is logical for the larger stones to be used lower down the wall. It may be 'brought to courses' (laid to arrive at the same level after every six, ten or twelve courses), and it can be laid in more or less regular courses, with larger pieces roughly squared on their top and bottom sides. Rubble work is an economical kind of masonry because it does not require skilled labour to prepare the stone and because there is no wastage: it uses all the stone brought out of the quarry, no matter how small or misshapen. It appealed to Victorian architects for its picturesque and 'homely' qualities. For P.F. Robinson, choosing rubble for 'humble dwellings' was both a socio-economic and aesthetic statement. In *True Principles*, Pugin suggested that using small, irregular stones was 'the strongest mode of construction' and counted this as another good reason for copying medieval building practices. Thirty years later, the aesthetic argument predominated once more, Kerr declaring that 'rough stone, and this perhaps of a variety of colours' was 'quite in character' for houses in the Gothic style.

Flint walling is rather a special case. Flint is found in chalky soils, especially in East Anglia, the South Downs and along the South Coast. It occurs in lumpy, chalk-coated nodules, which have to be split open or 'knapped' to reveal the dark grey, smooth and glassy interior. A skilled knapper can chip away at the edges of the flint to square off the edges, but in most domestic buildings the flints are used as they come to make a rubble wall faced with the smooth sides of the split flints. Bricks or stones are used to make straight edges where these are required at corners and openings. There is a high proportion of mortar to stone in a flint wall, and to build or repair flint masonry requires great skill.

The persistence of local traditions gave a distinctive character to Victorian towns and cities in stone-building areas. Many Glasgow tenement buildings were constructed of warm red sandstone, and Aberdeen is famous for its granite buildings, but neither of these materials is used in similar quantity south of the border. Granite is so hard to work that it tends to be used in large blocks which, together with its sombre grey colour, convey a brooding monumentality that can be oppressive – although the little flecks of mica in the stone sparkle delightfully when they catch the light after a shower of rain. The difficulty of working this very hard stone accounts for features such as crow-step gables, which are characteristic of 'Scottish baronial' houses: the stepped form could be achieved with the minimum of cutting. Granite from Scotland, and the paler Cornish variety, can be found as kerbstones in Victorian streets throughout Britain. It was also chosen for hard-wearing paving on quays and around the trapdoors of pub cellars, as the only paving tough enough to stand up to the constant trundling of heavy barrows and barrels.

The sharp and simple mouldings on Victorian houses in Yorkshire and Nottinghamshire bear witness to the difficulty of working sandstone. Millstone grit, a variety of carboniferous sandstone found in the north of England, was used extensively for the back-to-back houses of millworkers in Yorkshire and Lancashire. The more carefully considered housing of Saltaire, West Yorkshire, was built of a local variety of ochre-coloured sandstone.

Bristol is notable for its stone houses. Pennant sandstone is used extensively for rubble walling in the Victorian houses surrounding the Georgian heart of Clifton, and there is much high quality carving in the golden-coloured, close-grained Bath stone, which was readily available from several local quarries. The Victorian suburbs of Redland, Bishopston and Horfield are full of interesting examples of decorative stonework from the second half of the nineteenth century.

*Local availability of good-quality building stone shows in the ornamentation of several of the Victorian suburbs of Bristol; the carved panels on these houses illustrate* Aesop's *Fables.*

Stone was imported to parts of Britain that had no good building stone of their own, and used for decorative details and elements such as quoins and openings, window bays, doorcases and porches. Houses in classical style had stone in rusticated or vermiculated quoins, parapets, flattened doors and window pediments, and columns. 'Elizabethan' houses had stone drip moulds over the window and Tudor roses carved in the spandrels of their four-centred arched doorcases. Gothic Revival houses were given stone window tracery, crow-step gables and even gargoyles. While early nineteenth-century architects preferred the pale smoothness of white Portland stone, which complemented their chaste neo-classical designs, the mid-century fashion for polychromy created a demand for more richly coloured stonework. In his essay 'The Lamp of Truth', Ruskin asserted that 'The true colours of architecture are those of natural stone, and I would fain see these taken advantage of to the full. Every variety of hue, from pale yellow to purple, passing through orange, red, and brown, is entirely at our command; nearly every kind of green and grey is also attainable; and with these, and pure white, what harmonies might we not achieve?' The influence of Ruskin's writings can also be seen in the naturalistic garlands of flowers carved on window lintels and in the twining strawberry-leaf capitals of porch pillars. Other publications had a more direct practical influence. Owen Jones's *Plans, Elevations, Sections and Details of the Alhambra* (1836–45) furnished inspiration for Moorish interlacings, and choice motifs were lifted straight from the detailed engravings of medieval churches in Rickman's *Gothic Architecture*, Paley's 'practical little treatise on Gothic Mouldings' or Bloxam's popular handbook, *Principles of Gothic Ecclesiastical Architecture*.

Several patents for artificial stone were taken out in the nineteenth century. Most of them involved mixing Portland cement with brick or stone dust, and pressing the mixture into a mould to cast an imitation of dressed or carved stone. Gwilt's *Encyclopaedia of Architecture* (1888) lists several, including Austin's Artificial Stone (patented in 1838), used for 'statues, garden ornaments and chimney shafts', and Ransome's Siliceous Stone (1844) and Concrete Stone (1861), used for 'cast ornaments and moulded work'.

## Maintenance and repair

Keeping rainwater goods clean and repaired, controlling vegetation, protecting iron fixings with a coat of paint to prevent rust and maintaining joints with small pointing repairs as necessary will help to keep stonework in good condition, reducing repair bills in the long run. Neglect is not the only cause of problems, however. Because it became so easy for builders without specialist mason's knowledge to obtain stone, they did not always use it wisely. Many examples of Victorian stonework, particularly from the last quarter of the nineteenth century, now need repair to rectify 'built-in' problems.

Decay and damage to stone can be caused by a number of factors. Some problems are purely cosmetic, while others have serious structural implications. It is important to establish the nature of the materials you have to deal with: what kind of stone (or artificial stone), how it is used, and whether it is solid stone masonry or used in combination with other materials. Although strong, artificial stones are usually quite brittle, they weather differently from natural stones and may react differently to chemical treatment.

Next, analyze the nature of the problem. Among the most common causes of damage and decay factors are weathering, that is, erosion, flaking or exfoliation caused by atmospheric pollution or an aggressive climate, structural movement or settling, and water penetration, caused by rising damp, penetrating damp (driving rain) or poor

*Illustrations in Victorian architectural histories were a rich source for carved stone ornament. These late thirteenth-century diaper patterns are from the 1862 edition of Thomas Rickman's* Gothic Architecture.

*The romantic appeal of these Tudor style, mid-nineteenth-century cottages in Gloucestershire is enhanced by climbing plants, but climbers and creepers must be kept in check to safeguard the stone masonry.*

maintenance of gutters and rainwater goods. As moisture moves through the stone, it carries dissolved mineral salts. As the stone dries out, the salts crystallize, appearing as white 'blooms' (efflorescence) on the surface, or even causing pitting, powdering or flaking of the stone itself. Poor original detailing may be responsible for some problems: lintels that are too thin will crack; copper flashings used above limestone will cause run-off staining of the stone; iron cramps or window fittings fixed into the stone will rust and expand, causing stones to crack or joints to open up. The masonry may need repointing, especially if it is in a very exposed area, or if it has been covered with climbing plants, such as ivy, which have air roots that invade mortar joints. Even well-intentioned previous repairs can cause problems if they are carried out with the wrong materials or techniques, for example repointing with mortar that is too hard and causes cracking. There are also 'man-made' problems, including vandalism by spray painting, scratching and scraping stone or breaking off sculpted elements, and theft of decorative finials and garden ornaments.

Fortunately, the materials and skills exist to solve most of the problems likely to occur in stonework of the 'average' Victorian house. When considering whether to repair, replace or clean stonework, you need to consider the following:

• Will the repair work be in keeping with the age and style of the building? In particular, be cautious about stripping historic paint, plaster or render off stone walls to 'reveal the natural beauty of the stone', regardless of the quality of what is revealed. This applies as much to interiors as exteriors. 'Costwold cave syndrome' has damaged many fine Victorian and older buildings by uncovering inferior stone and workmanship that was never meant to be on show. In the nineteenth century even the humblest larder or privy was carefully plastered and whitewashed, and it is inconceivable that a Victorian family would have consented to dine or sit in a room with bare stone walls.

• Structural soundness. All buildings settle over time, so a slight variation from the perpendicular is to be expected in houses more than a century old, and probably does not require treatment. On the other hand, bulging walls, large cracks in masonry blocks or blocks pulling apart from one another may indicate subsidence or some other serious structural problem, and should be investigated by a suitably qualified surveyor or structural engineer.

- The root cause of the problem: is it in the stonework itself? Problems with damp, in particular, are often due to poorly detailed or inadequately maintained rainwater goods, by leaking roofs or plumbing, or by inadequate or blocked ventilation. It is pointless to spend time, effort and money on masonry repairs without eliminating the source of the problem.
- The finished appearance. This applies particularly where old stone is cleaned or new stone is used for patch repairs, and where walls are repointed.

Before starting any repair work, plan and budget for materials, labour and the extras associated with large-scale repairs to heavy materials. Hiring scaffolding, ladders and lifting gear for heavy masonry blocks adds greatly to the cost of stone repairs. Some cleaning processes require protective sheeting and special arrangements for the disposal of waste and run-off. Special permission may be required if footpaths or pavements have to be closed while the work is going on.

## Cleaning

In many cases the softening effect of a little dirt on the surface of the stone gives a pleasing sense of age. It deepens the shadows in carved or moulded stonework to good effect and helps the building blend in with its neighbours that have aged in the same way. A light spotting of lichen can be attractive and does no harm as long as it is kept in check. It has even been said that limestone is almost 'self-cleaning', since it is slightly soluble in acid rain, although excessive pollution leads to the formation of black sulphate crusts.

If you do decide to clean stonework, it is important to specify the kind of final result you want. It is easy to end up with a patchy or 'scrubbed' appearance through

*Brick quoins make it easy to achieve a strong, sharp angle at the corner of a stone wall. Here, repointing with strong, cement-based mortar mix has driven moisture out through the softer stone, causing it to flake away.*

uneven or over-enthusiastic cleaning. Whatever cleaning method is chosen, it should be applied to a test patch on an unobtrusive part of the building. Time should be allowed for this to dry out thoroughly and be assessed in all lights before the go-ahead is given for the process to be repeated over the whole building.

### Washing

The simplest method of cleaning stone, and one that works well on limestone and marble, is to dampen the surface of the stone with a fine spray of clean water, brush off the loosened dirt and rinse the stone clean. This will remove loose dirt, bird droppings and so forth, and may be sufficient to freshen the appearance of the stonework. It is important not to saturate the stone: too much water, or water used at too great a pressure, can cause uneven cleaning, staining, loss of mortar and damp. The ideal is a 'mist' or 'fog' of fine water droplets covering the soiled surface. Brushes should be made of natural bristles, or have bristles of bronze wire – never steel, which is too harsh and may cause rust stains. A water lance may be used to deliver water at high pressure, or water and fine aggregate at low pressure, but this should be used with particular care, as both methods can erode soft stone.

*The village of Edensor, on the Chatsworth Estate in Derbyshire, consists of high-quality stone houses designed by John Robertson in the early 1840s.*

## Mechanical/abrasion

Another approach is to rub the dirt off the surface of the stone using an abrasive. Compressed air or water containing calcite, glass bead, sand, grit slag or aluminium oxide powder (chosen according to the type of stone and the nature of the dirt) is blasted onto the stone. Both methods are messy, the 'dry' method in particular creating a lot of potentially hazardous dust. Operatives must wear protective clothing, including an 'air-line' helmet, and the site must be properly protected with screens and plastic sheeting. Windows and doors should be taped up; even so, some dust will get into the building, and the noise of pressurized air and water can be a problem.

There is a risk with all abrasives that some of the stone will be lost along with the dirt, leaving a pitted and vulnerable surface. Soft areas of stone will wear away more easily than hard. For this reason, abrasive discs should never be used to clean stone.

## Other cleaning methods

Chemical cleaners, such as pH neutral soap or very weak solutions of hydrofluoric acid, can be used on sandstone and unpolished granite. Various poultices are useful, especially for localized staining. Relatively new developments include laser techniques, used in conservation laboratories on fine stonework such as sculpture.

It should be clear from the above descriptions that cleaning stone is not a DIY job. All the available methods are messy, require specialized equipment and training, and have serious health and safety implications. Specialist contractors should be hired, and their work closely supervised at all times. An excellent summary of the available methods and their applications is contained in Chapter 5 of *Practical Building Conservation Volume 1: Stone Masonry* (see Further Reading, p.259).

### *Removing plant growth*

To remove moss, lichen or small plants, brush the stone with a bristle brush or plastic scraper to remove loose material. You can then spray the wall with a proprietary biocide applied with a garden spray or hose with spray attachment. Dilute the mix according to the manufacturer's instructions and wear protective clothing, a mask, gloves and goggles. Do not spray in strong winds, or near people or animals, and protect plants and grass growing beneath the building. Start at the top of the wall, covering the entire surface in a series of overlapping horizontal passes. After a few days, brush off the dead and dying material. It may be necessary to repeat the treatment until the wall is completely clear of vegetation.

Ivy and other clinging creepers look attractive on a stone wall but can do a great deal of damage, as much by concealing incipient problems and preventing regular maintenance as by penetrating masonry joints. Buddleia protruding from a parapet or rainwater head is a sure sign that maintenance has been neglected. Although few things are more satisfying than pulling large pieces of vegetation off an overgrown wall, the temptation to rush should be resisted, as you can easily pull out large chunks of masonry with the roots of well-established plants. It is much better to prune until you can see what you are doing and address each stem or root separately.

To kill ivy, cut it back to a main stem and allow it to wither before pulling it gently off the wall. Ivy stumps should be painted with a biocidal 'stump killer' paste to prevent regrowth. If you want to grow a climbing plant over a stone wall, choose plants that will not penetrate the masonry, such as roses or wisteria. Support the plant on wires trained through vine eyes that stand proud of the masonry surface, or on a trellis. These allow the surface of the wall to be ventilated and to dry out after rain.

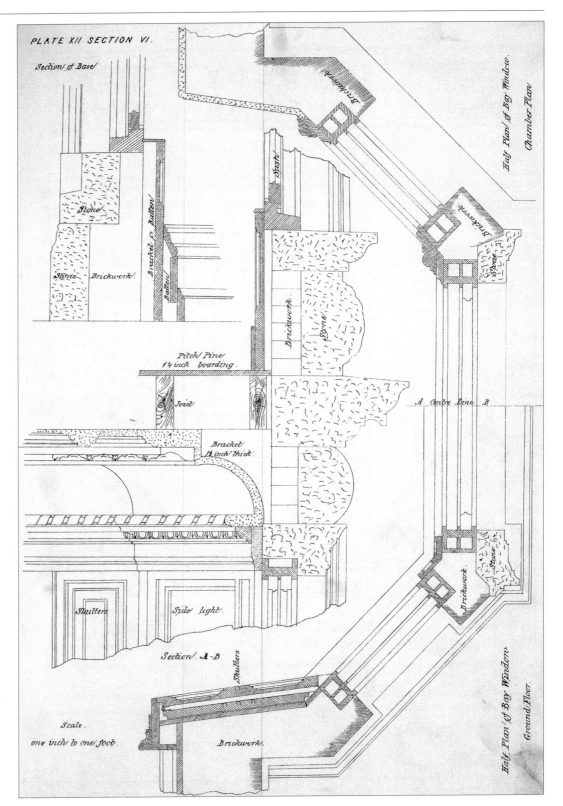

PLATE XII SECTION VI.

*A drawing of bay window construction from a builders' handbook of 1855 shows how brick construction was faced with stone for a handsome appearance at less cost. The projecting cornice shown in the centre of the page is angled slightly downwards, to throw off rainwater.*

### Repointing

Repointing should be done with a compatible mortar, mixed to match the ingredients, colour and texture of the original, and applied in a style that matches the original work. Special care must be taken when old mortar is removed, as it is easy to damage stone arrises and make joints wider than they should be. Detailed information about mortar mixes and pointing, much of which applies also to stone masonry, is given in Chapter 4, Brick and Terracotta. The general rule is that the finished pointing should be visually subordinate to the stone; when you look at the finished work, it is the shape, colour and texture of the stone that should dominate, not a network of cement lines standing proud of the surface. Careful repointing is especially important in rubble or flint walls, where there is a higher proportion of mortar to stone, and where particular skill is needed to avoid smearing the surface of the stone with mortar.

### *Masonry repair and replacement*

There are various techniques and materials that can be used to repair stone masonry, including removing rusted iron cramps and replacing them with stainless steel, repairing with mortar patches, redressing existing stones, and inserting new stones. Rubble walls can be stabilized if necessary by grouting, that is, filling voids within the thickness of the wall with liquid mortar, which bonds the internal stones of the wall together as it dries.

Sometimes it is necessary to cut out old stones completely and replace them with new. This applies particularly to structurally important stones or those that support or protect other elements (for example, copings, quoins, lintels and voussoirs) and have become too decayed or damaged to function properly. New stones should match the originals as closely as possible. They can be fixed into place with mortar, or pinned using stainless steel dowels and resin cement, before being pointed to match the surrounding work. Although new stones may present a patchwork appearance initially, they will weather to blend in with the original work surprisingly quickly, so it is not necessary to artificially dirty or 'distress' them.

All stone repairs require expert advice and workmanship. Some books and organizations that may be helpful in sourcing new stone and finding masons with appropriate skills and experience are listed in Further Reading, p.259 and Useful Addresses, p.266.

### *Protective finishes*

Gloss paint was a traditional finish for the sills, lintels and steps of houses in some parts of northern Britain, and limewash continued to be used on vernacular stone buildings in the Victorian period, but where exterior stonework appears in its natural state, it is best left that way. It is not a good idea to seal stone with proprietary water-repellent sealants: these alter the appearance of the stone, may discolour or peel over time, and can actually cause problems by trapping moisture within the wall and prevent the natural process of evaporation necessary to keep the wall from becoming damp. English Heritage have, however, acknowledged that silicone-, silane- or silicon-ester-based water repellents may be useful in extremely exposed sites, and to protect brickwork from staining limestone dressings.

# RENDER, STUCCO AND TILE-HANGING

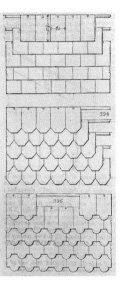

ABOVE: *Tile-hanging patterns from Loudon's* Encyclopaedia of Cottage, Farm and Villa Architecture *(1833).*

OPPOSITE: *an early Victorian house in West London. The stucco on the ground floor was built up around narrow timber battens which were removed once the stucco had dried, leaving 'incised' lines that imitate fine ashlar masonry.*

RENDER IS A GENERAL TERM for various kinds of plaster or cement coating applied in two or three layers to the external wall of a building. It can be used as an attractive building material in its own right, to protect the masonry from the weather, to provide a neat finish which will take a coat of paint if required, to cover poor workmanship, or to disguise cheap building materials. Used throughout the British Isles, its form varies according to climate, availability of materials and local traditions; the 'harling' of Scotland, the Welsh 'roughcast' and the pargeting of Essex and Suffolk are all types of render.

Before 1800 most renders were based on lime putty (see Chapter 4, Brick and Terracotta), to which animal hair or other fibres might be added for reinforcement, or sand and other aggregates for different textures. The 'weakness' and permeability of these lime-based mixtures were seen as disadvantages in the British climate, and various attempts were made to improve their strength and durability. In the eighteenth century it was discovered that certain limestone deposits containing a large proportion of clay could be used as the basis for much stronger, quick-setting cements. James Parker patented one of the first of these so-called 'Roman' cements in 1794; the name, with its helpful implications of nobility and durability, was suggested by the pinkish-brown colour, similar to the hue of render traditionally used in Italy. Several new formulas for 'artificial' cements, which involved adding clay to crushed limestone or chalk, were developed in the early nineteenth century. In 1811 James Frost patented the first artificial hydraulic cement, and in 1824 Joseph Aspdin took out a patent for the first Portland cement. Again, the name of the new product was suggested by its colour – a pale whitish-grey – thought to resemble Portland stone (and again, no doubt, the manufacturers were happy to exploit the association between the Portland name and dignified stone architecture). Aspdin's son William had cement works at Gateshead and on the Thames, from where in 1845 he supplied the cement for Osborne, the royal family's country house on the Isle of Wight. Isaac Johnson of Rochester improved the Aspdin recipe, and by 1852 had arrived at a formula virtually the same as that still used in making Portland cement today.

Roughcast is render with coarse aggregate such as gravel mixed in to make a porridge-like mix, which is thrown onto the wall where it sticks (similar to the twentieth-century variant, pebbledash). Its lumpy texture increases the surface area of the wall, thereby reducing rain penetration and providing a larger surface area from which water can evaporate once the rain has stopped.

A little stucco goes a long way towards creating the Tudor character of de Beauvoir Square, an early Victorian suburb in Hackney.

Stucco is external render with a smooth surface applied in deliberate imitation of fine stonework. Applied in three coats, each one is thinner and smoother than the previous one, and is finished with a wooden float to achieve a perfectly flat surface. It can be built up between timber laths fixed to the wall; the grooves left behind when the laths are removed mimic the wide joints between large blocks of stone. Stucco can also be scored to look like finely jointed ashlar, moulded for string courses and cornices, or incised with reed or key patterns. It has practical advantages besides its obvious role as a protective layer for masonry: white-painted stucco around doors and windows reflects light into the openings, and can disguise awkward joins where a bay window meets the front wall of the house.

As a cheap way of lending the appearance of stone masonry to brick and rubble walls, stucco was enthusiastically adopted by Regency architects, most notably John Nash, who applied it to the Gothic villas and classical terraces he built in and around Regent's Park in the 1820s. Although Robert Kerr disapproved, they were very influential. Starting in 1826, the young George Basevi used stucco for the dignified palace fronts of the terraces that make up Belgrave Square, built by Thomas Cubitt, who also used stucco for Eaton Square. Developments such as these established the conventional 'wedding-cake' house front that dominated the London townscape for the next thirty years. The repetitive, white-painted terraces of houses in Bayswater, Knightsbridge and Kensington bear witness to the longevity of the taste for stucco. Every other town has its share of Victorian stuccoed houses. Coastal towns in particular adopted stucco because of the extra protection it afforded from sea winds. Older resorts such as Brighton or Teignmouth were merely continuing a custom established in the Regency period; the towns that sprang up in the mid-nineteenth century to provide the newly-leisured middle classes with seaside holidays, such as Bridlington, Llandudno, Rhyll and Shanklin, adopted stucco with fresh enthusiasm.

In many cases the use of stucco was confined to eye-catching details on otherwise plain brick house-fronts. Two developments in London – De Beauvoir Square, Hackney (W.C. Lockner, 1834) and Lonsdale Square, Islington (R.C. Carpenter, 1837) – showed how window and door surrounds, gable edgings and drip moulds picked out in white stucco could endow a terrace or sequence of fairly standard urban houses with 'medieval' character.

The standard-issue townhouses of the Phillimore Estate, Kensington, built in the 1860s and 1870s, are distinguished by a clever use of stucco, which occurs wherever there is a feature – parapet, window frame, pillared porch or balustered balcony – that might draw the eye away from the background walling. The front elevation at basement and first-floor level is also stuccoed, in imitation of ashlar blocks. At street level the passer-by gains an impression of monumental stone masonry, which is only dispelled if an upward glance reveals the underlying yellow London brick of the upper storeys. This was a necessary deception, since the houses were destined for middle-class professionals who would not have bought houses made from humble, unadorned brick. Eastlake, faithful to the doctrine of honest construction, must have had houses such as these in mind when he lamented that 'Not only is plaster or cement used as a covering for inferior brickwork, but it is boldly employed for columns, parapets, and veranda balusters in place of stone. It is not at all an uncommon thing to see a would-be Doric or Corinthian shaft shorn of its base, and actually hanging to the side of a house until the pedestal (which, of course, will also be of cement) is completed. Plaster brackets support plaster pediments: stucco bas-reliefs are raised upon a stucco ground.' But even he had grudgingly to admit that they could often be 'palaces of comfort within'.

From about 1860 stucco gradually began to give way to 'truthful' materials. Mechanized manufacture and railway transport meant that builders everywhere could obtain real stone, good quality brick and the newly fashionable moulded and glazed terracotta. Once these 'real' materials became so cheap, there was no longer any need to resort to fakery. It was only by shedding its pretensions that render could become respectable again as a homely, vernacular building material in its own right.

The unpretentious qualities of render were thoughtfully exploited in the second half of the nineteenth century by Arts and Crafts architects, who loved roughcast for its softness, texture and vernacular associations. Though he made his name as an architect

*Drum-shaped window bays are enlivened by some rather meagre stucco detailing of the kind deplored by Pugin, who railed against 'the resistless torrent of the Roman-cement men, who buy their ornaments by the yard, and their capitals by the ton'.*

*Eaton Square, central London, was begun by Thomas Cubitt in 1826 but not completed until the year of his death, 1855.*

of large country houses, George Devey studied vernacular architecture and traditional building crafts in close detail, and used this knowledge in designs for cottages, lodges and ancillary buildings on his clients' estates. A pair of cottages at Penshurst, Kent, designed by Devey in 1850, have roughcast render at first-floor level, sandwiched between a ground floor of local ragstone and a steeply-pitched roof of clay tiles and weatherboarded gables. This work blended in so well with the genuine old cottages of the neighbourhood that it was difficult to tell which were new.

Devey's work inspired the next generation of architects, including Shaw and Nesfield. Shaw, the most influential of the Queen Anne architects, loved to contrast smooth render with undulating tile-hung walls, or roughcast with fine rubbed brick. In the semi-detached houses he designed for Bedford Park, West London, in 1877–8, he lightened the dominant red brick of the estate by using roughcast on coving, gables and window bays. Such combinations of render with timber, brick, stone and tile were copied in late-Victorian suburbs everywhere, for cheap and instant 'picturesqueness'.

C.F.A. Voysey, who worked in Devey's office at the start of his career, liked render, because 'A 9-in. brick wall, rough cast, was the cheapest weathertight wall that could be built'. So many of Voysey's houses of the 1890s, whether large country houses, new cottages for agricultural labourers, or his own house, The Orchard, at Chorleywood, Hertfordshire, were covered in roughcast that it can be considered an absolute hallmark of his work. In 1897 H.H. Statham outlined some of the aesthetic advantages of combining roughcast with brick or stone: 'it can be compounded of various colours, such as will harmonize with various tones of stone or brick, and it has a more effective surface, with more texture, than the smoother surface formed by the ordinary cement or plaster finish.'

The 'rediscovery' of these traditional renders was, inevitably, accompanied by attempts to achieve the appearance of hand-raised plaster decoration by cheaper, mechanical means. 'Stamped work' was a form of relief-patterned render used to adorn gables and front walls on mass-produced houses in many Victorian suburbs. Made with a very hard mixture of 5 parts of Portland cement to 2 parts lime and 2 parts sand, it was smoothed onto the wall in panels and then patterned with an incised stamp.

*This design for a house by Edgar Wood (1898) illustrates how Arts and Crafts architects reintroduced rendered finishes into the repertoire of respectable building materials by exploiting its vernacular origins.*

## Tile-hanging

Tile-hanging is an external wall covering of clay tiles hung on battens, often in combinations of shapes to make decorative patterns. Sometimes employed over an entire wall, it is more usually restricted to the upper floors, a bay window, a gable or the side walls of a porch. The technique was traditionally used in those parts of the country where clay tiles were made, notably East Anglia and the Home Counties. A variation found in Devon and Cornwall used local slates cut to diamond or scallop shapes. Loudon illustrated several variations of tile-hanging in the section of his *Encyclopaedia* devoted to 'Cottage Dwellings', remarking that 'It is very common to have two, three or more courses of ornamental tiles separated by a row of plain ones, which has a good effect.' The use of tile-hanging was restricted to vernacular or consciously picturesque buildings, and it hardly appears in mid-nineteenth-century urban and suburban housing. By the 1870s the association between tile-hanging and rural cottages was being explored by Shaw and his contemporaries, who added tile-hanging to their repertoire of picturesque effects. The technique crept into town from Surrey via the 'artistic' houses of Bedford Park, and by the 1880s no high-class suburban development was without its tile-hung gables or bays – an economical way of adding a fashionable touch of individuality to otherwise standardized designs.

*A Devon variant of tile-hanging is the use of cut slate in decorative patterns. This example is from Kingsbridge.*

## Maintenance and repair

Poorly mixed or wrongly applied renders tend to fail within months, but renders made with appropriate ingredients and applied in the right way can last a long time, only failing eventually because of external factors such as damp, building movement or inappropriate

77

*Scalloped shapes predominate in this attractively-weathered clay tile hanging on a house in Bedford Park, West London, designed by Shaw in the late 1870s.*

maintenance. The sudden failure of a Victorian render that has lasted well until recently needs to be investigated and rectified as soon as possible, both for the sake of the building's appearance and to preserve the protection the render gives to the underlying structure.

Damp is a common cause of problems. All masonry will absorb water in wet conditions and dry out again when conditions improve. Render needs to be able to 'breathe' with the wall so water within the wall can evaporate. Water trapped within the masonry will freeze and expand in cold weather, or cause salts within the masonry and mortar to swell until the render is blown off the wall. Leaking gutters, burst pipes and floods need to be remedied before any repairs to render are undertaken, as the damage will only recur if the underlying problem remains. Damp may also be trapped within the wall by recent repairs with the wrong kind of mortar or render, or by a new coat of impermeable paint. Lime-based renders have sufficient flexibility to cope with ordinary building settlement, so cracks and bulges appearing in the render of a previously sound, dry wall need to be investigated by a structural surveyor or engineer.

When repairing render, it is important to retain as much of the original material as possible. Where a patch of render needs to be replaced, take back the edges until you reach sound material with good adhesion to the wall. If the patch is large, continue stripping the render until you reach the nearest natural break in the covering – which could be a scoreline between 'blocks' of stucco, the edge where an infill panel of plaster meets part of a timber frame, or a corner of a roughcast building. This makes it easier to disguise the new work, as it is impossible to make an invisible join without any bump or shadow where new plaster meets old.

It is important to match any new render to the original material. A visual match is not the only consideration. The new material must match the old not only in texture, colour and thickness, but also in composition, flexibility and porosity. If an old lime render is patched with a hard modern cement, water which cannot evaporate through the modern material will be driven out through the old, causing it to fail at the edge of the repair. Brittle renders will crack, allowing water to enter and cause problems with damp. In the early nineteenth century lime mortar was used, perhaps with earth pigments such as ochre added to make a range of stone colours. By the 1850s, as we have seen, builders were starting to use Portland cement, often with a little lime in the mix to improve its elasticity. Most stucco can be repaired with the following mixes:

- base coat: lime putty/sand 1:2½; top coat lime putty/sand 1:3, or
- base coat: OPC/lime/sand 1:2:9; top coat 1:3:12

Thanks to the recent revival of interest in traditional building materials and methods, building lime is now easily obtainable. 'Roman' cement is no longer available, but a good match can be achieved with coloured sands and hydraulic lime mixed to match the original material. Remember that a wet mix will become paler as it dries; it may be necessary to experiment with different types of sand, and to allow time for each sample to dry thoroughly in order to achieve a good match.

A conservation architect or builder with experience of old houses should be able to identify the type of render you have and recommend suitable mixes and aggregates for the repair material. Detailed guidance is contained in English Heritage's and the SPAB's excellent publications (see Further Reading, p.259).

The wall surface should be clean and sound, and brushed free of any loose material before re-rendering begins. This is also the moment to check the condition of the masonry and to carry out any repairs that may be needed. Pointing should be raked out, or the wall surface scored to provide a key for the render. Features such as door and window openings, flashings and lean-to roofs should be protected from splashes and drips with plastic sheeting before work starts. The wall should be wetted to receive the new render; this prevents the dry wall from sucking out too much water from the mix and weakening the render. The first, or 'laying-on' coat of render, is applied and scratched before it has dried to give a key for subsequent coats, which are thrown or, if a smooth finish is desired, applied with a wooden float. In stucco work the top coat is scored or 'lined out' with a straight-edged rule while it is still wet and the excess smoothed away. If render dries too quickly it can shrink and crack, so the rate of drying should be controlled, especially in hot weather. Damp sacking hung over the newly-rendered wall, and screens to provide shelter in windy conditions, will help to slow down the drying process.

Roughcast was not usually painted, as the colour is integral to the material. A good basic mix for roughcast repairs is cement/lime/well graded aggregate and pebbles 1:2:8 or 9. Matching the size and colour of the aggregate is essential in roughcast repairs. Where roughcast has become stained or weathered so that the colour of the aggregate is showing through, it can be restored with a coat of limewash made with lime putty and water as described in the SPAB Information Sheet No.9 (see Further Reading, p.259). Any paints applied to old render should be permeable, so as not to trap moisture within the wall. Many renders derive their colour from the sand that formed part of the original mix. It is always better to match these by getting the right mix as described above; a superficial layer of paint will never be an exact match, and will eventually wear away, leaving a patchy appearance where the underlying material 'grins through'. If in doubt as to whether your house should be painted, seek the advice of a suitably qualified historic buildings consultant, or ask your conservation officer.

Render that was not self-coloured was painted. Stucco was usually painted with an oil-based paint. Modern taste decrees that it should be painted white or pale cream; such pale shades may even be specified in leases for particular addresses, to ensure a uniform appearance across a terrace or an estate. Since the point of using stucco was to make the house look as if it was made of stone, it is more logical and historically appropriate to choose a stone colour. Moreover, the bright brilliant white paint favoured (and sometimes specified in leases) today was not available to Victorian house-painters. However, this historical inaccuracy has to be balanced against the importance of achieving visual unity, and it is probably better to preserve a uniform appearance – and good relations with one's neighbours – than to be pedantic about colour. Where free choice is possible, take your colour from the palette of natural stone colours, ranging from creamy white through pale grey and honey to deep gold. The most convincing deceptions will be those that imitate locally available building stones. Branded 'exterior' paints containing cement should not be used, as they will alter the surface texture of the stucco and are unlikely to provide better protection than oil-based gloss paint applied to a properly prepared and undercoated surface.

If your house is not rendered, do not be tempted to apply a coat of render to 'smarten it up' or change its 'look'. Many Victorian houses have been irretrievably damaged by coats of 'Tyrolean' textured render, or stone cladding, which cannot be removed without damaging the underlying surface. Besides being historically inappropriate, such finishes can create problems by trapping damp inside the wall. Original materials and finishes are valued as authentic elements of historic buildings, and should always be preserved if possible. Altering them is likely to reduce the value of the house, as well as its historic interest.

### Typical patch mixes

These are examples of common patch mixes for render repairs, given for general guidance only. Consult an independent conservation architect or surveyor for advice on the exact mix that is right for any particular historic building.

### Lime plaster

base coat of lime putty/sand 1:2½

### Lime stucco

two coats of cement/lime/sand 1:2:9

### Roman cement

Render and floating coats masonry cement/sand 1:5½. Top coat hydraulic lime/brown and red sands 1:2½

### Roughcast (wet dash; harling)

Base coat lime/sand and hair 1:2½. Casting coat lime/sand and pea gravel 1:3, or Render coat hydraulic lime/aggregates 1:2½. Casting coat hydraulic lime/sand and pea gravel 1:3.

### Tile-hanging repairs

Tile-hanging develops similar problems to those that afflict tiled roofs (see Chapter 7, Roofs): decayed or loose battens, nail sickness, damage from the weather and from invasive creepers. Slipping tiles do not cling to the vertical surface for long, and decorative tile-hanging with tiles missing is particularly unsightly. If they are carefully removed, it should be possible to re-use most of them. Do not be alarmed if new tiles patched into old tile-hanging look garish to begin with. Like new bricks, they will weather to match their neighbours in a few years.

Replacement tiles should match the old exactly. The visual effect of hand-made tiles, with their individual shapes and imperfections, cannot be matched by machine-made tiles. Hand-made tiles cannot be fitted into geometrically-perfect patterns, and their undulations and variations are part of their charm. Particular attention should be paid to inner corners and the bottom edge of the tile-hung area, often supported from behind to achieve a bell-cast which throws rainwater clear of the wall below. Machine-made tiles, on the other hand, frequently found on post-1880 suburban houses, depend on accuracy and geometric perfection to achieve their desired effect.

# ROOFS

## HISTORY

In many early Victorian terraced houses the roof could not be seen from the street, but was hidden behind a parapet so that its sharp angles, ridges and gutters would not upset the rectilinear harmony of the classical façade. In terraced housing the party wall separating each house from its neighbour was extended upwards to enclose the flues that would otherwise clutter the roofline with separate chimneystacks and to support the rafters. The roof was at right angles to the façade and pitched down towards the centre of the each house in a V-shape. In the bottom of the V was a valley gutter, which drained into the parapet gutter at the front and straight into a downpipe at the back.

The elegant front elevation thus achieved came at a price. The V placed in the centre of the plan made it difficult to use the roof space, and the valley and parapet gutters were vulnerable to damage, which, because of their concealed location, might become quite severe before it was noticed. An alternative design aligned the ridge of the roof with the parapet, giving a usable loft space. If the roof was raised to a shallower pitch in the centre to make a 'mansard' cross-section, it became possible to insert attic rooms, with dormer windows looking out onto the parapet. Dormers seen from below were given an architectural treatment – segmental arches, pediments, or stucco surrounds supported on scrolled brackets – that related to the rest of the façade. In the absence of a valley gutter, the parapet gutter drained into a 'secret' gutter running under the attic floor to a downpipe in the centre of the rear elevation, thus avoiding the necessity for an unsightly downpipe at the front of the house.

An alternative roof type, brought into fashion by Nash and other Regency architects, had wide overhanging eaves derived from Italian villa prototypes (although in Britain the overhang proved more useful for throwing off rain than for giving shade). The outline of the roof remained simple: a low-pitched gabled or hipped shape supported at eaves level by deep decorative brackets springing from the walls. Kerr categorized such roofs as elements of the 'cottage style', which he tried to dismiss as an 'inferior sort of Rural-Italian', but later admitted had been 'extensively in vogue throughout the entire kingdom for many years, as the common model for small Country-Houses'.

Changing taste in the mid-century made the roof more visible, and Gothic architects began to make a positive feature of this part of the house, using hips and bays outlined with contrasting ridge tiles, gables on main and secondary roofs emphasized with crowsteps, scalloped bargeboards, terracotta crestings and cast iron finials. Novel

ABOVE: *perky dormers add to the rustic charm of a thatched roof on a pair of estate workers' cottages in Suffolk.*

OPPOSITE: *The complex, many-gabled roof of a Nottinghamshire vicarage, designed by the diocesan architect T.C. Hine in 1849, is typical of the Gothic Revival's delight in variety and asymmetry.*

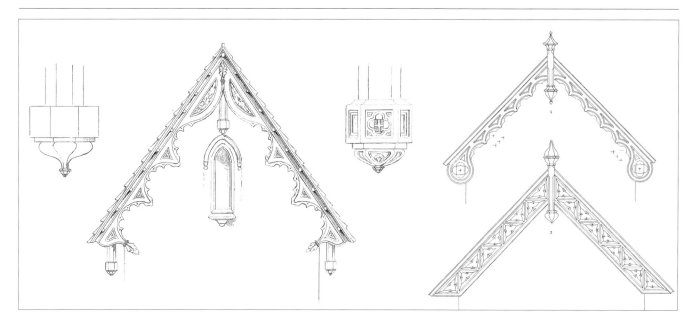

*Ornamental bargeboards: the example on the left, with finials, is by P.F. Robinson, who admired the 'fretted shadow produced on the face of the building ... very pleasing to the pictorial draughtsman'. On the right, 'Bargeboard (Gothic)' from a builder's handbook of 1855.*

shapes such as steep cones and pyramids were used as subsidiary roofs for staircases and water tanks at the corners of buildings. Roofs on Gothic houses often have barge-boards, long carved and moulded timbers that protect the exposed ends of the rafters at the gable eaves. These were fitted to gables on main roofs, dormer windows and porches, and had great decorative potential.

In the last quarter of the century plain clay-tiled roofs came back into fashion. Bright red roofs characterized the skyline of Bedford Park in West London, and were used in countless suburban villas and terraces in the 1880s and 1890s. Picturesque features like bell-cast eaves, catslide roofs and canted dormers were used to give individuality and a vernacular flavour to middle-class houses by Nesfield, Shaw and Voysey. Voysey liked to break up the eaves with dormer windows and make a feature of the gutter by carrying it across the front of dormers and supporting it on curved brackets of wrought iron, which emphasized the depth of the eaves as they sprang out from the walls. However, by far the most common type of roof throughout the Victorian period was the slate-covered, pitched roof.

### Roof coverings: slate

True slate is a metamorphic rock, making a tough, impermeable, quick-drying, frost- and pollution-resistant roof. Slate from North Wales, sometimes referred to as Bangor or Portmadoc slate, splits into smooth-faced, thin sheets of blue, purple or greenish-grey colour. They are dressed to standard sizes, most commonly 24 x 12 inches (610 x 300mm). Although much has been made of the romantic names traditionally given to the different sizes (princesses, duchesses, countesses and so forth), and these names were used in nineteenth-century specifications, slates nowadays tend to be prosaically specified by their dimensions. North Wales slate sheds rain very easily and can therefore be used on roofs of lower pitch. This made it ideal for the discreet parapet designs favoured early in the century, and it was used in London from about 1800. It makes neat, regular but rather characterless roofs, which many contemporary architects found unattractive. Later architectural writers, notably Alec Clifton-Taylor, have been very critical of the monotonous appearance of these roofs, which show slate 'in its least attractive guise'. On the other hand, the slates were readily available, easy to use and cheaper than tiles, and so found a ready market among speculative builders putting up standardized, mass-produced housing.

Westmorland slate, found in Cumbria, has a more grainy texture and is green or dark blue. Thicker and less uniformly flat than North Wales slate, it repels water rather better. It was supplied in random sizes, which the roofer would sort and use in diminishing courses, with the larger slates at eaves level and the smallest at the top of the roof. This meant that the part of the roof receiving the greatest amount of rainwater run-off had the best protection, while the weight of the bigger slates was carried by the external walls. Architects admired the colour, texture and character of Westmorland slate: it was used by William Burges on his own house in Melbury Road, Kensington in 1882, where its texture and beautiful grey-green aqueous colours are in striking contrast to those used on the neighbouring houses. Slates from Cornwall (Delabole) and South Wales were supplied in random sizes like Westmorland slate, but have a rather less grainy texture, a flatter, smoother surface, and are dark grey tinged with green.

## Tiles

Clay tiles are a traditional roof covering in the East of England, particularly in the south-east (notably London, Kent and Surrey), East Anglia, Lincolnshire and Yorkshire. Plain clay tiles, or peg tiles, are rectangular slabs of unglazed clay with a slightly convex shape that helps them to throw off rainwater. The back of the tile has two moulded projections, called 'nibs', which hang over battens on the roof and help to hold the tiles in place. Special sizes and shapes are needed for certain parts of the roof: half-round tiles cover the ridge, fan-shaped convex tiles called 'bonnets' are used on hips, and one-and-a-half tiles are laid in alternate courses to achieve a straight line at the edge of the roof. Other types of clay tile are half-round pantiles, which are laid with the convex and concave surfaces alternating, and 'Roman' tiles, which have one convex and one notched edge and interlock with their neighbours when laid on the roof.

*Roofing slates ready to be transported from the Llanberis quarry, now a museum of the slate industry.*

At the beginning of the nineteenth century tiles were made by hand, the tile maker throwing a lump of wet clay into a mould and removing any excess with a wire cutter. Dusting the mould with sand made it easier to release the sticky clay and gave a textured surface to the tile. Throughout the 1820s between 80,000 and 90,000 tiles were produced per year in England. The process was mechanized with pug mills, which ground the clay to a uniform texture with no air bubbles, and extruding machines, which produced a flat 'ribbon' of clay that could be sliced and stamped into shape ready for firing. Although architects with a taste for quaint, hand-made materials started to specify clay tiles as part of the vernacular revival in the 1860s, it was the availability of consistent, smooth-textured machine-made tiles in the 1870s that effectively challenged the dominance of slate.

### Stone

Stone 'slates' are made from fissile stones – usually limestones – found in many parts of the United Kingdom and used close to their source: Collyweston slates in Lincolnshire, Cotswold stone in Oxfordshire and Gloucestershire. Sandstone was used in Sussex and, in the form of millstone grit, in Yorkshire and Lancashire. Despite improved transport, the regional distribution of these characteristic roof coverings remained largely intact throughout the Victorian period. Stone slates are hooked over the battens with oak pegs, and always laid in diminishing courses. They shed water more slowly than true slates, and therefore need a steep pitch to work effectively.

*The roof of Foster's Almshouses, Bristol (begun 1861, by Foster & Wood) has a subtle geometric pattern of red and purple tiles, inspired by the late medieval architecture of Burgundy.*

*Slates laid in graduated courses and framed by terracotta pierced cresting and timber bargeboard. This is a finely detailed combination of 'honest' materials by the architect H.A. Darbishire in Holly Village, Highgate (1865).*

## Lead

Roofs with a pitch lower than about 25° and small roofs of complex shape, such as cupolas, need a continuous, flexible covering. Lead was most commonly used in these situations, as well as for the vertical sides of dormer windows, door hoods, flashings, soakers and internal gutters. Although zinc sheeting and tiles were cheaper, and extensively used in continental Europe, their use in Britain was restricted to the large, simple roofs of buildings such as railway stations and factories. It was felt that the relatively high cost of lead roofs was justified by their long-term durability and noble appearance.

Sheets of cast lead were made by pouring molten lead onto a casting bed covered with fine, damp sand. As it solidified within seconds, the metal had to be rapidly spread and smoothed to an even thickness. It was then cut into sheets and rolled up into cylinders for transport and storage. Milled lead, introduced in the 1830s, is made by rolling the metal between steel rollers, and it is this type that is most easily obtainable today.

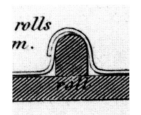

Detail of a lead roof, showing a cross-section through a roll joint. The joint is built up over a timber support and has a wide lap to prevent water seeping back up and underneath the lead cloak by capillary action.

Lead roofs had to be carefully designed to cope with the particular characteristics of the material. Lead can be easily bent or deformed, and it moves more than any other building material as it expands and contracts in response to changes in temperature. For this reason it was used in small sheets, joined with special rolled or stepped overlaps, which allowed it to move. New lead has a distinctive blue-black colour and a dull surface sheen that gradually weathers to a characteristic grey-white 'powdery' appearance.

### Thatch

The cottage roof covering *par excellence* has always been thatch. Thatch in Britain is of two main types: wheat straw, mainly used in the West Country, and water reed, found in Norfolk (although most modern supplies come from Middle and Eastern Europe). Thatch is an emphatically rural roof covering, and never used in urban or suburban settings because of the risk of fire. Its application in Victorian houses is restricted to a few picturesque lodges and cottages, and to 'fantasy' architecture such as summerhouses; a charming little thatched summerhouse at Osborne is attached to the equally whimsical Swiss Cottage.

### Glass

The most innovative roofing of the Victorian age was made of glass and iron, and was used in greenhouses, conservatories and lean-tos (see Chapter 12, Conservatories and Extensions). Glass was also used for rooflights (skylights), and even to make patent tiles designed to fit alongside conventional slates or tiles. Rooflights consisting of plain glass in an iron or timber frame were set parallel to the roof slope, and projected very little above the line of the roof covering. The condensation that inevitably formed on single-glazed lights was ducted into a small lead gutter that drained onto the flashing at the lower edge.

The V-section roofs on the houses in this London terrace of about 1830 remained a standard design well into the Victorian period.

*Cottages at Elmesthorpe, near Leicester, designed by C.F.A. Voysey for the Earl of Lovelace in 1896. This distinctive, rather exaggerated thatch was replaced by slates after a fire in 1914.*

# Maintenance and repair

## Safety

Safe access to the roof is vital. Never go up onto the roof if you are alone at the property. Use an extending ladder with a ladder stay to support the top edge clear of the gutter, and make sure that the ladder is safely angled and standing on a dry, level, non-slip surface. A roof ladder, which has a large hook to go over the ridge and wheels to move it up the slope of the roof, may also be useful. If your roof is more than one storey, leave it to professional roofers.

## Roof inspections

Some symptoms, such as sagging roofs or damp patches on bedroom ceilings, are unmistakable signs of trouble, but it is better not to wait until things get that bad before inspecting the roof. An annual inspection at the end of autumn will allow you to clear away any leaves or debris from the gutters and cut back any creepers threatening to invade the eaves or the roof covering. At the same time, you should be able to check the condition of roof coverings, chimneys, flaunchings, soakers, flashings, ridges, gutters, bargeboards, fascia boards, rooflights and dormer windows. Parapet gutters are easily accessible from dormer windows, but you will need a ladder to look at parapet and valley gutters where there is no direct access to the roof. Complete your inspection by checking inside the roof space, using a torch to look right into the eaves. Damp patches, powdery white or grey deposits on the timbers, obvious fungal growths, fresh beetle (woodworm) exit holes, wet or sagging timbers and musty smells are all symptoms that need to be investigated. If water is leaking through a bedroom ceiling, do not assume that the source of the leak is right over the drip; water can travel within the roof space, especially if it comes from a defective internal gutter. The fluorescent dye used for drain inspection can be useful in tracking leaks to their source.

Oak was considered the best timber for roofs, but the one most commonly found is slow grown, seasoned softwood, such as Baltic pine. This is of much better quality than most of the new building timber available today, and is very resistant to decay. However, if the roof becomes damp and is not properly ventilated, wet and dry rot or beetle infestation will quickly take hold.

*A conservation rooflight replicates the materials and profiles a Victorian original, and is much less obtrusive than a standard modern rooflight.*

Traditional carpentry techniques, in which roof timbers were slotted and pegged together using hardly any metal fixings, were almost entirely superseded in the nineteenth century by the use of iron bolts, straps and ties. These will invariably show signs of surface rust, but it is unlikely that they will be so badly corroded that they can no longer do their job. Do not unscrew, cut through or remove any iron fixings without first asking an architect, surveyor or structural engineer whether it is safe to do so.

### Small repairs

Always try to repair minor damage before it becomes major, as swift attention to small problems can postpone the evil hour when the whole roof must be replaced. Where slates are slipped or missing, check the condition of the battens. If just a few slates are loose or missing but the battens are sound, the slates can be refixed. Single slates, or the last slate in a small gap, can be refixed with a metal strap called a 'tingle'. One end of the tingle is nailed to the batten, the slate is slid into position, and the other end is bent upwards to clip the slate into place. Tingles can be made of copper, zinc or aluminium. Lead can also be used, although if it is sufficiently thick not to tear, it may be too thick to allow the slate to lie flat.

Junctions with other parts of the building or neighbouring roof slopes are particularly vulnerable. Broken chimney stack flashings allow water to penetrate, a problem that often manifests itself in damp patches on internal chimney breasts. Mortar fillets are not adequate substitutes for lead flashings, especially on exposed sites. BRE Defect Action Sheet No.94 (see Further Reading, p.259) deals in detail with chimney flashings and soakers. Loose ridge tiles can be refixed by bedding them in a mortar mix of cement/lime/sand in the proportions 1:1:6.

Never be tempted to use cement, bitumen or other waterproof coatings on the outside of the roof. They look dreadful and never last long. They are impossible to remove without damaging the underlying roof covering, and, by preventing adequate ventilation, may actually add to the roof's problems (problems which, incidentally, are harder to detect under a concealing cloak of tar). Large numbers of slipped, missing or delaminating slates mean that the roof needs to be replaced, and the presence of cracked and buckled old coatings merely confirms the diagnosis.

Caution should also be used when assessing expanded polyisocyanurate foam systems, which are sold on the promise that they will cure slipping slates and tiles from inside the roof. The spaces between the rafters are sprayed with a foam that expands on contact with the air and dries to form a rigid insulating layer which bonds to the underside of the roof covering. Although it provides good insulation and certainly glues the covering into place, the foam makes it difficult to inspect the roof fully and may conceal decay in the roof timbers. Installation is messy, the result visually unpleasant, and the material not easily removed, repaired or maintained. It cannot be recommended for use on historic buildings.

## Roof replacement

Well-laid roofs will last at least eighty years, and perhaps as long as a century. Eventually, however, slates may start to delaminate and absorb water, in one architect's words, 'like blotting paper'. Unrepaired leaks will cause structural timbers to rot and battens to fail. A Victorian roof will sometimes suffer from 'nail sickness' – the poetic name given by roofers to widespread rusting and snapping of the old iron nails that hold the slates or tiles in place.

Once it becomes clear that complete replacement of the roof is the only option, a few considerations may help soften the blow. If you are buying the house, a surveyor's report that specifies roof replacement can be used to negotiate a lower price. Renovating the roof provides an opportunity to inspect the roof structure and replace any decayed timber or apply any necessary insecticide or preservative. It is also an opportunity to install or improve insulation: the roof accounts for 25 per cent of heat loss in uninsulated houses. Remember to leave the space underneath the water tank uninsulated, and make sure the insulation does not block ventilation within the roof. If the roofline is disfigured by TV aerials, it may be possible to bring them into the roof space. It may also be appropriate to think about extending the living accommodation into the roof, or simply making a loft more usable with flooring, lighting and a fixed ladder.

*Dated decorative rainwater head and 'gargoyle' hopper in The Park, Nottingham. Cast iron rainwater goods should be retained or replaced 'like for like' wherever possible.*

You may be able to save money on materials by re-using the old roof covering. Tiles and slates can be salvaged if they have intact nail holes and no serious cracks, pitting or crumbling areas, and if they are not encrusted with old cement or bitumen. Roofers should be asked to strip the roof with great care and lower the tiles to the ground before sorting and stacking them according to size, thickness and shape. With care, it is sometimes possible to salvage 60–75 per cent of the roof covering.

When buying new roof coverings, match materials like for like wherever possible. Match new slates to the size, colour, texture and thickness of the old. Thickness is particularly important, as slates that are much thinner or thicker than their neighbours will not lie flat and the wind will lift them. Not all the slates on the house will be the same size, so do not rely on a single sample but take several slates from different faces of the roof before ordering. If you are combining old and new materials on the same roof, use the new materials on rear and inner faces of roofs where they will not be so noticeable. They will eventually weather to match the original materials. Real slate is expensive but looks good and will last, whereas artificial slates never look like the real thing, and their durability has not been proved.

Since seasoned, slow-grown softwood is not easily obtainable, the 'like for like' principle can be stretched to accommodate new timbers, which should have been pressure-treated with preservative to protect them against decay and insect attack. You can also improve on iron nails for fixing tiles and slates: copper alloy nails do not rust, but can be gradually drawn out by constant shifting in high wind or as battens dry out. Stainless steel, galvanized tin or aluminium alloy nails are all acceptable.

### Repairs to lead roofs

Lead is among the most durable of roof coverings, as long as it is properly installed and carefully maintained. The most common cause of problems is incorrect installation. Sheets that are too large, or over-restrained, will rip or buckle with thermal movement. Flashings poorly bedded into the masonry or inadequately clipped will tear. Accidental damage is a big problem: falling slates, dropped nails which later get trodden in, and even careless roofers treading heavily on gutters and vulnerable joints to get to where they are working – all these can make holes in lead roofs. Water leaking from a structural lead gutter can be disastrous for the fabric of the building, as few places are more conducive to dry rot than the unventilated void beneath a broken valley gutter.

Small cracks can be repaired by lead burning (welding), using lead as a filler. Large cracks can be similarly patched. Mastics and bitumen should not be used to seal cracks – they contract and expand at a different rate and may therefore actually exacerbate the problem. They are also unsightly and difficult to remove prior to proper repair.

Sheet lead is available in various thicknesses, ranging from 1.32mm to 3.55mm, and coded according to its weight per square foot. Thus a square foot of 'Code 7' lead weighs about 7lb. Flashings are generally made of Code 4 or Code 5 lead (1.8mm or 2.24mm thick). Gutters are made of thicker Code 5 or 6 lead (2.24mm or 2.65mm) and sheet roofing is thickest of all – Code 6, 7 or 8 (2.65mm, 3.15mm or 3.55mm). Code 4 lead is the one commonly stocked by builder's merchants and the one builders tend to use for repairs unless specifically instructed otherwise. Roll joints may be built up around a wood core, or hollow. Hollow rolls are said to be more durable, because there is no timber to trap moisture. However, they will be damaged by anyone stepping on them, so should not be used in locations where people are likely to tread, for example, a balcony, or a gutter accessible from a dormer window.

The use of heat to make or repair lead roofs is a serious fire risk and should only be undertaken by trained workers. Plumbers should follow the codes of the Lead Sheet Association (see Useful Addresses, p.266). Any heating equipment or torches should be turned off an hour before work stops and the site should be carefully inspected before it is left at the end of the day, to guard against the possibility of smouldering fires.

### Rainwater goods

Cast iron was the commonest material for rainwater goods in Victorian houses. Eaves gutters were half-round or ogee shaped, attached to the rafters or the fascia board with cast or wrought iron brackets. Ogee section gutters are liable to fail sooner than half-round because of the angle between the flat back and the bottom of the gutter. Joints between lengths of gutter can be patched, but when the bottom of the gutter has rusted through, the whole section must be replaced. Cast iron costs two or three times as much as plastic (uPVC), but is better looking and far more durable. Cast aluminium is lighter and more durable, although more expensive than cast iron. It needs painting and is vulnerable to acid attack from pigeon droppings. Extruded aluminium, which is thinner, should be avoided: it looks mean and is not sufficiently durable. The cheapest option is glass-reinforced polyester, which is self-coloured so that it does not need to be painted, but synthetic substitute materials should be avoided if possible. For most houses 100mm (4 inches) half-round is suitable, but ogee gutters should be replaced with the same shape.

Lead was used for rainwater heads and downpipes in more expensive houses. The heads might be cast or bossed (beaten) into a shaped profile, or carry cast decoration such as Tudor roses, the date or the owner's monogram. Repairing lead rainwater systems is a job for a specialist plumber. The Lead Development Association (see Useful Addresses, p.266) has information on contractors and suppliers.

At the end of the nineteenth century there was a brief vogue for copper guttering among Arts and Crafts architects, who liked the green patina that this metal develops. Copper is long-lasting and does not need painting, but it is expensive and difficult to repair. Having been especially chosen for its colour and texture, it should be preserved if at all possible.

### Roof conversions

The high cost of housing is a great incentive to make the most of any potential living space by extending the accommodation into the roof. You need to look carefully at the size of the roof space and the structure to see whether it is suitable for conversion, and consider the effect on the external appearance of the house. If the scheme requires the roof to be raised, the shape of the roof to be changed or the insertion of lots of new openings, it is likely to result in a top-heavy design that fundamentally disrupts the proportions of the house. Having enough roof space to extend into is only part of the equation. You must also consider access into the roof from the rest of the house, insulation (including sound insulation under the new floor), installation of services and fire safety.

If you do decide to go ahead, then plan, design and cost the conversion, and get all the necessary permissions before starting work. You will need to consult an architect or surveyor, or a builder with experience of converting roof spaces. There are building companies that specialize in loft conversions. Before engaging any professionals or contractors, make sure they can deal with the necessary planning permission, listed building or conservation area consent and building regulations approval on your behalf.

Roof conversions should not interfere with the scale or shape of the roof, nor change the roof covering. New openings are a particularly vexed question: obviously, they must not damage the roof structure, but they must also be in scale and in keeping with the rest of the house. Dormers should be sensitively designed, modestly scaled and carefully sited so as not to jar with the existing architecture. This is particularly important on the front elevation, but applies also to the side and rear of the house. The same care should be taken over the choice and siting of rooflights. The aim should be to have as few as possible, matched in shape and size (and as small as possible – small skylights can provide a surprising amount of light) and aligned with one another, and with the existing windows. Double-glazed rooflights that replicate the proportions, glazing bars and profiles of Victorian iron rooflights are now available.

Services should be planned so as to disrupt the external appearance as little as possible. Where an extra bathrooms is being installed, the need for extra soil pipes can be avoided by using a 'Saniflo' type toilet, which connects to a small bore pipe. Details make a difference: care should be taken to matching joinery in new doors and staircases, and in the siting of fire alarms.

# 8

# CARPENTRY AND JOINERY

*The quality of the internal finishes was directly related to the status of the house.*
OPPOSITE: *custom-made oak panelling in the entrance hall of a house in St Albans, Hertfordshire, designed by the Arts and Crafts architect F.W. Kinneir Tarte in 1895.*
ABOVE: *these off-the-peg softwood skirting boards offered by the timber merchant Alfred Lockhart in the 1890s had minimal mouldings and were destined for the cheapest housing.*

PETER NICHOLSON, AUTHOR OF *The Practical Carpenter* (1836) and *The New and Improved Practical Builder* (1837), defined the carpenter's job as 'the art of applying and joining rough timbers so as to give the greatest degree of strength', and that of the joiner as 'uniting and framing wood, for the internal and external finishing of buildings', adding that, in joinery, 'it is requisite that all the parts should be much more nicely adjusted to each other than carpentry'. Put another way, the carpenter made the structural timbers that are usually invisible in the finished house, and the joiner was responsible for all the woodwork that shows.

Timber was used to support the entire structure of the Victorian house: trusses and rafters in the roof, joists and floorboards, staircases, and window and door frames are obvious examples. Less noticeable are the sills and lintels, stiffening timbers and studwork built into the masonry and plastered over, or timber stud walls covered with lath-and-plaster (the latter, only found in non-load-bearing locations, can be detected by the hollow sound they make when tapped). There are also many instances where timber is used for decorative effect, for example in plain or carved panelling or inlaid flooring.

The Victorian builder had one tremendous advantage over his modern counterpart: he had access to high quality, slow-grown, well-seasoned wood not readily available today. This is one good reason to preserve as much original timber as possible when restoring a Victorian house. It is also usually much cheaper to conserve existing materials than to replace them, and it may be difficult or expensive to replicate the craftsmanship that went into the original working and fitting of the wood – to say nothing of the environmental arguments against discarding sound building materials.

## Floors

Oak was acknowledged to be the best timber for floors and was reserved for the best quality housing and for floors in places where carpet would be inappropriate, such as ballrooms. Even more exceptional were floors made of mahogany or patterned with marquetry in a variety of exotic timbers. There was a vogue for parquet in the early years of Victoria's reign. This was affordable in the best middle-class housing, if only in the form, recommended by Loudon, of a decorative border showing around the edges of a carpet. In mid-century interiors the floors of reception rooms were usually covered; when Ralph Wornum suggested in 1851 that 'we have a good floor already in our wooden boards', he

95

was expressing quite an advanced view. Parquet, and exposed wood floors generally, came back into fashion in the 1870s, by which time it was possible to buy ready-made parquet flooring by the square yard. It was laid down like a veneer over the existing floorboards.

Fine wood floors were polished and left bare so the quality of the timber and craftsmanship could be admired. Most houses (and most rooms in even the grandest houses), however, had deal floors, made of imported Baltic or Scandinavian pine. This cheap timber was never left in its raw state. If it could not be decently covered with a carpet, it was painted, or stained and varnished. Deal floors in bedrooms were scrubbed with sand and limewater until they gleamed white.

Eighteenth-century floorboards were hand-sawn, and not expected to be all the same width. The introduction of steam-powered saws in the 1830s made it easy to produce floorboards of identical size. The traditional method of fixing was to lay floorboards edge to edge, with dowels inserted horizontally to ensure they fitted closely without warping, and to nail them to the joists. An alternative was tongue-and-groove, but cutting tongues and grooves by hand was laborious and expensive before the introduction of specialized machines simplified the task. Thin metal plates inserted into grooved boards were used in some cases. Boards were laid so that they would meet end to end over the centre of a joist. Nails were placed in the edges of the boards and driven into the joists at an angle of 45° so that the next board would conceal the nail head. The cheapest floors were made by laying straight-edged boards side by side and nailing them into the joists from above with no attempt to hide the nails.

Throughout the nineteenth century the tendency was for floor structure to become lighter. Better scientific understanding of the structure led to the use of smaller joists, and the use of powered machines to cut wood to precise dimensions encouraged the use of more, narrower boards. By the early 1900s narrow boards of as little as 3 or 4 inches and not more than 6 inches (80–100mm or 150mm) in width were considered a sign of a good quality floor.

*Sheet of joinery details by E.W. Godwin, 1873.*

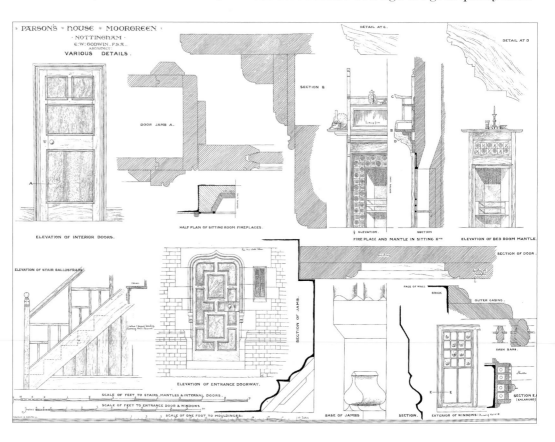

*A cast-iron baluster and
newel post combined
with softwood staircase
and mahogany
handrail in a house of
1869. A delicate raised
profile enhances the
tread ends and frames
the fixing plate of each
baluster pendant.*

## Staircases

Victorian houses had staircases made of stone, cast iron, timber or combinations of
these materials. By far the most common are timber staircases made up of one or more
straight flights linked by landings or half-landings. In small houses, particularly those
with no entrance hall and an entrance opening directly into the front room, the staircase was sometimes placed between the two principal rooms on each floor. This was
economical because no balustrade was required and because the support provided by
brickwork on both sides (or one wall of brick and one studwork partition) meant that
less timber was needed in the construction of the stairs themselves, but it resulted in
cramped landings and bedroom corridors. The classic terraced house staircase, nearly
always towards the back of the hall and against the party wall, is a more imposing and
elegant compromise between economy and convenience.

There were two ways of achieving the necessary dog-leg turn between flights. In
early Victorian houses the 'wreathed string' method developed by Georgian builders
was favoured and remained in use for better quality houses throughout the nineteenth
century. This involved building the curved part of the string out of fan-shaped pieces of
timber glued together to follow the shape of a timber former. When the glue dried, the
former was taken away and the face of the string was veneered to cover the joins and
match the rest of the string. The winding handrail was made out of several pieces of
timber carved to shape, fitted together, and stained and polished to match the straight

97

The rich decoration of the dining room at 18 Stafford Terrace, Kensington, is framed by timber mouldings, including deep skirtings, a dado rail and a plate rail supported on tall, thin brackets, added to display a collection of blue and white oriental porcelain.

*The carpenter who carved this distinctive lion's paw terminal to a mahogany handrail was presumably inspired by furniture designs.*

*Skirting boards 18 inches (450mm) high with composite mouldings, destined for use in the reception rooms of high-class housing.*

runs of handrail. The other way to make the dog-leg was to have a short, straight section of string joined at right angles to the straight runs, an option more widely adopted as it became cheaper to produce the newel posts necessary for the corners. Only the costliest houses had 'geometric' staircases, winding without a break around an open well to make an impressive feature in a large entrance hall.

At the beginning of the Victorian period, when all the components of the staircase had to be made by hand, it was common to have decorative balusters only on the principal flight, between the ground and first floors, and to have simpler balusters or even plain square-section sticks on flights leading down to basements or up to attics. Once steam-powered woodcutting and moulding machinery began to take over in the 1840s, bundles of turned balusters could be bought very cheaply and there was no longer any economic motive for such distinctions. Balustrades on long flights could be strengthened with the insertion of cast iron balusters at intervals. Made to match the wooden balusters, and painted the same colour, these look just the same as their timber neighbours, but can be identified with a magnet or by touch: the iron is appreciably colder than wood, and sounds when struck lightly with metal. Many wooden staircases were entirely fitted with iron balusters. The foot of the principal flight was usually given a wider, rounded tread to the bottom step and a thick, decorative newel post in carved or inlaid wood. In good quality housing the handrails were made of polished hardwood, such as mahogany, which both looked good and felt smooth and warm to the touch.

## Mouldings

Architectural mouldings developed as an attractive solution to several practical problems. They owe their origin to the need to hide unsightly joins in the construction of the house – for example between the bottom of the wall and the floor. They can also accommodate slight changes in the shape of the house due to expansion and settlement. In situations such as door and window frames, they provide fixing points for hinges and other fittings, and they protect vulnerable plaster and wall-coverings.

Early mouldings were simple enhancements of structural timbers: chamfering the corner of a timber beam to make it less vulnerable to damage, or carving it to turn a necessary part of the structure into something decorative. Applied mouldings, made separately and then fixed to the structural parts of the building, proved more versatile, and a range of profiles and sizes was developed for use in different situations. During the eighteenth century the number of profiles, many of them copied from Antique examples, increased enormously, and a complex set of rules was developed to govern their use in 'polite' architecture.

Despite occasional excursions into exotic architectural styles – Indian, Chinese, Egyptian and Moorish – Regency taste on the whole preferred understated, flatter mouldings enlivened with fluted, reeded and incised decoration. The 1840s saw a decisive shift in taste: interior joinery became bigger in scale, mouldings fatter, and ornament generally more elaborate. Mechanization led to a simplification of the shapes available – although simple elements could be combined to create an infinite variety of rails and architraves. In fact, the basic vocabulary of mouldings current in the 1840s remained constant; it was the scale and the way in which they were combined that changed. Elements such as door and window surrounds were made in various degrees of elaboration, matching the status of each room and establishing a continuity of style between various parts of the room, so that doors, shutters, architraves and skirting all related to one another.

The proportions of the wall were changed in the 1870s by the reintroduction of the dado rail, an Aesthetic device that became enormously popular. Indeed, the use of dado and picture rails to divide the wall into 'dado, filling and frieze' became a cliché of 'artistic' interiors in the last quarter of the nineteenth century. By 1900 the dado had been abandoned in favour of a deeper frieze, created by lowering the picture rail, which descended in some cases as low as the top of the doorframe. In some houses a plate rail – a wooden shelf about 3 inches (80mm) wide, supported on shaped brackets, which could be used to display ornaments – was installed. Once the Arts and Crafts movement had brought wainscot back into fashion, plate rails were also found to be a useful way of topping-off panelling that stopped two-thirds or three-quarters of the way up the wall.

## Repair and reinstatement

### Timber decay

It is well known that damp is the greatest enemy of timber, and that damp, warm, unventilated timber provides a perfect breeding ground for rot. Wet rot attacks softwoods and hardwoods, and appears as a fan of blackish-brown strands that spread over the surface of the affected timber and across neighbouring walls. The affected wood turns dark brown and cracks along and across the grain. Dry rot has spectacular rust-red fruiting bodies with white edges, and produces masses of white, furry mycelium, which sometimes secretes 'dewdrops' of moisture, and dries to a mat of thin, grey strands. Wood attacked by dry rot is light brown in colour, has deep cuboidal cracking and feels dry and brittle. In summary, the treatment for timbers affected with rot is to remove and burn all the affected timber and, in the case of dry rot, remove the plaster on neighbouring surfaces. Fungicide is then applied to the affected area and to neighbouring timbers. The destroyed timber is replaced with new, well-seasoned wood that has been pretreated with preservative. It is essential also to eliminate the source of the problem. If you put new timber back into a damp environment, it will simply become a new source of food for the decay fungus. The importance of ventilation cannot be overstressed: airbricks and air vents must be kept clear, and any new insulation must not impede the free flow of air. Decay organisms and approaches to repair are described in detail in the English Heritage Technical Handbook Vol.5: *Wood, Glass and Resins*, and in *Timber Decay in Buildings* by Brian Ridout (see Further Reading, p.259).

The ground floor of most Victorian houses is suspended over a basement or a shallow void. If there is no basement, the space under the floor is ventilated with airbricks, or ducts covered with iron grills, which are set into the external walls above the damp-proof course and below the joists. In many terraced houses the back parts of the ground floor are laid directly onto a solid floor consisting of a thick bed of concrete, a damp-proof layer of asphalt and a levelling screed, which was ideal for tiled floors in kitchens and sculleries. In suspended floors joists carry the floorboards and support the ceilings of any rooms below. Joists are supported by the walls. In the best quality housing the walls were built to a decreasing thickness in each succeeding storey, so that there was a little shelf of brickwork at each level for the joists to sit on. The most basic support was a socket created by leaving out a couple of bricks in the inner face of the wall. As long as the wall remains dry, the joists will stay sound, but if the wall becomes damp (and a solid external wall will certainly contain moisture), the joists will begin to decay from the ends inwards. One way to avoid this problem was not to fit the ends of the joists too tightly into the masonry, but to leave a pocket of air to ventilate the timber. Sometimes the joists rest on a timber wall plate, a method that frequently leads to decay of the joists and the wall plate.

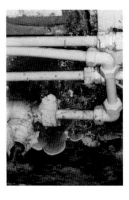

*Leaking pipework has provided the ideal damp conditions for dry rot to thrive.*

*The dining room at Standen, Sussex (1890–92, by Philip Webb), has exquisitely detailed panelling painted a distinctive, soft shade of green.*

### Floor repairs and finishes

Parquet, tongue-and-groove and secret-nailed floors are difficult to lift and replace without damage; they should be repaired by specialists. Straight-edged floorboards are easy to repair or replace with new, matching timber. Replacing the fixing nails with screws will usually cure a creaking floorboard. Overloading of old floors is a danger, especially where large houses have been converted into flats, and rooms that formerly contained a bed and a wardrobe are required to house far more furniture. Books are particularly heavy. Information on this aspect of structural safety is given in the English Heritage advice note, *Office Floor Loading in Historic Buildings*; detailed advice on the repair of old floors is given in the SPAB publications listed in Further Reading (p.259). New wiring or pipework should be carefully planned and discussed with the electrician or plumber to minimize the damage to the floorboards. Pipes and cables should never be run in notches cut into the top of the joists because of the risk of puncturing them with nails in the future; they should be passed through holes drilled at a minimum of 50mm (2 inches) below the top of the joist. The holes should be as small in diameter and few in number as possible because of the risk of weakening the joists.

One Victorian floor fashion that has returned to favour is polished floorboards. But not every old timber floor should be revealed: cheap softwood boards laid edge-to-edge with knots and nailheads showing, and with gaps where shrinkage occurred after fitting, would never have been exposed to view. At the very least the gaps would have been filled with slivers of timber, the surface planed smooth and the timber stained to hide its giveaway yellow colour and open grain. Painting with oil paint was another popular finish: in 1881 Edis recommended painting 'a margin of 2 or 3 feet [610 or 915mm] wide all round the room in four or five coats of dark colour'. If the timber was good enough to be seen, it was waxed and polished or varnished to achieve a subtle sheen.

Wood laminate flooring is sold as a quick and easy way to install a timber floor, but it is best to consult a decorative flooring specialist, especially if you are contemplating installing a wood block, parquet or inlaid floor, as many laminates are too pale, too yellow in colour and made up in strips too narrow to fit convincingly into a Victorian interior. Laminate floors have to be laid on top of an existing, sound substrate. Unskilled fitters will often apply an edge of quadrant beading where the new flooring meets the old skirting board, advertising that the floor is not part of the original structure but a superficial and recent addition.

### Staircase repairs

A common problem with Victorian stairs is that the treads and risers become loose, causing the stairs to bend and creak underfoot. This may be because the timber has shrunk so that the component parts of the staircase have become loose, or because the old glue has lost its adhesive power. The cure is to strengthen the blocks and wedges holding the treads and risers firm. This repair is relatively straightforward if it is easy to get at the underside of the stair. Basement flights are often open underneath, and it is usually possible to get at the underside of the ground-floor flight from the understair cupboard. If the underside of the stairs is enclosed and plastered, it will be necessary to remove the plaster and reinstate it when the staircase is mended – not something to be undertaken unless the staircase really does require major structural repair.

Blocks and wedges usually become loose because the original glue is no longer doing its job and nails alone cannot keep them in place. It may be sufficient simply to refix the triangular blocks underneath the leading edge of each step. If the glue has failed, it is easy to gently prise these off, clean them or cut replacements, reglue them and fix them back into place. For a more thorough repair you need to remove the blocks and investigate the long timber wedges that run behind the riser and under the tread at both ends of each step. These are driven into channels in the housings on both sides of the staircase, but once they become loose they are easy to prise out. They can usually be cleaned of old glue, reglued and driven back to fit more snugly. If they have shrunk significantly, you may need to cut new, slightly oversized wedges. Then refix the blocks. Make sure that any new blocks or wedges are cut from timber that matches the existing material: softwood staircases should be repaired with softwood, hardwood with hardwood. An exception to this 'like for like' rule can be made in the case of the glue: modern PVA wood glues are easier to use and more flexible than traditional animal glue.

Another problem affecting old timber stairs is that the treads, and particularly the nosings, become worn away underfoot. Slight dips in the treads can be packed with felt or rubber underlay beneath the carpet. Make sure the packing is fixed in place, otherwise it will buckle and shift under the pressure of use, causing bumps or patches of uneven wear in the carpet. A sheet of thin plywood nailed over packing onto the tread and concealed by the carpet is an alternative solution. Worn nosings can be prised or cut off the front of the tread and replicated in new timber, morticed and screwed into place. Make sure the cut-off point is in front of the riser, because the tread needs to rest on the riser for support. If the damage extends beyond the noser onto the tread, the whole tread should be replaced.

Wobbly balustrades are very hazardous. They may be caused by loosening of the joints between handrail and newel post, weak joints between sections of the handrail itself, or loose and broken balusters. Handrails are usually attached to newel posts with dowelled mortice-and-tenon joints, which can be dismantled and reglued with relative ease. If the problem is in a joint between lengths of handrail, you will need to look at the underside of the rail to one side of the joint to find the plug or patch of veneer that conceals the internal railbolt. The railbolt is a specially designed screw that tightens with a notched nut to pull the two sections of rail tightly together. It can be tightened using a screwdriver in the notches. Balusters are fixed into treads and handrails in various different ways, according to the quality of the house, the type of string (closed or open) and the skill of the original carpenter. Sometimes a baluster will split diagonally without breaking. This can be repaired by working some wood glue into the split with the flat of a knife blade and squeezing the two pieces together. Wipe away any excess glue that oozes out and bind the repair tightly with string or sticky tape until the glue has dried. Remove the binding, and repaint the baluster if necessary. The simplest repair for a loose baluster is to reglue the loose joint and strengthen it with a woodscrew running diagonally through the end of the baluster into the tread or handrail. If this is not sufficient, the baluster will have to be removed entirely, a job that can be as simple or complex as the construction of the staircase itself. If you need to replace missing or broken balusters, go to a specialist joiner's shop to get replicas made. It is practically impossible to obtain a perfect match for Victorian balusters 'off-the-peg', and a baluster that does not quite match will be irritatingly noticeable.

Sagging staircases, or stairs separating from strings, are symptoms of more serious problems. Structural settlement or failure may cause a wall flanking a staircase to bow outwards, pulling the string away from the treads. A weakness in the construction of the staircase, such as a failing joint between a string and a newel post at the top or bottom of the flight, will cause the staircase to sag. Damp masonry can cause decay in the joists and bearings that hold the staircase up. In such cases the staircase should be propped safely, used as little as possible and a properly qualified and experienced professional should be consulted about the best method of repair.

### Repairs to timber mouldings

You may be lucky enough to discover original wooden mouldings hidden behind hardboard or wallpaper. Because many timber mouldings play both a structural and decorative role, they are rarely stripped out completely when a room is redecorated, although they may be heavily disguised. Thus, although turned staircase balusters and the mouldings on panelled doors cannot easily be removed (because they support the handrail and the panels), they were often boxed-in under sheets of painted hardboard, perhaps to achieve a 'streamlined' look in the 1950s, or during conversions of large Victorian houses into flats in the 1980s. Box shutters are often nailed back and painted into place, and many owners of houses with sash-type shutters may not even be aware that the shutters are there, sealed into the thickness of the wall by many layers of paint on the window sills. It is a relatively simple matter to uncover joinery that has been hidden in this way.

*Detail of a handrail joint. The handrail was carved in the carpenter's workshop in several sections, and the on-site carpenters assembled it by matching the Roman numerals carved on the underside. The circular plug below the joint conceals the railbolt.*

Where joinery and mouldings have been removed, it can be difficult to determine how to reinstate them. Original skirting and rails that survive in one part of the house can sometimes provide clues to the scale and quality of mouldings missing from elsewhere in the building. During redecoration, look for traces of lost mouldings left in old wallpaper or paint schemes, or appearing as scars in the plaster where the fixing nails went in. Where new plaster has been applied, the faint line left by a missing dado or picture rail will sometimes show up under an oblique light. It is occasionally possible to discern the profile of a moulding by partially stripping the paintwork on the side of a door or window architrave; the outline of a skirting, dado or picture rail may be preserved in the old paint layers.

The best guides for sympathetic replacements are original mouldings on a neighbouring house of similar age and style to yours. Ask permission to carry out a survey, using a profile gauge and tape measure. Do not assume that the details found in the living room will be replicated in the rest of the house, but compare as many different rooms as possible, especially in a house built before about 1880, when the mouldings are less likely to have been standardized.

Where no such clues survive, you will have to design your scheme of architectural decoration from scratch. In determining the height of skirting and rails it is important to consider the effect of each on the proportions of the wall as a whole. A room of the 1870s, with the wall divided in dado, filling and frieze, requires narrower rails and lower skirting than a room of the 1840s, in which a deep cornice and tall skirting balance the expanse of a wall with no dado.

Before deciding to replace a damaged Victorian moulding, investigate the possibility of repair. Although repairs can be troublesome and time-consuming, they are invariably cheaper than the cost of ordering replacements made to the standard of the originals, and made of better-quality timber than that available today. A competent joiner will be able to replace damaged sections of timber with new wood cut to match the original. Many of the mouldings available 'off the peg' are suitable for use in Victorian houses. If the precise design you want is not available, joinery workshops will cut 'specials' to order. If you have to replicate large quantities, it may be worth buying or hiring a router, with which you can cut your own mouldings. Do not be tempted to skimp: sticking four rectangles of beading onto a plywood door does not convincingly replicate a proper panelled door.

### Redecoration

Turned and moulded timber can lose its fine detail under very few layers of paint. However, before removing the old paint, consider whether you need to have a record of what the original colour was, and if necessary employ a specialist to analyze the original paint finishes – once stripped, that historical evidence can never be recovered. Be aware of the need for caution when stripping old paint, especially if you suspect it may contain lead. The Health and Safety Executive has published advice on how to remove lead-based paint (see Useful Addresses, p.266).

All the timber elements in Victorian interiors (except those made from expensive woods such as oak or mahogany) were always painted. The knots and irregular grain of bare pine were never exposed to view, even in the kitchen. Whatever colour is used, it should be in a matt or semi-gloss finish; high gloss paint, particularly brilliant whites, are not generally appropriate for old houses.

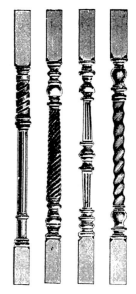

*The introduction of steam-powered machinery for converting timber into joinery elements made a huge number of patterns available very cheaply. The examples shown here are a fraction of the range available from the builders' merchants Young & Marten in the late 1890s.*

# WINDOWS

AGGRESSIVE MARKETING by the replacement window industry has led to the loss of many nineteenth-century windows which, with the right care and repair, might have provided many more years of service. Original windows contribute greatly to the special interest of old houses, and efforts should be made to retain them and extend their working lives wherever possible. Repairs and maintenance can appear tiresome and expensive, but research by English Heritage has shown that they are often cheaper in the long term than wholesale replacement. Original windows can also increase the resale value of an old house. Fortunately, the skills and materials for repair and reinstatement still exist, although persistence may be required in tracking them down. The levels of insulation and draughtproofing house owners now demand can be achieved through benign methods of upgrading existing windows.

The sliding sash window with a softwood timber frame is the predominant type in nineteenth-century housing. Sash windows were introduced into England in the 1670s; early versions often had one fixed and one sliding sash, and were characterized by thick glazing bars separating up to two dozen small lights (panes) in each sash. Several refinements were introduced in the eighteenth century: double-hung sashes, which enabled both upper and lower lights to be opened, thinner glazing bars and larger panes of glass. The early nineteenth-century fashion for verandas and balconies caused many Georgian windows to be enlarged downwards so that the sill was at floor level.

The basic mechanical layout of the sash window has hardly changed since its introduction. The sashes, separated by a central vertical parting bead, slide in grooves formed in vertical stiles on each side of the window. These stiles in turn form the inner faces of tall boxes, which contain the counterbalance weights; the weights are attached to the sides of the sashes by cords that run over pulleys at the top of the boxes.

In 1832 Robert Lucas Chance perfected the manufacture of Improved Cylinder Sheet glass – the glass that would later be used in the Crystal Palace for the Great Exhibition of 1851. The availability of large sheets of good quality, cheap glass had an immediate effect on window design: individual lights became larger, and the Georgian convention of six or more lights to a sash was abandoned. Sashes with four or two lights became commonplace, eventually to be superseded by single-light sashes.

To cope with the extra weight of the glass and compensate for the loss of the internal glazing bars, which had helped to keep the sash rigid, the remaining joinery became thicker. Whereas the meeting rails of a Georgian sash window were often made as thin as possible so as to be indistinguishable from the other glazing bars when the windows were

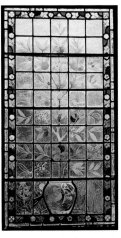

ABOVE: *panel of painted glass with Aesthetic decoration, installed in the garden door of 18 Stafford Terrace, Kensington, in the 1870s.*

OPPOSITE: *the drawing room of an early Victorian house in South London. The floor-length windows give access to a cast iron balcony, continuing the Regency fashion for blurring the boundaries between house and garden.*

107

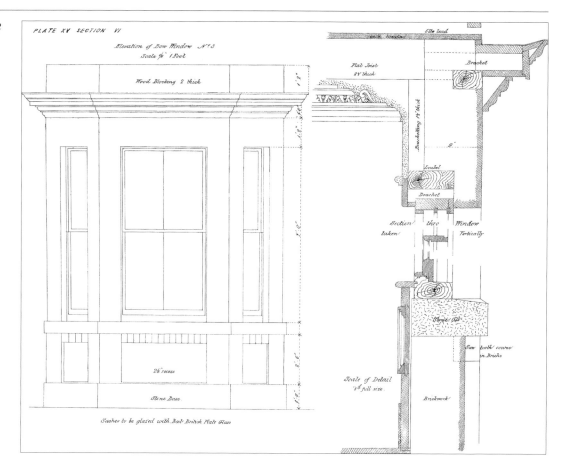

*The construction of a typical bay window, from a builder's handbook of 1855.*

closed, the meeting rails of large-paned Victorian windows are thicker, clearly dividing the upper and lower halves of the window. The sashes had to be strengthened with full mortice and tenon joints at the corners, which entailed extending the stiles beyond the corner of the sash: hence the 'horns' that appear on sashes after about 1840.

The cost of windows dropped as the work of the skilled joiner was taken over by machines. Several patents for machines that could cut mouldings were issued from the 1840s onwards. The delicacy and individuality of the hand-made window inevitably gave way to a certain standardization of design and detail, but there was still plenty of scope for innovation. The square-headed sash could be adapted to round-headed or pointed openings by simply filling in the spandrels with timber and providing a void in the wall above the window opening for the corners of the top sash to slide into when closed. A large void above or below the window opening could also accommodate a window extended downwards to create a 'garden sash', with sufficient headroom for people to step out of it. Too heavy for cords, the larger sashes were often hung on chains over cogged pulleys. Meeting rails were sometimes rebated, to prevent a knife being slipped between the sashes to open the catch.

Sashes were associated with the regularity and symmetry of classical architecture. The mullioned casement was a vital ingredient in picturesque, early nineteenth-century cottage architecture, and joined the architectural mainstream as the Gothic Revival gained ground. Gothic houses, especially where a rustic effect was required (perhaps in estate cottages or almshouses), might have iron casements, following the example set by Pugin at his own house in Ramsgate, although few architects would go as far as Pugin in permitting plate glass only 'in those windows which command a sea view', and having quarried glazing in all the others. Metal windows were usually of cast iron, but sometimes had wrought iron or bronze frames with cast tracery in hexagonal, ogee or diamond designs to mimic the lines of leading in medieval windows. Some cast iron window frames copied the proportions of multi-paned sashes, with four or six internal lights opening on a pivot.

In the 1870s interest in seventeenth- and eighteenth-century English domestic architecture led to the reintroduction of timber-framed, small-paned sash and casement windows. Prominent, white-painted window joinery, a hallmark of the Queen Anne revival, was widely used by speculative builders in terraced houses in the 1880s and 1890s. Often the expensive glazing bars would appear in a single row across the top of an upper sash, lending charm to a window that was otherwise simply – and economically – glazed with large single panes. H.H. Statham liked the mullioned casement window, and thought it a mistake to attempt to combine mullions with vertically sliding box sashes.

The revival of the art of stained glass, prompted by the demand for church windows, led to the use of leaded lights, which could be used where a clear view was not essential. Frosted or rolled glass could be used in bathrooms to achieve privacy without loss of light. Acid etching, bevelling and brilliant-cutting were used to achieve decorative effects for staircase windows or front door panels.

*Figured rolled glass by Chance Brothers & Co. of Birmingham who claimed that, 'The White is of exceptional purity of colour, which, together with the perfect impression of the pattern in relief and the brightness of the reverse surface, produces an effect of great brilliancy.'*

## Ironmongery

Bright brass window catches and sash lifts, or wrought iron casement bars and catches, completed the fittings of the Victorian window. Catches might incorporate pins or screws to prevent a knife blade being slipped between the sashes, or be decorated with cast brass detail or ceramic knobs. Hand-made fastenings of wrought iron were a feature of Arts and Crafts windows. Voysey's distinctive heart-shaped designs were widely imitated at the turn of the century, and wrought iron casement bars with curled ends, inspired by Arts and Crafts models, were popular until the mid-twentieth century.

*Architects used mullioned windows with leaded lights to impart medieval character to houses. These Gothic door and window details are from a design for four connected cottages by P.F. Robinson (1836).*

## Shutters and blinds

Many Victorian windows were fitted with internal shutters of panelled timber that folded back into spaces at either side of the window or within the depth of the window bay. When closed they were fastened with an iron bar. Another type is the internal sash shutter, which works on the same principal as the sash window but drops down into a panelled dado below the window. Internal shutters should be preserved wherever possible: apart from being an integral part of the original design, they provide unrivalled thermal and sound insulation and excellent security.

Victorian householders were very concerned about the damaging effects of too much sunlight on brightly-coloured decorations and furnishings, and so – besides an impressive array of curtains, sub-curtains and blinds on the inside – windows were often fitted with external 'bonnet' blinds on spring-loaded rollers or with chains and pulleys that could be cranked up and down with a handle. Although the fabric – a canvas with a colourful stripe, or green to filter the sunlight – has usually disappeared, along with the roller mechanism, any blind boxes that remain are worth preserving.

*When not in use, sash-type internal shutters are concealed by a hinged windowsill.*

## Maintenance and Repair

When old windows need attention, each window should be examined separately and decisions about any treatment or repair taken on a case-by-case basis.

When assessing the need to repair a window, it is wise to survey the opening in which the window sits. Dropped bricks in the arch or cracks and bulges in brickwork or masonry may indicate decay of the timber lintel above the window or serious structural problems. These faults need to be investigated and sometimes require large-scale remedial treatment before repairs to the window itself are undertaken.

In some cases the window opening has settled into an irregular shape but no further distortion will take place. If the top sash refuses to fill the frame when closed, it may be possible either to plane the top rail to fit the deformed frame or to insert a shaped fillet into the frame to close the gap.

The worst enemy of windows – whether of timber or metal – is damp. Horizontal ledges are vulnerable to fungus attack; dry rot can be concealed in pulley and shutter boxes, wet rot can attack sills, bottom rails and the bases of jambs, mullions and glazing bars. A penknife or screwdriver can be pushed into the timber to test for soundness. If only a small area is decayed, the frame can be cut back to sound timber and a patch repair carried out with a proprietary wood filler. The filler should be built up to stand proud of the surrounding timber so that it can be planed and sanded smooth when dry. Filler repairs will degrade in sunlight, so they should be painted even if they match the colour of the surrounding frame. Larger cavities can be repaired by letting in a new piece of wood, aligning its grain with the surrounding timber. The cavity should be thoroughly cleaned out, and both the old and new timber treated with fungicide. The edges of the repair should be filled with putty and allowed to dry thoroughly before repainting.

If a sash has become unstable at the corners, an L-shaped steel strap can be fitted into the angle, countersunk, and filled and painted so that it does not show. Exterior repairs should be carried out using galvanized or stainless steel straps and screws. Where whole elements such as sills or bottom rails of sashes are too decayed to be treated with a patch repair, it should be possible to replace the decayed part, rather than jettison the whole window. A joiner should be instructed to replicate the existing profiles and joints in any repair work.

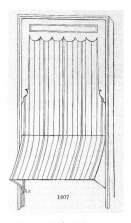

*A bonnet blind for use on the exterior of a window, illustrated by Loudon (1833). Although the canvas has usually rotted, the painted timber blind boxes can still be seen, particularly on early Victorian houses.*

OPPOSITE: *Panelled timber shutters with original wrought iron hinges, bar and latch provide unrivalled security and insulation, and fold back into wedge-shaped embrasures at the sides. The stripped finish reflects modern taste; the Victorians always painted this kind of softwood joinery.*

### Removing paint and putty

Softwood window joinery needs a protective layer of paint, and should never be left bare, or stripped and varnished. If layers of old paint have built up to such an extent that they clog the mouldings or cause the sashes to stick, it will be necessary to remove some or all of them before repainting, but take care not to strip away useful evidence of earlier colour schemes or special woodgrain finishes you might want to replicate.

Old glass, with its characterful imperfections, should be preserved if possible, but removing old putty for joinery repairs is difficult to do without damaging the original glass. Traditional putty is made of whiting mixed with linseed oil, which hardens as the oil oxidizes. It can be difficult to remove, but household bleach or a commercial paint stripper such as Nitromors may soften the putty to permit its removal. Covering the stripper with cling-film will stop it from drying out and thus prolong its softening action. Heat is also an effective softener, but must be used with great care, as it can cause the glass to crack.

### Mechanical faults

Wear and tear will eventually damage even the best-quality windows. Where windows do not operate correctly, it is a good policy to correct the fault before people get into the habit of forcing or wedging the window, putting extra strain on the frame, mechanism and fasteners. Windows can seize up as a result of paint build-up; missing or worn beads can cause misalignment or jamming, rattles and draughts; and sash cords become brittle with age or rotten with damp. If the bottom sash opens easily but the top is a struggle, it may be that the weights hit the bottom before the top shuts tight because the cords have stretched, rubbish has built up in the bottom of the box, the pulleys do not run smoothly or the weights do not balance. None of these problems is serious, and do-it-yourself repairs are possible, if time-consuming.

*The characterful imperfections of Victorian plate glass provide lively reflections that cannot be replicated in modern glass.*

SASH·OPEN·TO·EXTENT·ALLOWED·BY·SAFETY·FASTENER· | VIEW·SHEWING·THE·SASH·OPEN·FOR·CLEANING·&c

## Reglazing

Old glass should be preserved if at all possible, but if you have to reglaze, it is worth looking for an alternative to the dull, flat perfection of modern float glass. Several companies now specialize in providing glass suitable for historic buildings, and it is possible to get crown glass, plate glass or curved glass (even curved double glazing). Curved glass is made in a metal mould shaped precisely to the dimensions and curvature of the window frame: the sheet of glass is placed on top of the mould and put into a glass kiln. As it softens in the heat of the kiln, the glass sags into the mould and is brought out to cool. Great skill is required to judge exactly when the glass is at the right temperature for each stage of the process. The most expensive part of the process is making the mould; most manufacturers have a large stock of moulds, and you may be lucky enough to find one that fits your window.

*The nineteenth-century equivalent of the modern Simplex system made it easy to clean the exterior of sash windows.*

## Upgrading

Old windows built with traditional methods and materials are likely to require some upgrading to meet modern standards of thermal insulation. Sash windows in particular are prone to develop rattles and draughts because the parting bead and meeting rails become worn, thus creating gaps. Draught stripping is available in various guises. Self-adhesive foam strips are cheap and effective short-term solutions. Rubber or neoprene gaskets and low-friction brush strips last longer, and there are several proprietary systems on the market, some of which can be recessed into the window frame so as to be invisible when the window is shut.

All improvements to house insulation must be balanced against the need for adequate ventilation to prevent problems with condensation and other forms of trapped damp, especially in bathrooms and bedrooms. There is little benefit in making a window completely airtight if it subsequently receives a daily soaking of condensation.

113

### Reinstatement

Where the original windows have been removed, it is sometimes possible to work out what they looked like and to get copies made. The first step is to see whether any original windows remain on the property. If the principal windows on the main elevation have been removed, there may still be old windows at the back, or in less significant rooms or outbuildings, which could give clues as to the mouldings used for the frame and sashes (there have even been cases where the original windows have been found in the garden, being used as cold frames). In terraces or semi-detached developments the neighbouring houses may still have the original windows. In getting windows reinstated, attention to detail is the key to authenticity. Points to note include:

- The depth of the frame and its relationship to the surrounding brickwork: the current fashion for windows set flush with the front face of the wall is at odds with most Victorian practice.
- The extent to which the frame is visible or hidden within the brickwork of the surround.
- The presence and shape of horns.
- The number and proportions of lights in each window.
- The thickness and profile of glazing bars, stiles and sashes, and the angle of the putty fixing the glass in place.
- The design of pulls, catches and other ironmongery.

Collections such as the Brooking Collection or the English Heritage Architectural Study Collection (see Useful Addresses, p.266) can be useful sources of detailed information on window design and installation. The fitting of new windows provides a good opportunity to improve draught insulation and security, and these should be discussed with window suppliers at an early stage.

It is now possible to buy timber windows that are described by their makers as faithful to original Victorian designs in every detail, except that the individual panes of glass are double glazed sealed units. However, the inclusion of double glazing requires the window design to be adjusted in several ways which, although they may be minor in themselves, have the cumulative effect of making the window significantly different from an authentic Victorian single-glazed window. Because the sealed units are thicker and heavier than single panes, the glazing bars have to be deeper and sometimes thicker; the extra weight requires a sturdier frame; the inside edges of the sealed unit are sometimes coated with a conspicuous silver finish; and the glass creates disconcerting double reflections and does not have the 'liveliness' of imperfect Victorian glazing. The levels of sound and thermal insulation given by double glazing can often be matched by draughtproofing original windows and using thick curtains or internal shutters.

*Secondary glazing is cheap, effective, reversible – and, if carefully designed, unobtrusive.*

### Secondary glazing

A cheaper, reversible way of achieving similar benefits to those offered by double glazing is to install secondary glazing. At its simplest this is a pane of glass or clear plastic in a frame that is screwed or clipped to the inside frame of the window. This type of fixed secondary glazing is not suitable in locations where there is no alternative means of escape in case of fire. Other types of secondary window are designed to open either on hinges which swing the window inwards, or (more usually) by sliding horizontally or vertically. The major internal divisions of secondary windows should correspond to those of

*Original window ironmongery, such as this early Victorian espagnolette bolt in brass, should be preserved if possible.*

115

the exterior windows to minimize the visual impact. The large gap between the primary and secondary panes offers better sound insulation than most sealed double-glazed units, and secondary glazing has the great advantage of being reversible in most cases.

### Maintenance

Once windows have been restored, it is important to maintain them properly to prolong their useful life. As described above, it is essential to keep the frames and the moving parts in good working order.

Regular painting, especially of the exteriors, is essential to protect the timber. The sequence of preparation and painting windows is widely described elsewhere (see Further Reading, p.259), but there are a few points that help to achieve a satisfactory result and that are worth noting:

• Ideally, sashes would be removed from the window frame before painting, to prevent the paint from sticking them to the frame. Fittings such as sash pulls should be removed to prevent painting over.

*The spandrels of this 'arched' sash slide up into a void within the wall when the window is closed. As the nearby flat roof could provide a means of access to intrepid burglars, this upper-storey window requires the same security fittings as a ground-floor window.*

- Primer, undercoat and top coat should all be from the same manufacturer to ensure compatibility.
- If the window needs to be completely stripped, this should be done by hand using a proprietary paint stripper (which should be kept off the putty if possible). Windows should never be sent away for 'dip stripping', since this raises the grain of the timber and weakens the glue and fixings holding the components together.
- Make sure the underside of the bottom rail and all the exposed end grains are coated.
- A small brush with the ends of its bristles cut obliquely will make it easier to paint corners properly.
- White was by no means the only colour used on Victorian windows. Purple-brown, dark red and green were all widely used, and wood graining (a paint effect that imitates expensive timber such as oak or mahogany) was also popular (see Chapter 19, Paint Colours and Finishes).
- In many conservation areas there are controls over the colours that can be used, so it is wise to check with the local conservation officer before committing yourself to a colour scheme.

### Security

The crime prevention officer, who can be contacted through your local police station, will be able to advise on the most effective kinds of locks; but any locks should be discreet as well as effective. It is worth taking the trouble to install flush-fitting locks so as not to clutter up the window with obtrusive, surface-mounted security devices

Sash stops, morticed into the upper frame, have hinged wedges which can be left flush with the frame when the window needs to be fully opened, or flipped outwards and latched into place to stop the lower sash being raised more than a couple of inches for ventilation. Dual screw bolts, consisting of a threaded steel bolt which screws into a sleeve and socket fitted on the meeting rails (or, in a casement window, into a socket on the frame), are also effective. However, they require a key to open them and do not offer the option of opening the window a little way.

# 10

# DOORS

## FRONT DOORS

The main entrance to the house was usually the most impressive feature of the façade. The established Georgian composition of a classically-inspired doorcase surrounding a solid timber six-panelled door was still used in the early Victorian period, especially for large houses in classical taste, but it was supplemented by a variety of front door designs. One popular design, echoing the Regency taste for slender, upright elements and visual fakery, had two long, vertical panels separated by an incised line of beading, which imitated a pair of double doors. An innovation was the four-panelled door, rarely seen before 1830, but the most common type by 1850. Front door designs were varied to denote status: the more expensive the house, the deeper and more elaborate the mouldings used to frame the panels and on the doorframe. In common with mouldings used elsewhere in the house, these became progressively heavier throughout the 1840s.

The Gothic Revival led to a definite move away from the classical doorcase with a flat top. Specially shaped doors were needed to fit the ogee and four-centred arched openings of Gothic-style houses. Gothic doors were usually unglazed and made of thick planks joined by raised mouldings in vertical panels, or tongue-and-groove planks arranged in a herringbone pattern, to emphasize the robust medieval character of the entrance. Great attention was paid to the architectural surround to the door. Doorcase columns and pilasters were adorned with capitals of carved or cast foliage, or disappeared altogether behind porches of timber, brick or stone.

Glass was introduced into the upper panels of the door itself and into its surround in the form of narrow sidelights and transom lights. The latter were sometimes fitted with integral lanterns for gas lights. The lower panels of the door were always made of solid timber and were usually thicker than the upper panels, to withstand kicks and scuffs. They might be too thick to take a raised moulding and be defined merely by a line of beading flush with the surround. The upper panels, however, were frequently filled with decorative glass, especially after about 1860. Acid-etched glass has a frosted appearance, used in contrast with brilliant-cutting or polishing to create elaborate swirling patterns of flowers or foliage – the kind of work used to such exuberant effect in pub interiors. Such glass is hard to replicate or replace and should be carefully preserved. After 1870 the cheaper sandblasting method was used to give glass a frosted appearance.

By far the most popular kind of decorative glazing was stained, painted or textured glass set in leaded lights. Sometimes these were simple geometric patterns, but they often incorporated roundels of painted glass. Ruskin had pleaded for an architecture of

ABOVE: *the front door of a West London house of about 1840 has been grained to resemble oak.*

OPPOSITE: *the door of the drawing room at 18 Stafford Terrace, Kensington, painted with Aesthetic sunflowers and butterflies by Edward Linley Sambourne as part of an evolving scheme of decoration he carried out over two decades from 1874.*

119

colour and variety, using motifs drawn from nature, and his wish was fulfilled in the stained-glass panels of suburban front doors in the 1870s and 1880s. Birds and flowers, landscapes and leaf sprays were hand-painted onto squares, discs and lozenges of plain glass and carefully framed in lead. Mass production led to the standardization of designs (which would not have please Ruskin), and so by the 1880s whole terraces were being supplied with front doors whose upper halves consisted almost entirely of elaborate leaded patterns of coloured glass divided by narrow glazing bars.

Unless they were made of an expensive hardwood such as oak, doors were invariably painted. Wood graining, a paint finish imitating the colour and pattern of expensive polished timber, was popular, but it attracted unfavourable criticism because it was at odds with the design reformers' insistence on the 'honest' use of materials. Nevertheless, wood graining remained in widespread use in modest houses until the 1920s. Towards the end of the nineteenth century the artistically inclined owners of Queen Anne revival houses emulated the taste of the eighteenth century and chose dark green or white paint for their front doors and the surrounding joinery.

Oak – whether grained imitation or the real thing – came back into fashion in the 1890s. The structure of the door and the ironmongery with which it was fitted were also given a renewed importance. Thick plank doors were adorned with wrought iron hinges and other fittings that drew attention to their hand-crafted quality. The influence of architects such as Philip Webb showed in the use of multiple small squares or circles of glass to make up larger lights. Towards the close of the century, Art Nouveau, which otherwise had little impact on the design of the average British house, had a powerful influence on the stained glass used in doors; many front doors installed at the turn of the century still have their original panels of swirling, whiplash-patterned glass.

ABOVE: *late nineteenth-century door with sunflower panels in leaded glass.*

RIGHT: *Oak plank doors complement the robust Tudor style of carved stone doorcases in these domestic Gothic doorways from a mid-nineteenth century builder's handbook.*

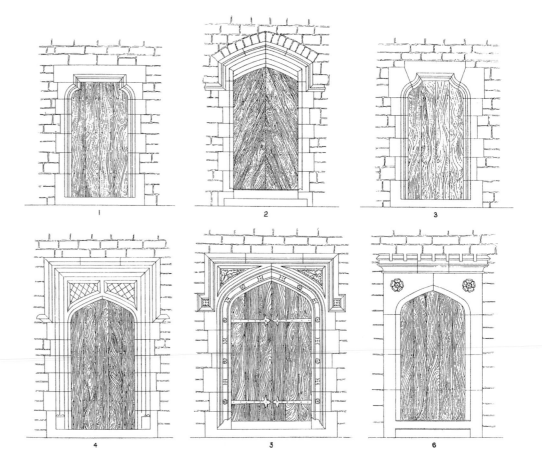

Doors would be more or less elaborate according to their location: for security reasons the front door was always the heaviest; because it was displayed to the street, it was also designed for maximum architectural impact, with the deepest and most complex mouldings. Many Victorian front doors, especially in smaller houses, have elaborately framed panels on the outside but relatively plain backs in which the panels are simply delineated with a line of beading; this means that a good stout thickness of timber can be maintained, but also ensures that no decorative effort is wasted on a surface that will not be seen and appreciated. No matter how elaborate the front entrance, the back door would have solid timber panels, or perhaps a couple of lights at the top, fitted with cheap rolled glass. The hierarchy continued right down to sheds and outhouses, which were given simple ledged-and-braced doors – a type revived in the cottages built by Voysey and his imitators at the end of the nineteenth century.

*Painted glass roundel in the centre of a panel of leaded, coloured glass, typical of the panels fitted to thousands of suburban front doors in the 1870s and 1880s.*

## Front door furniture

The introduction of the penny post in 1840 led to the use of letter plates for the first time. Many of the old two-panelled doors were damaged by the placing of letter plates across the central bead, destroying the illusion of paired doors. It was easier to fit a letter plate on a four-panelled door, especially since the plates were small compared to modern ones. Problems can sometimes occur when an original Victorian letter slit is enlarged to accommodate modern, larger envelopes and the old letter plate is replaced with a correspondingly larger plate. In doors made after 1840, however, the lock rail (the centre muntin) was widened so that the door could accommodate the letter plate and still retain pleasant proportions. Elaborate letter plates combined with pull bar handles or door knockers were produced, some with the word 'letters' cast into the flap.

Regular postal deliveries also required that houses be individually and conspicuously numbered for the first time. Oval number plaques of glazed ceramic or enamelled iron still survive on some houses. An alternative was to paint the number on the door or on the surround. Professional sign writers were sometimes employed to paint elaborate gilded and shadowed numbers on the interior face of the transom light – in mirror-writing, of course, so that the numbers would read properly when seen from the other side.

Only the wealthy could afford solid brass door furniture. Most letter plates, handles and knockers were of wrought or cast iron with a 'japanned' (lacquered), 'Berlin black' (stove-enamelled) or bronzed finish, or painted to match the door. Even in the late 1890s the difference in price was significant: the builders' merchants Young & Marten sold a dozen Gothic doorknockers in japanned iron for 12 shillings (60p, or 5p each); a single knocker of the same pattern cost 4s 1½d (21p) if made in polished brass.

Mortise locks were fitted on many exterior doors. As early as 1784 Joseph Bramah had invented a secure, small lock operated with a small key, rather than the large and heavy keys that worked the old-fashioned rim locks. Jeremiah Chubb invented another type of burglar-proof lock in 1818, and the Yale lock, named after its inventor, the American locksmith Linus Yale, Jr., was introduced in the 1850s.

*Householders who could not afford hand-made répoussé metal fittings could add fashionable furniture to their doors with mass-produced, stamped and polished brass finger plates, which mimicked the craftsman-made examples at a fraction of the cost.*

## Internal doors

Throughout the nineteenth century, four-panelled doors were the most popular style for internal use. Double and folding doors were sometimes used to divide paired reception rooms. Subtle variations in the design denoted the relative importance of different rooms: the most complex mouldings would be found on the main reception room doors; bedroom doors would have simpler mouldings; while doors in the servants' quarters

121

would be entirely plain – a point to bear in mind when replacing original panelled doors.

In the first half of the nineteenth century doorknobs were simple brass, turned wood or glazed china spheres, perhaps adorned with grooves in the metal or a gold line painted onto the china. Fingerplates and escutcheons were equally plain. Later designs could be more elaborate and reflected the prevailing fashions in interior decoration – whether Japanese, Rococo or 'Louis Quinze' – although the cost of these fashionable items ensured they were only used in expensive houses. Arts and Crafts houses were often fitted with remarkable wrought, pierced, repoussé or stamped fittings using a variety of metals, including iron, brass and copper. Notable examples include the pierced brass 'sunflower' finger plates designed by Philip Webb for Standen in Sussex and the repoussé copper door furniture specified by Edgar Wood for his houses in Birmingham.

## Restoration and maintenance

Simple maintenance tasks that require little skill can do a great deal to prolong the life of a door. Locks and hinges should be lubricated to prevent squeaking and sticking: use powdered graphite rather than oil, as the latter traps grit and fluff, which wear away the mechanism faster in the long run. If the door sticks in damp weather, make sure it is not absorbing water from an undetected leak, and sandpaper or shave the sticking edge until it closes freely.

Before deciding to replace a damaged Victorian door, it is important to investigate the possibility of repair. Although repairs to doors can be troublesome and time-consuming, they are invariably cheaper than the cost of ordering replacements made to the standard of the originals. Weatherboards at the bottom of external doors are designed to protect the body of the door from the effects of rain and from scuffs and kicks; they should be inspected regularly and refixed, repainted or replaced as necessary. More serious problems in the structure of the door require professional expertise. A competent joiner will be able to replace damaged sections of timber with well-seasoned wood to match the original material.

Some advance planning may be necessary: if a repair requires an external door to be taken off its hinges, have ready a cheap but sturdy replacement that can be fitted temporarily, so the house can be kept secure while the work is carried out.

Porches and hoods should be regularly inspected for signs of damage from water ingress, particularly at the join between the porch and the front of the house. Cracked lead flashings should be repaired promptly. The temptation to glaze-in an open porch should be resisted – it spoils the appearance of the house, and by cutting the free flow of air it can trap moisture, leading to problems with condensation. Because the external face of an open porch was not originally designed to contain a door, any that are subsequently fitted will be inappropriately exposed to the elements; many such doors have begun to show signs of rot within a few years of being fitted.

### Replacing missing doors

If the front door is damaged beyond repair or has been replaced with an unsuitable modern design, the best possible model for a sensitive replacement is an original door on a neighbouring house of similar age and style. A joiner can be instructed to copy their measurements and moulding profiles.

Architectural salvage outlets can be a useful source of original doors, provided you buy with care. Doors that still have their paint or those that have been stripped by hand should be acceptable. On no account buy a door (or any other timber item) that

ABOVE AND OPPOSITE: *carefully restored doors of the late 1880s in Hackney, East London, seen from both sides and in detail. The glass panels in No.33 were damaged and incomplete, and were repaired following surviving examples on neighbouring houses.*

has been stripped by total immersion in a tank of caustic solution. Tank stripping raises the grain of the timber and dissolves old animal glues, leading to the joints beginning to widen and the door warping or falling apart in use.

Although it is likely that a salvaged door will have to be planed or have an edge of timber pieced-in in order to achieve a perfect fit in its new home, avoid buying a significantly over-large door in the hope of cutting it down to fit your doorway. Cutting down damages the proportions of the door and can cause structural weakness by slicing through the wedges securing the mortice-and-tenon joints in the frame.

## Painting

Exterior doors should be repainted every three to five years, depending on the degree to which they are exposed to the elements. Some people admire a build-up of paint on a venerable door as a sign of great age and evidence of the care expended on the house by previous owners; besides this, the many layers are a record of previous generations' taste in colours and finishes, and as such may be a valuable part of the history of the house, not to be discarded lightly. Others prefer the crisp look of mouldings that retain their sharpness under the minimum three or four coats of paint necessary to protect the timber and achieve a good depth of colour. Before stripping off layers of old paint, however, consider keeping a sample patch intact under the new paint, as a historical record, and consult the local conservation officer before altering the paint finish of a door on a listed building.

The Victorians always painted softwood doors; the knots and irregular grain of bare pine were never exposed to public view. Dark blue, chocolate brown, deep red and olive green were popular colours until the Aesthetic movement of the 1870s created a fashion for black (to suggest ebonized wood) or white (but always 'broken' with a touch of black or yellow, and never brilliant white, as this did not appear on the market until after World War II). Whatever colour is chosen, a matt or semi-gloss finish will replicate the dull sheen of a traditional lead-based exterior paint better than a high gloss.

Occasionally the removal of hardboard coverings from internal doors will reveal panels decorated with hand-painted designs, pieces of embossed and gilded wallcoverings cut to fit or printed papers specially shaped to fit the panels. These rare survivals should be retained wherever possible. If they do not fit the proposed scheme of decoration, they can be left *in situ*, protected by a layer of acid-free paper and concealed behind a piece of thin plywood fixed behind the panel moulding and painted to match the rest of the door.

Although it may require a persistent search, it is possible to find appropriate glass to replace lost or broken panels. The repair of leaded lights is a job for an expert. Thanks to the recent revival of interest in the craft, people skilled in glass repair are not hard to find. New etched, sandblasted or leaded lights can be designed and made to order.

## Choosing door furniture

As a general rule, door furniture should be regarded as a subordinate accessory to the door itself (the highly decorative, hand-forged wrought iron hinges and other ironmongery sometimes found on Gothic Revival and Arts and Crafts doors are exceptions). The door should not be treated as merely the background to a glittering array of elaborate, oversized knobs and knockers in lacquered brass.

Original door furniture should be retained wherever it survives. Victorian fittings can be found in antique shops and salvage yards, and some good reproductions exist, including cast iron knockers cast from original moulds.

If you have to buy modern door furniture, simple designs in unassertive materials and finishes are preferable to ornate 'Victoriana' of doubtful authenticity. Fittings can be painted black to make them less visually obtrusive. Door furniture should always be fitted to the structural members of the door, never into the panels.

House numbers need to stand out from their surroundings in order to be readable from a distance. It is not easy to find appropriate numerals: most of the brass house numbers on sale in the DIY stores are too big and in modern typefaces. You can com-

*Appropriate door furniture, including a rare surviving ceramic number plate, enhances a Gothic front door in Lonsdale Square, North London (R.C. Carpenter, 1837)*

mission a sign writer to paint a house number in a roundel on the front wall of the house or a porch column, on the door itself, or on a transom light. Whatever form the numbering takes, it should be in a script appropriate to the age of the house.

Plain round doorknobs in brass, porcelain or wood are a good choice for all internal doors. The grooved brass design sometimes called a 'beehive' is particularly suitable for houses of the 1880s and 1890s. Lever-style handles are not suitable for Victorian interiors. Fingerplates and escutcheons should be made of the same materials as the doorknobs.

### Draughtproofing and insulation

There are several unobtrusive and reversible ways of upgrading the insulation of a front door. A simple way to cut down draughts is to fix a draught excluder to the inside of the door and/or frame. Complete kits of narrow brush strips and fixings are available from any DIY store. Cover the letter slit with a brush strip draught excluder on the inside of the door. The white plastic edge of the strip can be painted to match the back of the door.

Glazed doors can be double glazed with glass or Perspex cut to size and fitted on the inside of the door with beading, improving security as well as insulation. The transom light can be double glazed in the same way.

The Victorian solution to draughty doors was to fit a portière, or door curtain, to the back of the door. Portière rods, which can be bought from specialist soft furnishings suppliers, have one fixed bracket that goes on the outer stile of the door, and one hinged bracket attached to the door frame on the hinge side. The hinge allows the rod to move with the door when it is opened, and the brackets hold the rod above the door, ensuring the curtain cuts out draughts from the top of the doorframe. A cheaper alternative is to fit a short length of curtain track to the back of the door at the top, and have a curtain heading that stands up at least 50mm (2 inches) above the top of the door. The portière should be of thick material, lined, and large enough to cover all four edges of the door. The hem can be weighted so it will not blow aside in a draught, and bound with canvas or carpet tape to prevent fraying from brushing over the floor each time the door is opened or closed. A portière will also trap a lot of the gritty dirt that comes into the house.

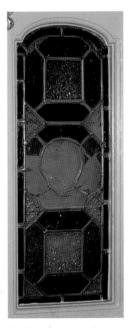

*Leaded glass panels are potential security risks. Safety can be improved by double-glazing the back of the panel with security glass or Perspex.*

### Fire Safety

The conversion of large Victorian houses into multiple dwellings raises the problem of fireproofing internal doors. The Fire Precautions Act requires doors to be at least 44mm (1¾ inches) thick and to be able to withstand fire for half an hour. It is often possible to upgrade original doors, even those with thin panels, to meet these requirements. If the stiles and rails are 44mm or thicker, the panels can be built up to the required thickness, or split and sandwiched with a layer of fireproof material. It is advisable to check whether this will satisfy the building control and fire inspectors before proceeding. If doors are required to be self-closing, an 'invisible' closer, fitted within the thickness of the hanging stile, is a discreet alternative to an obtrusive spring box on the doorframe.

# 11

# IRONWORK

CAST AND WROUGHT IRON, in such elements as gates, railings, balconies, finials and boot scrapers, add character to Victorian houses. Even humble rainwater goods may provide distinctive decoration. Iron has a tough image but has proved very vulnerable. Many railings were lost during World War II, when they were ripped out in the mistaken belief that the metal they contained could be reprocessed into weapons. Much more has been lost since then, either through neglect, inadequate repairs or transient fashions for modernization. Where original ironwork remains, it should be prized and preserved. Where it has been lost, reinstatement or repair will enhance the house, and may even improve its value.

## History: ironwork

Before the mid-nineteenth century, most architectural ironwork was executed in wrought iron, a very pure form of iron that is strong under tension and resistant to fatigue. Wrought iron lends itself to graceful, curvilinear designs with elaborate naturalistic decoration based on foliage and flowers. The decorative potential of the material was fully exploited by the great artist-blacksmiths of the seventeenth and eighteenth centuries, who established a strong British tradition of fine ironwork. The introduction of Henry Cort's rolling mill in 1730 made possible the production of very regular wrought iron bars in a wide range of sizes, simplifying the making of plain railings. In general, however, the skilled and intensive labour involved in the production of wrought iron made it very expensive, and only the wealthy could afford to commission large decorative pieces. Thus most of the architectural ironwork seen on Victorian houses is mass-produced cast iron.

The most expensive part of the cast iron process is making the original pattern from which the mould is taken. But once the pattern has been made, an infinite number of identical elements can be produced very cheaply. Cast iron is less pure and more brittle than wrought iron; it cannot be worked by hand, and will break under impact. It can, however, support heavier loads, and is better able to resist fire.

The nineteenth-century building industry created an unprecedented demand for architectural ironwork, particularly railings. Most consisted of straight standards set with lead directly into the pavement or into the stone coping of a low wall, linked to a cross-bar at the top and finished with decorative finials. This style was established by the mid-eighteenth century and predominated for the next hundred years. It was common to mix wrought and cast iron in sets of railings by brazing or 'casting in' finials of cast iron onto wrought iron standards, or screwing cast iron embellishments, such as

ABOVE: *molten ore being poured into moulds in the foundry to make cast iron.*

OPPOSITE: *Newly cast doorknockers cooling off in their mould of fine, damp sand. The links formed by the molten metal as it filled up the mould will be broken off and the stumps 'fettled' or filed to a smooth finish.*

127

rosettes, onto the face of wrought iron gates and balconies. This practice continued into the mid-nineteenth century, but as technical advances brought down the price of cast iron, it became more common to use it for every part of the railing.

Many of the classically inspired motifs used in eighteenth-century wrought ironwork could easily be adapted for cast iron finials. Anthemions, spikes, arrow and spear heads, in various proportions and degrees of elaboration, continued to appear throughout the nineteenth century. Urn or acorn finials were used for emphasis where railings ended or turned corners. Many designs were adapted from published pattern-books such as Lewis Nockall Cottingham's hugely influential *Smith and Founder's Director* (1824), which contained hundreds of drawings for gates, railings, finials and balconies. Classical motifs remained popular throughout the early Victorian period, but after about 1850 softer and more elaborate designs based on leaves and plants were preferred; narrow arrow heads were abandoned in favour of fleshy acanthus, fleur-de-lys and scrolling 'baroque' or 'rococo' foliage.

Economic and technological developments also influenced the design of railings. The Nielsen blast furnace, which increased output and reduced fuel consumption, was introduced in 1828, and had an immediate effect on the industry. As the price of iron dropped, manufacturers made their railings thicker and taller. Sharp angles are hard to cast cleanly, so standards with round sections supplanted the rolled, square-section type. In 1858 Henry Bessemer produced a wrought iron substitute that came to be known as mild steel. Although widely produced by the 1880s, it did not supplant iron until much later – and it is not recommended as a substitute or repair material for old ironwork today.

The design of railings also changed to accommodate new types of house plan. Until the late 1860s it was usual for large terraced houses to have basements, the front door being reached by a flight of stone steps over the area. Thus railings and handrails not only defined property boundaries and conferred status on the house, but also acted as vital safety barriers. From about 1870 houses without basements became more common and railings that were no longer needed for safety were supplanted by more purely decorative boundary markers. Developers found it easy and inexpensive to build a low wall of brick, perhaps faced with stucco scored to resemble ashlar, and to top it with the new 'butterfly' railing – a horizontal bar supported every few feet by a small post with curlicue brackets – to achieve an elaborate decorative effect with relatively little material. Railings were bedded into stone copings with lead, or fixed into place with iron bolts passed through lugs incorporated into the design.

Decorative cast iron was also used for doorknockers and (after the introduction of the penny post in 1840) a letter plate. Boot scrapers, which might be free-standing, incorporated into the gate support or set into the wall by the front door, were necessary, especially in new suburban developments, where the unpaved roads and footpaths over neighbouring fields soon turned muddy in wet weather. Bay windows received adornment in the form of small rails to hold flowerpots and window boxes in place. These designs were advertised in foundry catalogues as 'flower pot or tomb rails', illustrating how one item could be used for two very different purposes. In the same way, a cast iron panel might be sold for use as a baluster for entrance steps, for the front of a balcony or a rail above a flat-roofed window bay, or as an element in a front railing. Cast iron crestings were used to enliven roof ridges, and the roofs of larger houses might be fitted with finials and lightning conductors in the shape of crosses or fleurs-de-lys.

Not much structural ironwork is found in Victorian houses because most were built using traditional masonry walling and timber for floors and roofs, although one conspicuous use of iron is in tie rods – wrought iron rods that run through underfloor voids and screw into cast iron plates visible on the exterior of the house. The tie plates may be circular, sometimes with lettering or other decoration, or in the shape of a cross or a capital 'S'. The new (and initially expensive) technology of building with prefabricated cast iron elements was perfected by Joseph Paxton in his design for the Crystal Palace in 1851, and the structural use of iron in Victorian architecture is mainly associated with large commercial, industrial or public buildings. In domestic settings the material really came into its own in garden buildings, where the semi-

ABOVE: *The projecting course of bricks above this iron tie-plate has been carved to accommodate the curve of the 'S'.*

LEFT: *Catalogue components were used to create this splendid cast iron gate in Castle Cary, Somerset. The name of the house has been added to order, and appears in a neoclassical plaque that is curiously at odds with the 'Japanese-y' Aesthetic design of the gate.*

industrial look of cast iron was more acceptable than in the house. Greenhouses and conservatories were supported on pillars and brackets, heated by gratings let into the floor and ventilated by rooflights – all made of cast iron.

Cast iron was used for many of the items essential to the efficient functioning of the house, such as rainwater goods and covers for drains, inspection pits and coalholes. Gutters were cast in semicircular or ogee sections and fed into circular or rectangular downpipes. The circular shape of coalhole covers lent itself to elaborate geometrical decoration, featuring concentric bands, stars, overlapping circles or flower shapes. Many such items carry their maker's names as an integral part of the casting.

Decorative cast iron was a key element in the design of urban and suburban housing throughout the nineteenth century. Its eventual fall from favour came about for several reasons. Disciples of the Arts and Crafts movement were taught to despise it as 'dishonest' if it mimicked hand-made wrought iron. Mass-production was also thought to stifle fresh and inventive design. Timber fences and gates had an old-fashioned, bucolic appeal, whereas cast iron's 'citified' associations disqualified it for use in Queen Anne streets and garden suburbs. At the same time a revival of interest in traditional building craftsmanship brought wrought iron back into fashion; besides enjoying the prestige associated with hand-crafted objects, the material lent itself particularly well to the swirling lines of Art Nouveau.

*Cast iron railings with a bottom rail designed to save the trouble and expense of setting each upright into the coping at the top of the wall. Paint samples taken from old ironwork show that black was by no means the only colour used on railings – as the set in the background of this picture indicates.*

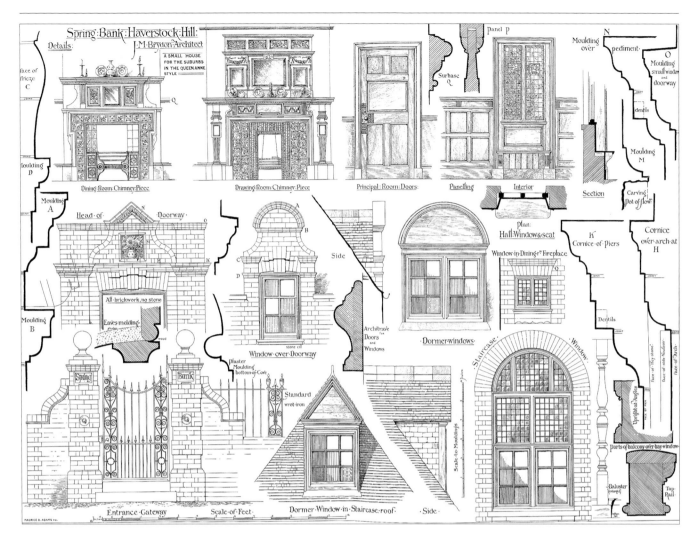

The various labels on the illustration read:

Spring·Bank·Haverstock·Hill
Details:
J·M·Brydon·Architect
A SMALL HOUSE FOR THE SUBURBS IN THE QUEEN ANNE STYLE

Dining·Room·Chimney·Piece
Drawing·Room·Chimney·Piece
Principal·Room·Doors
Panelling
Interior
Section

face of frieze C
Moulding D
Moulding A
Moulding B

Head·of· · ·Doorway·
All·brickwork, no stone
Eaves·molding
Window·over·Doorway·
Plaster Moulding bottom·of·Cove

Spring
Bunk
Standard wrot·iron
Entrance·Gateway
Scale·of·Feet

Side
Architrave for Doors and Windows

Dormer·windows·
Window·in·Dining·r⁰ Fireplace
Plan: Hall·Windows & seat
Scale·to·Mouldings

Dormer·Window·in·Staircase·roof·
·Side·
Staircase·
Window·

Panel p
Surbase Q
Moulding over
pediment·
Moulding small window and doorway
dentils
Moulding M
Carving Pot of flower
Cornice over·arch at H
Cornice·of·Piers
Dentils
Upright at Angles
Parts of balcony over bay window
Baluster
Top Rail

MAURICE B. ADAMS del.

## Maintenance and repair

Many potential problems can be avoided by regular inspection and maintenance of the iron parts of a building. They should be inspected annually for signs of rust, and be cleaned and repainted as soon as any deterioration of the paintwork becomes evident. Litter, dead leaves and other debris that can trap water should be cleared away from rainwater goods and the base of railings. Loose fixings should be repaired as soon as possible, because wobbly elements very quickly work loose, setting up stresses the material cannot withstand. Moving parts such as gates are particularly vulnerable. Gates should not be allowed to sag on their hinges or scrape over the ground as they open. Small cracks in ironwork can be filled with linseed oil putty as a temporary measure until permanent repairs can be carried out; the putty prevents the crack from trapping water and developing into a major problem.

Close examination of the ironwork will enable you to make informed decisions and understand what potential problems need to be taken into account. It is also helpful to take photographs of the problem areas: clear snapshots will aid accurate reinstatement if any parts need to be dismantled or taken off-site for repair. You need to know whether you are dealing with wrought iron, cast iron or a combination of the two. Investigate and record any old paint layers before cleaning, to glean any information about previous colours. A good principle is to do the minimum necessary to maintain the ironwork in good order, and retain as much of the original material as possible. For example, one cracked gutter or downpipe is no reason to throw out an entire cast iron rainwater system; it may be cheaper to buy one new cast iron element than to replace the lot in plastic.

*Suburban Queen Anne in a house of 1874 by M. Brydon. The wrought iron front gate and railings are as carefully considered as every other detail of the house.*

131

If rust has been allowed to develop, even to twice the thickness of the underlying iron, there is no need to panic. Rust can cause iron to expand to more than ten times the volume of the original material, so there may be enough sound iron remaining under the rust to make replacement unnecessary. Some areas are particularly vulnerable: upward-facing angles, crevices and grooves in ornamental leaves, and horizontal members all shed water slowly, and may be difficult to paint properly; they therefore provide more opportunities for rust to develop. As it expands, rust will push apart neighbouring iron elements and masonry. Railings are traditionally set into masonry with lead, which is soft enough to cope with a little expansion. In some cases, however, Portland cement has been used for repairs, and this is unable to accommodate expansion. It cracks and may cause the masonry in which it is set to crack as well.

Some small repairs can be carried out on site. Cast iron eaten away by rust but still reasonably sound can be made good using a steel and epoxy resin filler. Heads and finials can be fixed into place with a stainless steel dowel or a threaded fixing. The broken pieces of a straight-edged element can sometimes be discreetly strapped together with a steel plate fixed with screws and painted to match the surrounding iron. Broken cast iron can occasionally be repaired by welding, but this should only be carried out by trained staff.

### Replacing lost ironwork

As many standard designs are still in production, it is often possible to buy replacements for missing parts 'off the shelf'. If this is not possible, a mould can be taken from an existing original. Because newly-cast iron shrinks as it cools, it may be necessary to have a new pattern made for large or interlocking pieces. The cost of this will probably be too great for the average house renovation project, but in small pieces, such as railing heads or finials, the size difference is negligible.

*The railings are gone, but it should not be too difficult to establish the basic scale, profile and spacing of any replacement railings from the remaining evidence.*

Where sets of railings are missing, a little detective work can often provide useful clues to what was originally there. Look for original coping stones that retain the sockets into which the railings were fitted. From these, the spacing, section and thickness of the uprights can be deduced. Look also for evidence of thicker support posts every few feet, and of buttress posts, which are set back one or two feet behind the line of the railing for extra support at key points such as gateposts. Sockets or hinge supports set into the sides of piers and gate posts are evidence of the height, and possibly the section, of the cross-rail. Circumstantial evidence is also helpful: neighbouring houses may retain their original railings.

Several companies supply architectural iron castings and may be able to recommend designs to suit a particular age or style of house. Archive collections of founders' catalogues may also be consulted. If there is no historical evidence to help you choose the right design, a good rule of thumb is to choose the sturdiest designs you can afford, and to keep the size, architectural style and status of the house in mind – delicate Gothic tracery will not suit a robust, neoclassical villa. However elaborately decorative Victorian cast iron might sometimes have been, there was always a functional purpose underlying its use, so the temptation to clutter the exterior of the house with irrelevant 'Victoriana', such as standard lamps, bollards, name plates and fake insurance plaques, should be resisted.

### Paint finishes

The best way to protect iron once it has been cleaned is to give it a sound coat of paint, and the key to successful painting is correct surface preparation. There is no need to strip all the existing layers of paint back to the bare metal – if they are sound, they can be simply rubbed down with abrasive paper or steel wool and used as the basis for a metal. Small patches can be cleaned using a wire brush to remove loose flakes, and steel wool to prepare the surface for repainting. Chemical strippers in liquid or paste form may be used on small items and should be cleaned off with white spirit, as the use of water encourages rust.

Shot blasting should only be carried out by a skilled operative, and a test section should be submitted for inspection before the go-ahead is given for the whole job to be completed. Each part of the work should be test-cleaned, as cast iron is often combined with wrought iron or cast lead, both soft metals that can be permanently damaged by indiscriminate cleaning. Too strong a pressure may fracture cast iron, distort wrought iron, leave a pitted appearance or blur the fine detail. Wrought iron can be flame-cleaned, but cast iron may crack under extreme and rapid changes of temperature. Whatever cleaning method is chosen, appropriate safety precautions must be taken and proper arrangements made for dealing with any waste, dust or run-off created by the work.

Cast iron should be primed straight after cleaning so as to give rust no time to develop. English Heritage recommend the use of two coats of primer before an undercoat or 'binder' coat of micaceous iron oxide is applied. This is followed by up to four applications of the top coat. The wide choice of paint systems on the market can be confusing, so it is a good idea to consult the paint manufacturers' own literature or consumer advice department about compatibility of paints, especially where new paints are to be used over old.

Existing layers of old paint can be examined to determine the original colours of old ironwork. However, it takes expert knowledge to be able to distinguish topcoats from undercoats, or varnish from layers of dirt, so a casual scrape with a penknife cannot be relied upon to provide a reliable colour sample. The convention that prevails today, of painting all exterior cast iron with black gloss paint, is not historically correct, and the notion that this was done as a mark of respect following the death of Prince Albert in 1861 is a sentimental myth. Victorian householders chose from a range of paint colours considered appropriate for ironwork: green was used throughout the mid-Victorian period but dark blue, red and chocolate brown were also popular. In the 1890s iron garden furniture was sold ready-painted in green or chocolate brown. Some estates followed the practice of painting all exterior ironwork in their own livery to identify properties belonging to a particular landowner.

Traditional paint formulations are widely promoted for use in the interior decoration of old houses, but they may not be so appropriate for exterior items. The use of lead-based paint is now restricted by law, and the desire for authenticity must be set against the practical need to protect against the British climate. Nonetheless, something of the texture of a traditional lead-based paint finish can be achieved by using an eggshell paint in a final, sacrificial coat over gloss paint of the same colour. The eggshell, which is not formulated for exterior use, breaks down on exposure to the weather and mimics the powdery appearance of old paintwork.

Gilding details and finials was only done at very smart addresses and is probably best avoided in modest houses. Where it does appear appropriate to gild ironwork, it should be done with real gold leaf, not gold paint.

## Security

Decorative cast iron is now highly prized and therefore vulnerable to theft. Bolt heads can be fixed to prevent gates from being lifted off their hinges, and loose items such as benches, urns and decorative coalhole covers can be bolted into place. Even so, it is wise to photograph such items and note their measurements and any maker's marks, so they can be described in case of theft.

# CONSERVATORIES AND EXTENSIONS

ABOVE: *the Nottinghamshire architect T.C. Hine relaxing in his conservatory. The practical, waterproof floor tiles and the lush tropical planting are typical of Victorian conservatories. The armchair has been brought in especially for the photograph; since fine furniture suffered in the hothouse atmosphere, chairs made of wicker, rattan or metal were more usual.*

OPPOSITE: *the interior of a carefully restored conservatory at the rear of a terraced house in East London retains its original plain clay floor tiles.*

HE GLASS-AND-IRON CONSERVATORY must rank as one of the most innovative features of Victorian domestic architecture. A building type derived from industrial and agricultural prototypes, it used industrially-produced materials in daring new designs. It looked harmless enough but was a quietly subversive addition to the house: its glass transformed watery English sunlight into tropical humidity, its iron glazing bars added the tang of the factory and machine to the bland domestic flavour of the suburban villa, and the lush fruit, scented lilies and waxy orchids that could be grown in it upset the cycle of the seasons, offering a disturbing alternative to the clipped familiarity of the flower garden. At first the conservatory was seen as a female preserve where the wholesome hobby of gardening could be pursued in inclement weather. By the 1880s, however, a more naturalistic approach to gardening had become fashionable, and the conservatory was a symbol of artificiality and hence decadence.

The conservatory had its origins in the eighteenth-century enthusiasm for orangeries and other plant houses with a large proportion of galzing, where an artificial environment, could be sustained to protect delicate and exotic plants. Early glasshouses tended to be free-standing structures, but they did not remain in functional isolation for long. In 1816 the landscape gardener Humphry Repton published a design for a conservatory to link the house to the garden and bring light into a previously gloomy parlour, and in the 1830s the architect J.B. Papworth designed rooftop conservatories for large London terraced houses.

It was Loudon who did most to promote the conservatory in the early nineteenth century. His design for wrought-iron glazing bars made it possible to have a curved, glazed roof that would make the most of the sun throughout the day, and was a great improvement on the existing timber frames. Using the London firm of W. & D. Bailey as his contractors, Loudon set up a design-and-build company to supply conservatories, and erected a particularly complex example at his own house in Bayswater to drum up custom. Bailey's went on to build numerous glasshouses in the 1820s using Loudon's glazing bars, including one for Loddige's plant nursery in Hackney, enclosing a 1000-foot-long (300m) walk.

The other great innovator was Joseph Paxton. He was endlessly inventive in his pursuit of glasshouse perfection, developing a glazing bar machine and an innovative ridge-and-furrow roof system in order to speed up the building of conservatories for his employer, the Duke of Devonshire. Paxton's need for speed was due to his determination to grow the water lily *Victoria regia*, which had been brought to England in 1837

*Lean-to greenhouse illustrated in Thomson's* Gardener's Assistant *(1838). The plant pots are placed on stands with cast iron supports, heating is provided by pipes running around the walls at floor level, and ventilation is via toplights.*

Fig. 3.—*LEAN-TO GREENHOUSE.*

and for ten years had failed to thrive in Kew Gardens. In August 1849 Paxton planted a small specimen in a specially-constructed 'tank' (a heated pond house with a glass roof) at Chatsworth. Within six weeks the lily had outgrown its accommodation and the size of the tank had to be doubled. The lily grew – and flowered – prodigiously, and by the following spring it had to be moved again, to a much larger new house. It is possible that the ribbed structure of the *Victoria regia* leaf inspired Paxton's greatest glasshouse project, the Crystal Palace in Hyde Park, which he designed to house the Great Exhibition of 1851; it is certainly true that Paxton's proven ability to build quickly in glass and iron helped to win him the job.

The Crystal Palace, the Palm House at Kew (Richard Turner, 1845–8) and the numerous exhibition halls and winter gardens built in their wake inspired private householders to acquire their own private conservatories. The expense, and the land required, meant that only the wealthy could afford to build on any scale. The conservatory at Flintham Hall, a country house in Nottinghamshire designed by T.C. Hine in 1851, is a magnificent two-storey stone structure with a barrel-vaulted roof in glass and iron and an internal first-floor balcony. In 1894 Frederick Horniman ordered for his home, Coombe Cliff in Croydon, what must have been one of the last great Victorian conservatories, from the iron founders Walter Macfarlane of Glasgow. This impressive addition to the house, 60 feet (18m) long and covering 1,500 square feet (139 square metres), also served as a billiards room. It was restored in the 1980s and can be visited at the Horniman Museum (see Places to Visit, p.264).

Conservatories were also available to less wealthy householders in the form of kits of parts, which could be assembled on site by local builders. Among suppliers of 'flat-pack' conservatories in the 1880s were Hereman and Morton of Pall Mall, the only authorized distributors of Sir Joseph Paxton's designs, and Messenger and Co. of Loughborough, who hired Maurice B. Adams and E.W. Godwin to design their conservatories; Godwin supplied particularly striking designs in the 'Anglo-Japanese' style he had helped to make so fashionable.

Although iron enabled architects and engineers to design structures of dazzling inventiveness, timber was by no means abandoned as a material for framing glasshouses. It was not as resistant to condensation as iron, so it tended to be used for cold frames and unheated greenhouses in the garden and for temperate (not tropical) conservatories. An all-wood frame did not have the structural strength of the iron equivalent, thus timber conservatories were usually built on dwarf walls of brick or stone, or onto the back wall of the house as a kind of extended bay window or glazed-in balcony. Stained glass, which would have struck a jarring note in the technically advanced structures of Paxton and other exponents of iron-and-glass houses, was used extensively in late Victorian wooden conservatories, fitting quite naturally between conventional moulded and painted glazing bars.

The decoration and furnishing of conservatories were largely determined by the need for materials that would neither fade in bright light nor decay in a moist atmosphere. Glazing bars and frames were regularly repainted to prevent rust or rot. Floors were paved with colourful and moisture-resistant geometric or encaustic tiles. Furniture was made of non-absorbent materials, such as cast iron, marble, wirework, rattan, wicker, bamboo, and even glazed earthenware.

Heating and ventilating the conservatory tested the ingenuity of heating engineers, ironmongers and glasshouse merchants to the utmost. Coal-fired furnaces sent heated air through complex systems of wall flues or underfloor pipework. Hinged or swivelling skylights operated by pulleys, ratchets or screw threads provided ventilation. Pools kept the atmosphere at the ideal humidity for raising tropical plants, and were prevented from stagnating by fountains and waterwheels. Mechanization could only go so far, however, and maintaining a large conservatory was extremely labour-intensive. In the twentieth century, when it became hard to maintain large numbers of domestic staff, conservatories were seen as an unjustifiable extravagance and were dismantled or left to decay.

## New conservatories and extensions

Extending an existing building is one of the most difficult architectural challenges, and when the building in question is one of historic interest, the challenge is magnified. It takes imagination, tact and restraint to design new accommodation in sympathy with a historic house. The new work does not have to be a slavish copy of the existing building, nor is it essential that it should look as though it has always been there, but it must look 'right'. Naturally, that rightness is a question of scale, architectural style and materials, but it also involves attention to detail and a willingness to seek out original and interesting solutions to the problem of providing more space rather than settling for the standard builder's solution.

ABOVE: *exterior of the conservatory shown on page 134, which extends over the basement at the rear of the house. Dark colours, and especially green, help timber and iron frames blend into a garden setting.*

OPPOSITE: *the imposing conservatory at Flintham Hall, Nottinghamshire, has a fountain to help maintain humidity.*

One way of extending is to build extra accommodation at the back of the house. An infill of the 'L' formed between the back wall of a terraced or semi-detached house and an existing kitchen extension, or building one or more storeys above the kitchen extension, are typical approaches. Another common type is a garage added to the side of a semi-detached or detached house. Before extending any part of your house, it is vital to obtain the necessary planning consent. If the work involves altering the sewer, you will need to arrange for this to be inspected and approved. And, of course, the extension must conform to current Building Regulations.

The extension should be on a smaller scale than the rest of the house, both in plan and elevation. In a single-storey ground-floor back extension the roof should not clash with the first-floor windows on the back and elevations. Extensions to front and back walls should be set back behind the original building line. This may lose a few centimetres of floor space within the extension, but the external appearance will 'read' much better. The slight break in the line of the wall will also help to make the visual contrast between the old and new materials less jarring.

Mimic or exploit the shape of the existing building in the extension. Extensions with lean-to, hipped or double-pitched roofs nearly always look better than flat roofs. The roof should pitch at the same angle as the roof of the main building. An effective way to link an extension to a low building is to continue the roof without interruption, making a catslide that covers the new construction. In most extensions to modest Victorian houses it is best to avoid gimmicky shapes such as quadrant or triangle plans, ogee roofs or cupolas, which call attention to themselves. In this case reticence is more appropriate – and cheaper.

Materials and finishes should match those used in the house. New bricks should be the same size, shape, colour and texture as the old, and laid in the same bond with matching mortar. Details such as courses of contrasting brick should be replicated in the new walling. If the main house has a slate roof with terracotta ridge tiles, use slate and terracotta for the extension. Do not be tempted to apply artificial ageing treatments to the new building; natural materials such as brick and stone will 'weather down' in a surprisingly short time. The detailing at the junction between the old build-

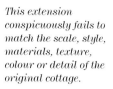

*This extension conspicuously fails to match the scale, style, materials, texture, colour or detail of the original cottage.*

*A two-storey extension to
a detached suburban
house is a successful
small-scale replica of the
mother building, and is
modestly set back from
the original building line.
Care has been taken to
match the colour, style
and pointing of the
brickwork, and to copy
details such as the design
of the bargeboards.*

ing and the new requires particular attention. On vertical joins the new wall must be soundly tied into the new structure, and horizontal or sloping roof joins must be properly flashed with lead.

Pay attention to the details: if the extension covers the back door, it may be possible (and will certainly save money) to re-use the door in the new exterior wall and buy a new door for the interior opening. Infill extensions often enclose the soil pipe and drain, which are usually located in the angle between the original back and kitchen walls. With careful planning these can be concealed within built-in cupboards or shelves, yet remain accessible for inspection. Door and window furniture is important, too; if you have got every aspect of the basic design right, it is a shame to spoil the effect with inappropriate modern fittings.

One of the most attractive ways to extend a Victorian house is with a new conservatory in a style appropriate to the house. And one of the least attractive ways is with an over-sized glazed box bought off the peg as a cheap alternative to a solid wall extension. The current revival of interest in conservatories began in the 1980s as a consequence of rising property prices and aggressive marketing by the double glazing industry. Thus many shiny aluminium and glaring white plastic structures were slapped onto the back of Victorian houses to which they were totally unsuited in scale, design and materials.

It is possible to obtain a conservatory extension that will enhance your house, but you should be prepared for it to cost as much as a well-designed, convincingly-detailed solid wall extension. A conservatory assembled from a kit of standard parts designed for an 'average' modern house cannot be expected to match the style and detail of a nineteenth-century house: this is one case when only made-to-measure will do.

Conservatories are partly transparent but they are not invisible, and it is important to get the scale right, as discussed for solid wall extensions above. The ratio of glass to

141

The spectacular
conservatory built in
1895 for Frederick
Horniman, using cast
iron components from
Walter Macfarlane's
Saracen Foundry in
Glasgow. The doors are
teak, which is resistant
to humidity.

solid structure is particularly relevant. Domestic conservatories in the nineteenth century usually had small individual panes of glass, with plenty of detail in the glazing bars, but strong, flawless glass is now so cheap that modern conservatories tend to be designed around large frames with uninterrupted blank glazing. The temptation to use large sheets is particularly strong in double-glazed designs, because the cost of several small sealed units is so much higher than the cost of one. This has led to the use of 'glazing bars' that are simply cut out of a flat piece of wood and stuck onto the face of the glass in a parody of proper window joinery. If you want to use your conservatory as a living room, you will need double glazing to prevent condensation and conserve heat, so consider reducing the amount of glazing in the walls to avoid the 'blank sheet' effect.

Materials are particularly important in a conservatory. Make sure any new walling, whether stone, brick or rendered, matches the rest of the house. The frame should be in cast metal or timber (not extruded aluminium, which has a skimpy appearance, or plastic) and should always be painted. Victorian conservatories were never painted brilliant white, for the simple reason that the colour did not exist before the mid-twentieth century. Broken whites were used, and green and brown were considered particularly appropriate for garden buildings. A conservatory can be visually anchored to the house if the joinery on both is painted the same colour.

# PART III
## *Services*

# FIREPLACES AND CHIMNEYS

T HE FIREPLACE WAS MORE than just the sole method of domestic heating for most of the nineteenth century. It was the focus of architectural interest in most interiors, and, as the centre of family life, it made an important symbolic contribution to the character of the house. Many chimneys were blocked and fireplaces removed in the 1960s and 1970s when central heating was installed. House owners are now opening up blocked fireplaces and buying second-hand or reproduction grates, or refurbishing original ones in order to restore the architectural character of their houses.

## History

The technology of the fireplace was refined and improved throughout the Victorian period. In early Victorian houses most fireplaces had square or rectangular openings, and were fitted with hob grates. These had horizontal bars to hold the burning coal in place, and flat metal plates on either side on which pans and kettles could be heated. Neoclassical motifs, incised or cast into the metal, provided restrained decoration. However, there were problems associated with this type of fireplace. The flame was high above the floor, so that cold draughts ran across the room at ground level. The bottom of the grate was open and the flue very wide, creating an unnecessarily strong draught that carried most of the heat straight up the chimney. Very little heat was reflected out into the room, and the wide fireplace opening made it difficult to control the draught or stop smoke from coming into the room.

The problem of fireplace efficiency had been addressed as early as the 1790s by the American technologist Benjamin Rumford. He recommended lowering the fire and placing it further forward in the opening, narrowing the throat of the flue, reducing the overall size of the opening and lining it with firebrick, and splaying the sides of the fire surround. These measures would provide better draught control and throw more heat out into the room, but the British were reluctant to tamper with the established style of fireplace, and it was not until nearly a century later that all these proposals were adopted as a matter of course. At first, existing fireplaces were 'Rumfordised' – that is, the throat of the flue was narrowed and the fire basket was lowered to a few inches above floor level. The register grate, introduced in about 1850, was the first step towards a standardized design that included all of Rumford's improvements. It consisted of a cast iron surround with an arched top and a metal plate above the fire, which blocked off the flue. A small metal trapdoor in the back plate enabled the flow of air to be

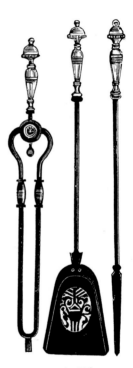

ABOVE: *a set of 'fire irons' was the essential accessory to every Victorian fireplace.*

OPPOSITE: *dining room fireplace in a house of 1869. The arched-top grate is typical of mid-century grates, and the dark marble surround was considered appropriate to the 'masculine' character of the dining room.*

147

*The design-conscious Linley Sambourne removed the standard-issue cast iron grate from his drawing room fireplace, preferring the less efficient but more fashionable Queen Anne style of tiled opening with free-standing basket grate.*

adjusted. It was opened wide when the fire was first lit to create sufficient draught to get the fire going. Once the fire was well established, the trapdoor was closed until there was just sufficient space to allow the smoke to be sucked out, but not enough to draw all the heat of the flames up the chimney.

In the 1870s a new style of cast iron fire surround began to replace the arched-top variety: a square opening, with splayed 'cheeks' ornamented with glazed tiles that reflected heat forward into the room. The bars holding the fire were cast in one piece and dropped into a slot at the front of the grate, or held in place by integral hooks that fitted into special housings on each side. A decorative panel in front of the ash pan controlled the draught via a louvred or sliding grill. As successive models moved the grate further forward, it became necessary to introduce a projecting metal plate above the fire to guide the smoke into the flue. These smoke hoods – which, incidentally, provided another flat surface for cast or tiled decoration – became quite common from about 1880.

Changing tastes sometimes undermined the quest for efficiency: when Edward Linley Sambourne renovated his drawing-room in 1884, he removed the standard grate, lined the fireplace opening with tiles and stood an open fire basket with brass fire dogs in its place. Although this must have burned more fuel and produced less heat, it paid the homage to eighteenth-century interior design that contemporary fashion demanded.

The late nineteenth-century interest in English vernacular architecture led to a revival of traditional English forms of fireplace. The inglenook, reintroduced by architects such as Shaw for dining rooms in the country houses of wealthy clients, eventually appeared in scaled-down versions for suburban houses, brick arches and hoods of beaten copper, supplying the necessary Olde Worlde touch.

### The fire surround

The most common style of fire surround in the early Victorian period was a simple arrangement of flat jambs and a lintel supporting a mantelshelf. This design was produced in timber, plaster and marble, and could be enriched with a variety of mouldings. Foundries such as the Coalbrookdale and Carron companies offered cast iron surrounds that could be combined with their grates; the smaller models were often cast with the grate and the surround all in one piece. Unless it was made of marble or an expensive hardwood such as oak, the surround was never left bare. Timber and plaster were invariably painted, and cast iron was either painted or black-leaded. Surrounds made of cheap Welsh slate were often painted to imitate complex coloured marble inlays. Illustrations in builders' merchants' catalogues showed how standard fireplace elements (cast iron grate, ceramic tiles, slate surround) could be combined to create different effects. The imitation marble paint finishes available included 'red limestone with black mounts' and 'Spanish brocatella with gilt lines'.

The design of surrounds reflected the customary manner of using the house, as well as fashions in interior decoration. Paterae (roundels) or rosettes were used to adorn the angle between the jambs and lintel during the Regency period, and remained popular during the early years of Victoria's reign. They were superseded by ornate brackets in the form of acanthus leaves or garlands of flowers. In middle-class houses of the mid-Victorian period, the arched-top grate in the dining room might have a surround of black marble, or slate painted in imitation marble inlay, to reflect the 'masculine' character of the room, while the drawing room had a white marble surround. Believing that 'there is perhaps no feature of even an ordinary dwelling-house which is capable of more artistic treatment than the fireplace of its most frequented sitting-room', Eastlake demanded 'picturesque and interesting' fireplaces, and cited Nesfield and Shaw as architects who might supply rich clients with inglenooks of herringbone brickwork or carved stone containing free-standing fire dogs, or householders of lesser pretensions with oak-panelled chimneypieces surrounding openings lined in blue and white tiles.

Less money was invested in fireplaces in other rooms. The family bedrooms had painted timber surrounds, while the attic bedrooms, if they had fireplaces at all, would be fitted with the smallest 'Student' grate with an integral cast iron mantelshelf.

### Fireplace accessories

The number of tools and fittings required to maintain a Victorian hearth could be considerable. A fender kept ashes and hot coals from falling onto the carpet. A set of poker and tongs was used to tend the burning fire, and a dustpan and brush to keep the hearth clean. Extra coal was kept to one side of the hearth in a polished brass scuttle or a 'purdonium', an ornamental coalbox with a hinged lid and a shovel-holder at the back, named after its designer, Mr Purdon.

Besides these essentials, there were any number of optional extras: screens protected delicate drawing-room complexions from the heat of the flames, while upstairs in the nursery, meals were served up with the aid of trivets and toasting forks. Embroidered or beaded valances were tacked along the edge of the mantelshelf, clocks and other ornaments were symmetrically arranged along the shelf, and gilt-framed mirrors filled the chimneybreast, reflecting the elaborate chandelier or gasolier that hung from the centre of the ceiling.

During the summer months the empty fireplace was always decorated with a painted or embroidered screen, a paper fan, an arrangement of flowers or a miniature

The main bedroom at 'Sunnycroft', Shropshire, has a shuttered grate designed to control the temperature of the room and, in particular, to be closed at night to prevent draughts.

151

Fireplace in Summer, drawn by Thomas Crane to illustrate his daughter Lucy's lectures on Art, and the Formation of Taste (1882).

garden of ferns, the only plants guaranteed to thrive in such a dark spot. In 1856 Mrs Beeton described 'very pretty modes' of ornamenting grates and fireplaces, such as 'the eternal crinoline, fringed out and adorned with ivy and real or artificial flowers'. A mirror fitted into the opening, reflecting potted plants on the hearth, was 'nice, but expensive', whereas everyone could afford a basketwork trellis, up which jasmine or clematis might be trained. By 1882 tastes had changed, and Lucy Crane was recommending a return to the simpler style of the eighteenth century.

The illustration that accompanied this plea for simplicity is a little snapshot of Aesthetic taste. It showed a mantelshelf supporting an artfully asymmetrical arrangement of blue-and-white pots, a Japanese fan, an eighteenth-century drinking-glass and a Regency mirror. The Aesthetic influence also made itself felt in chimneypieces designed to cover the entire chimneybreast, from mantelshelf to picture rail. Influenced by the 'Japanese-y' furniture of designers such as E.W. Godwin, these consisted of multiple shelves, cupboards and compartments of ebonized wood lined with tiles, mirror or embossed and gilded wallpaper – a suitable background for ornaments carefully chosen and arranged to express their owner's refined good taste.

Managing the fire was a duty that usually devolved upon the humbler members of the household. Male servants filled the coal scuttles but it was the housemaid's job to empty the ash cans, lay the fire and sweep the hearth before the family descended for breakfast. Such was the drudgery of maintaining fires that in households with no servants, the fire in the front parlour might never be lit except for very special occasions.

Sweeping the chimneys was the first stage in the annual spring clean, as recommended by Mrs Beeton. The careful housewife would empty the room and cover any immoveable furniture before the work started, and take care to see that the brush was 'sent up through the top of the chimney'. Sweeps employed apprentices, or 'climbing boys', who had to crawl into the complex interconnecting flues of large houses.

Gas fires were developed in the 1860s, and in 1870 a firebrick made with asbestos, which could withstand the intense, localized heat of a gas burner, was introduced. Although gas fires were widely installed in institutions, they did not become popular for domestic use until the 1920s. Electric fires made their appearance at the end of the Edwardian period. Very occasionally, early gas or electric fires are found when boxed-in fireplaces are opened up. They are worth retaining as curiosities, but it is rarely possible to restore them to safe working order.

Central heating by underfloor hot-air systems was used in some large country houses, for example Cragside, but it was regarded as unhealthy by Britons accustomed for generations to chilly bedrooms and draughty corridors, and was not fitted into ordinary suburban housing until the middle of the twentieth century.

## Maintenance and Repair
### Flues and chimneys

Each fireplace has a separate flue, which connects with others on its upward progress so that one chimneystack contains several outlets. Flues became narrower during the nineteenth century. Early Victorian flues measured about 9 x 14 inches (230 x 350mm), but by 1850 the average size was 9 inches (230mm) square. In terraced houses the back of the chimney is built into the party wall and shares masonry with the neighbouring house. Before fitting a grate or lighting a fire, ask a chimney sweep to clean and inspect the flue. A smoke test will show whether the flue is blocked. Smoke escaping into upstairs rooms or the neighbouring house indicates cracks in the internal

*Composite chimney stack above a Flemish gable on a Suffolk farmhouse of 1874 by Frederick Barnes.*

masonry of the flue. Loose bricks or mortar in the soot brought down by sweeping indicate that the internal masonry is crumbling.

Internal damage to a flue is usually inaccessible, but it may be possible to reline the flue, either with a flexible steel sleeve liner dropped into the flue and fixed at both ends, or with self-setting foam. To install the latter, an inflatable rubber lining is dropped into the flue from the top and fixed at both ends. A chemical foam is then poured into the space between the lining and the internal face of the flue. This hardens into a heatproof and rigid shell around the new flue, and prevents further deterioration of the internal masonry. However, many conservationists, including the SPAB, do not recommend this type of relining, as it is irreversible and in some cases may prevent proper ventilation of the flue.

Check the condition of the masonry on the chimneys above the roofline. A pair of binoculars will enable you to make an initial inspection if you cannot get onto the roof.

153

*Doulton's decorative
terracotta chimneypots
modelled on
Elizabethan brick
chimneys were among
the impressive ceramic
building products
displayed at the Great
Exhibition of 1851.*

The pointing, soakers (lead flashings at the junction of the chimney and the roof) and the flaunching (the slope of mortar in which the chimney pot is bedded to the stack) should be sound (see Chapter 4, Brick and Terracotta, and Chapter 7, Roofs). Some 'Tudorbethan' style houses have elaborate 'barleytwist' chimneys, which require skilled repair.

In houses where fireplaces have been sealed off, chimneypots may have been capped or removed altogether, or chimney stacks may have been reduced in height. Redundant chimneys should never be completely sealed at the top, as this prevents ventilation and may cause condensation to form within the flue. An airbrick inserted into the masonry of the chimney stack will ensure a free flow of air if the top of the stack has been sealed. If you are reopening a chimney, the airbrick should be removed and replaced with bricks to match the rest of the chimney.

Terracotta chimney pots were produced in many different sizes and patterns, glazed and unglazed. Many have been removed but it is possible to buy replacements, either newly made or from salvage yards that sell them as garden ornaments. Elaborately moulded terracotta pots can be reproduced as 'specials' to order, but this is an expensive business. If a tall building overshadows the chimney, it may be necessary to raise the height of the chimney or install taller pots in order to maintain a good draught. A variety of caps and cowls is available to prevent wind, rain or nesting birds from entering the open chimney.

### Opening up a blocked fireplace

Having established that you have a sound and serviceable flue and chimney, you will need to investigate how the fireplace opening was sealed. If the surround is still in place, it is likely that the opening was merely fitted with a plywood panel. If the surround is gone and the chimney breast has been plastered and redecorated, the opening was probably sealed with brickwork or breezeblock, which will have to be hacked out. There should be a ventilator grill just above the skirting to ventilate the chimney: remove this and insert a lighted spill into the void. If the flame burns well, and is drawn inwards and upwards, the flue is clear. If the flame is still, there is a blockage somewhere in the flue or the builder's opening that will have to be removed before you can fit the fireplace. In either case, it is essential to have the chimney swept before you go any further.

Step-by-step instructions for fitting replacement fireplaces are given in DIY manuals, the Solid Fuel Association publishes a series of excellent guides (see Further Reading, p.259), and there are many specialist contractors who will fit a fireplace for you. Whichever route you choose, it is as well to understand how the fireplace opening was constructed. The large, square opening in the brickwork of the chimneybreast, into which the fireplace is fitted, is known as the 'builder's opening'. The top of the builder's opening is formed by an iron bar or a brickwork arch. Do not remove or disturb this, as it is holding up the brickwork of the chimney breast above. The constructional hearth is a concrete slab forming a barrier between the fireplace and the combustible elements in the room such as timber floors and carpets. It must project a minimum of 500mm (20 inches) in front of the chimney breast and at least 150mm (9 inches) on either side of the builder's opening. On top of this goes the decorative hearth of brick, tile or marble, which must be 48mm (1¾ inches) thick, and must project not less than 300mm (12 inches) beyond the open fire. Behind this, the floor level is raised flush with mortar to make the back hearth; in modern installations a piece of glass fibre rope is laid between the two to form an expansion joint.

In some Arts and Crafts houses the builder's opening was lined with good quality brickwork in a herringbone, basketweave or other decorative bond. In Queen Anne revival interiors the opening was lined with tiles in the early eighteenth-century manner. Most Victorian fireplaces, however, were fitted with cast-iron grates.

When lighting your first fire in a newly-installed grate, or in a grate that has not been used for a long time, start slowly. You need to start with a small fire of paper and fire-lighter to warm the chimney and help the fire to draw properly. Keep a low fire going for a couple of hours before piling on the (smokeless) fuel and blazing away.

Coal effect gas fires are convincing substitutes for a real coal fire and are a labour-saving way of bringing a fireplace back to life. The gas fittings should be placed with care, however: nothing ruins the illusion more than a gas supply pipe snaking round the front of the grate to an obtrusive on/off tap. Only a purist could object to the fakery of a coal effect fire – although owners of such fires will have to decide whether to go as far as fitting out the hearth with fire irons and a full coal scuttle in order to sustain the illusion.

ABOVE: *Distinctive moulded terracotta chimneys on a Suffolk farmhouse (1874).*

LEFT: *An early-Victorian fireplace has a white marble surround with finely carved acanthus leaf corbels.*

### *Repairing and replacing grates and chimneypieces*

It can be difficult to choose the right style to replace a missing fireplace. Traditional designs remained popular for many years, and revivals of historical styles complicate the picture. The best guide would be an original fireplace from a neighbouring house of similar age and date, which has escaped modernization. The status of the house, and of the room in which the fireplace is to be fitted, should be taken into account when choosing the style and materials of any replacement. An elaborate grate will be oversized and pretentious in the living room of an artisan's cottage and equally out of place in a maid's bedroom in a mansion. A drawing room full of classical mouldings in an Italianate house is obviously unsuited to a Gothic fire surround. Victorian grates are available from architectural salvage yards, and reproduction grates are now widely available. Many of the reproductions are cast from original patterns, and they are ideal for use in the principal rooms of Victorian houses (the modern product ranges rarely include small grates for secondary rooms such as bedrooms).

Sometimes the original fireplace is there but parts are missing; projecting elements such as the ash pan, the hood or the bars were often removed in order to install a sheet of hardboard flush with the surround. Finding replacements for these is likely to be a hit-and-miss affair. Look for a manufacturer's name or model number, and make a note of the method of fitting the missing parts to the main fireplace, including the dimensions of any slots, lugs or bolt holes. Ash pans usually sat on the backhearth, bars fitted into slots or grooves in the front of the grate, and hoods were usually bolted to the inside of the moulding that frames the opening. Then take the information to an architectural salvage or fireplace specialist to see whether they stock suitable replacement parts. If parts of the fireplace have rusted into place, clean off the loose dirt, rust and soot with a stiff brush and apply a lubricant such as WD40. With patience you should eventually be able to work the parts loose.

Rusted and dirty cast iron can be brushed down with wire wool and cleaned with a rag dipped in white spirit (not water). A chemical paint stripper (e.g. Nitromors) will remove paint from cast iron. Do not use a blowtorch: cast iron can crack if subjected to sudden changes of temperature. Use a wooden or plastic spatula to remove the softened paint, and a nylon bristle brush on the details. Metal scrapers and wire brushes will scratch the metal. Rub the metal clean with white spirit. Alternatively, find a firm in your area that can blast-clean the metal *in situ*: look under 'metal finishers' and 'metal polishers' in the Yellow Pages.

If the quality of the casting is good and you like the surface colour when you have finished the stripping, you could apply a thin coat of WD40, rub it in well in to prevent rust forming, and stop there. Ideally, however, the bare metal should be protected with polish or a coat of paint. The traditional finish for cast iron grates was the dull sheen imparted by black lead polish. This is now sold in a safe, lead-free formulation under the trade name Zebo. The trick is to apply the cream very sparingly and elbow grease generously. A labour-saving finish that mimics the effect of black lead is a thin coat of stove black (heat-resistant) paint applied over a coat of red oxide primer and polished when dry with a sparing application of wax.

Rusty steel can be cleaned with a rust remover such as Solvol Autosol and brought to a bright shine with fine wire wool dipped in oil. Although some grates and surrounds incorporate brightly polished metal elements – beaten copper hoods, brass finials or moulded decoration in polished steel – an overall glitter of white metal is not an authentic Victorian finish for a cast iron surround. Brass and copper fittings can be polished with a proprietary cleaner such as Brasso.

## The surround

The surround should be in proportion to the height of the wall and the width of the chimney-breast. Look for the outline of the former surround under the wallpaper; it may even show up through the wallpaper if the chimneybreast is examined under a raking light. Salvage yards and fireplace specialists usually stock surrounds. If you need a timber surround, avoid the self-assembly kits sold in DIY stores: their proportions and detailing are not convincing, and it is better to get a joiner to copy an original than to resort to an off-the-peg compromise.

To clean light stains off a marble chimneypiece, try a very weak solution of ammonia (half a cup in a bucket of water). Bell's 1966 cleaner is a strong, general purpose cleaner for stone and Bell's 1967 is suitable for marble. Bell also manufacture a special cleaner for badly marked marble. Stubborn stains can be tackled with a poultice made with fuller's earth, talc, sepiolite or powdered chalk. Mix one of these absorbent materials with distilled water to form a creamy paste. Wet the stone and before spreading the paste over the stained area to a thickness of at least 1cm (½ inch). Cover the poultice with Clingfilm and leave it to dry. Once dry, it can be scraped off with a plastic spatula. For organic stains (e.g. food spills) make the poultice with a solvent such as ammonia or 2% hydrogen peroxide instead of distilled water. For grease or oil-based marks, use acetone (nail polish remover) or white spirit instead of distilled water. For smoke or soot stains, first brush off all loose material and then apply a poultice with a powdered alkaline cleaner such as washing powder or baking soda, and distilled water. Weak acid solutions, for instance lemon juice, may also be effective.

Be prepared to poultice a badly stained area several times, experimenting with different solvents until the stain is finally lifted out. It is best to start with a mild approach and work up to stronger solvents. Residual stains can be lightened with a weak solution of household bleach – but never use bleach and ammonia together: the two combine to produce a toxic gas. After each of these treatments, the area should be rinsed with clean water and dried.

Paint can be removed from slate and marble by a proprietary stripper such as Nitromors or Kwik Strip. Never use abrasives, sanders or disc grinders. Wear protective clothing, gloves and goggles as necessary when carrying out any of these procedures. Once cleaned, the marble can be given a protective coating of microcrystalline wax polish, for example Renaissance, sparingly applied and well buffed.

## Paint finishes for fire surrounds

Softwood fire surrounds were invariably painted. The 'stripped pine' look was anathema to Victorian householders, who would demand that even the best quality pitch pine be stained and varnished. Another way to achieve the appearance of good-quality timber was to paint cheap deal with a woodgrain finish so that it looked like oak, mahogany or ebony. A solid colour to match the rest of the interior joinery or otherwise suit the decoration of the rest of the room was the most usual finish. The modern eggshell finish is a good substitute for the gloss paints available to the Victorians, which usually dulled with time. Marbling on slate surrounds should be retained if possible and expertly restored if necessary; matching specialist paint effects is not a DIY job.

## Security

Fire grates and surrounds are attractive to thieves. Be vigilant about security, especially when building or decorating work is going on. Take photographs of your fireplaces and record any distinguishing features, such as maker's names or pattern numbers cast into the metal, so that your property can be identified or replaced if necessary.

31. Gerard Hoet

49

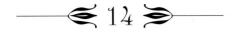

# LIGHTING

ONE OF THE MOST fundamental changes in British home life in the nineteenth century was the adoption of cheap and convenient artificial light. Illumination by oil, gas and finally electric lamps encouraged the tyranny of long hours and night shifts in Victorian offices and factories, but in the home it opened up new possibilities for work and leisure, changed the way rooms were decorated and furniture arranged, and liberated families from the need to huddle round a single precious candle before going early to bed.

Like other innovations, new methods of lighting developed in fits and starts and were adopted piecemeal. Urban areas tended to use gas and electricity before others because it was more profitable for companies to install their equipment in densely populated areas where demand would be high. Early supplies were erratic, and people were naturally reluctant to abandon tried and tested forms of lighting and leave themselves at the mercy of an unreliable system. Thus different methods of lighting were in use simultaneously in most houses throughout the century. A parlour lighted entirely by firelight and candles in 1800 might by 1838 have acquired one expensive oil lamp to supplement the candlelight. By 1870 the same room might have been lit with gas fed to a central gasolier or to brackets on the walls, but still have oil lamps at the table for reading and sewing. By the end of the century the gas fittings would have been adapted to electricity and the old oil lamps banished to the attic; the candlesticks displayed on the mantelpiece remained merely as sentimental witnesses to a vanished age.

## Rushlights and candles

In the 1830s most houses were lit by oil lamps and candles. The cheapest form of candle was a rushlight: the green outer leaf was peeled off a rush, exposing the spongy interior of the stem (a narrow strip of green was left to stop the stem drooping). The peeled rush was then soaked in a tallow of rendered animal fat (usually mutton). It solidified into a long, thin, wickless taper. Rushlights were stored in cylindrical tin boxes that hung on the kitchen wall. Placed in a spring-clip holder, each one would give a dim, yellowish light for about fifteen minutes. They were messy and smelly, and had to be regularly trimmed to prevent them from producing alarming quantities of sooty smoke.

Candles came in various guises: dipped or moulded, and composed of different fats, oils and waxes. Many households made their own for everyday use, reserving 'shop' candles for special occasions. Small candle-making firms supplied local demand for better-quality candles, and wax candles remained a luxury well into the nineteenth

ABOVE: *An oil lamp designed by W.A.S. Benson for Morris & Co. in about 1895 combines a conventional brass pedestal stand with a futuristic shade of overlapping copper blades.*

OPPOSITE: *an Argand lamp of the 1850s on a bronze and ormolu stand with frosted glass shades. The oil reservoir has been incorporated into the design in the shape of an urn.*

159

*The same tubular brass frame is the basis for each of these pendants for incandescent gas burners of the 1890s, but the addition of a 'Superior Silk' or 'Aurora Tinted Glass' shade rings the changes. The inverted dishes hanging above the lamps are 'smoke bells', designed to prevent smuts from blackening the ceiling.*

century. Like soap, candles were kept for as long as possible before use so that the wax would harden and burn longer; good housekeepers took care to buy 'cold weather' candles, as it was known that candles made in winter lasted longer.

Tallow candles were cheap but almost as smelly, dirty and fast-burning as rushlights. Beeswax candles burned evenly and cleanly, required little attention and had a pleasant smell but were very expensive. The most luxurious candles were made from fragrant white spermaceti, but by 1820 the sperm whale had been hunted almost to extinction and the search was on for substitute fuels. In 1823 the French chemist Chevreul succeeded in isolating the fatty acid stearine from tallow, and by 1829 it was possible to synthesize stearine.

Two English tallow dealers, William Wilson and Benjamin Lancaster, saw the potential of stearine for candle-making on an industrial scale and opened a candle factory in Battersea in 1830. The business, which they named Price's, received an immediate boost with the abolition of the candle tax in the following year. Soon there were two Price's factories in London and one in Liverpool, each with its own quay to take delivery of materials from all corners of the Earth. The introduction of paraffin wax in the 1850s was smoothly absorbed into the business, and by 1860 the Battersea factory employed 9000 people, producing 100 tons (£7,000 worth) of candles every week. The Battersea works still uses moulding machines made to a patented design of the 1880s. A series of racks, each containing seven dozen metal moulds, is threaded with wicks and filled with molten wax. Cold water is piped in to cool the moulds, and when the wax has hardened enough to keep its shape, the rack is cranked so that the newly-made candles pop up, ready for their wicks to be trimmed.

Although in 1820 Cambacère had invented a 'snuffless' candle with a wick requiring no trimming, and William Palmer patented a four-wick 'Magnum' candle in the 1830s, candles were low-tech products that resisted improvement. In their efforts to increase sales, candle makers became masters of niche marketing and product diversification:

infants were comforted by night lights on the nursery mantelpiece, while at the other end of life's journey, funerals were lit by wake candles sold in packets with black-bordered wrappings. 'Boudoir candles', hand-painted with pretty nosegays, cast a flattering light over the dressing table; piano candles were packaged with images of handsome tenors singing soulful ballads; and parties were made brilliant by 'Parastrine' and 'Best Ballroom Sperm' (i.e. spermaceti) candles.

Candle holders were made in a variety of materials and designs. A common design took the form of a saucer with a short cylindrical candle holder riveted to the centre and a metal loop for a handle. These were produced in wrought iron, pressed tin, enamel ware and brass, and were used in kitchens and bedrooms, the handle making them easy to carry upstairs at night.

Candlesticks based on various forms of column and baluster were made in a wider range of materials, including brass, pottery, glass and silver (or its imitators, Sheffield plate and Britannia metal). Designs tended towards the traditional, and only changing proportions and details distinguished Victorian silver column candlesticks from their Georgian ancestors. Pewter and brass baluster candlesticks can be hard to date accurately, since they have been in continuous production from the early eighteenth century to the present day, and rarely carry meaningful marks like the hallmarks on precious metals. Some sticks were fitted with sliding mechanisms to push the candle up the holder, ensuring that only the smallest possible stub of candle was left unburnt.

More elaborate candlesticks and chandeliers were made to complement all the fashionable styles in interior decoration, including some that were, to say the least, eclectic in style. Examples in bronze, iron, ormolu, glass and even gilded papier-mâché were shown at the Great Exhibition of 1851. The Coalbrookdale Company exhibited an 'Elizabethan looking-glass' in cast iron painted white and gilded, with six branches for candles. Potts of Birmingham were praised for their candle lamps (tall, tubular candle holders with push-up mechanisms and glass shades), including one with a 'pedestal composed of elephants' heads, very skilfully wrought'. Osler of London and Birmingham exhibited a fifteen-light candelabrum of pure crystal and standing 8 feet (2.4m) high, which they had made for Queen Victoria. The Medieval Court contained brass chandeliers designed by Pugin and made by Hardman & Co. of Birmingham.

The Gothic Revival made brass acceptable again as a material for candlesticks and chandeliers in genteel interiors. From about 1860 Arts and Crafts designers made particularly beautiful candlesticks and sconces in brass and copper. A pair of copper candlesticks designed by Philip Webb in 1861 had push-up mechanisms and wide drip pans on squat conical bases with bands of simple cross-hatching and punched holes for decoration. Cheltenham Art Gallery owns a pair of wall sconces by Ernest Gimson in pierced and polished brass.

Living by candlelight required special skills and tools. Wax tapers were used to carry a flame from candle to candle when lighting a chandelier, and conical extinguishers to put out candle flames without spreading droplets of wax; snuffing – trimming a wick to prevent it from growing too long, falling over and melting the candle – was done by special scissors with a little box mounted on one blade to catch the trimmings. Friction matches or 'lucifers' were invented in 1827, but well into the nineteenth century servants who set up candles were instructed to light the 'cotton' (i.e. the wick) to burn off any excess length and then extinguish it so that it would relight easily when it was needed – a refinement that dated from an age when steel, flint and tinder were required to start a flame, and candles were lit with tapers held to the fire.

*A copper candlestick, one of a pair designed by Philip Webb for Sir Edward Burne-Jones in about 1860, demonstrates the Arts and Crafts movement's interest in humble materials.*

# Oil lamps

Simple oil lamps, consisting of an oil-saturated wick protruding from an oil reservoir, were used by the ancient Romans. Exactly the same principle was used in Victorian oil lamps – although disguised by such refinements as a glass, porcelain or metal reservoir, a rack-and-pinion mechanism to raise and lower the wick, a glass chimney to protect the flame and a shade to diffuse the light.

In 1784 the Swiss scientist François-Pierre Ami Argand had patented a new kind of oil lamp. The Argand lamp had a tubular wick that admitted air directly into the centre of the flame, and was enclosed in a glass chimney, so that, in the words of Webster and Parkes' *Encyclopaedia of Domestic Economy* (1844), 'every part of the thin circular flame is between two currents of air, which supply the combustion with oxygen so

*Expensive light fittings would be adapted to new technology rather than replaced: this ormolu and opaque glass pendant lamp started life in the mid-nineteenth century as an oil burner, and is now lit by electricity.*

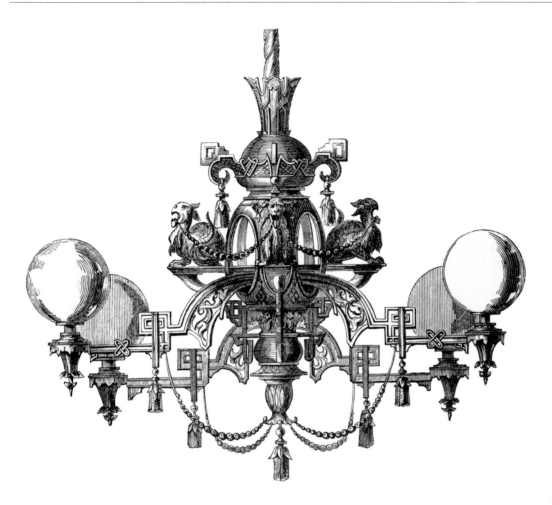

*Gas chandelier by Potts of Birmingham. This was exhibited at the Great Exhibition of 1851, and described in the catalogue as 'a bold arrangement of curves, and angles ... altogether a beautiful example of metallurgical and manufacturing art'. The pendant tassel on each branch operates the gas tap.*

much as to create a heat that is sufficient to consume the smoke and convert it into heat and light'. The oil reservoir was higher than the burner and attached to it by a branching tube so that the oil was gravity-fed to the wick; the flow was controlled by a screw valve. Versions designed to hang from the ceiling had a central, urn-shaped reservoir with branches radiating out to separate burners. Argand lamps were cleaner than candles or conventional oil lamps, needed less attention, were controllable and gave a comparatively brilliant light. But a problem remained: the shadow cast by the oil reservoir. The 'Astral' and 'Sinumbra' lamps, developed in the 1820s, solved this by containing the oil in a ring-shaped reservoir that supported the shade.

Good quality, smoothly flowing oil – the best whale oil or, more usually, colza (rape seed), palm or olive oil – was required to make Argand lamps burn efficiently. There were various attempts to make lamps that would burn cheaper, thicker fish oils or even lard, and yet give as much light as an Argand. Most of these had a mechanism to force the fuel from the reservoir to the wick under pressure: the French 'Carcel' lamp, invented in 1800, employed clockwork; the 'Moderator', patented in 1825, had a spring-driven piston. 'Solar' lamps applied the heat from their own burners to the reservoir in order to soften the viscous oil to a good flowing consistency. New lamps and old were used alongside one another according to need and convenience; in the 1840s one might have found, for example, a moderator lamp supplementing the firelight in the drawing room, and an Argand fitting hanging in the hall where there was more gloom to dispel. In most houses the use of lamps was reserved for the best rooms, and so there would still be candles for each member of the household to carry up to bed.

*A hall lamp in coloured, leaded glass. The gas was delivered via hollow tubes in the brass frame. In the 1890s consumers were offered identical lamps with oil or gas fittings; the latter were cheaper by about one-third.*

All naked flame lights had to be shaded or carefully placed to protect them from being accidentally blown out. Hall lamps were particularly vulnerable to draughts, and were usually enclosed in a glass cage with a glass disc or 'smoke bell' on the chain above to protect the ceiling from the smoke.

In 1850 a chemist named James Young patented paraffin oil, a new kind of lamp fuel he had distilled from coal. Sales of lamps designed for the new fuel increased rapidly after 1859, when the Pennsylvania oilfields were opened up and the price of oil dropped. The new thin, free-flowing liquid fuels were easily absorbed into the wick by capillary action, thus solving the problem of getting the fuel to the burner. Hinks's 'Duplex' burner, a double wick that increased the amount of light produced by a paraffin lamp, was introduced in 1865.

The dirty and smelly business of trimming wicks, cleaning chimneys and refuelling was carried out in the scullery, well away from furniture that might be damaged by oil spills, and certainly not in the kitchen, where the hot stove was a fire hazard and the smell of paraffin might taint the food. Large houses had lamp rooms entirely dedicated to this work. The points to observe when keeping lamps in good working order included rubbing the screws with beeswax so that they would move easily to raise or lower the wicks, thinning wicks to fit small burners by pulling out some threads (never by cutting), and levelling the wicks of circular lamps by singeing them with a red-hot poker.

Paraffin did not entirely supersede all other kinds of lamp fuel. Lamps were expensive, high-status items, and their owners were reluctant to discard them. Many Argand lamps were adapted for paraffin, but some continued to be used with colza oil. Some retailers specialized in nothing but lamps, and their addresses indicate that the top end of the trade could be very smart indeed: Smethursts, established in Southwark in the early 1800s, later had premises in New Bond Street, then Piccadilly and finally Grosvenor Square.

In theory, any old bottle could be made into a paraffin lamp, but in fact manufacturers competed to produce more beautiful lamps than ever before. The classic shape of a reservoir on a pedestal underneath a burner in a clear glass chimney was quickly established for table lamps. The glass globe that shaded the burner appeared in myriad guises – etched, coloured, cut, pressed, moulded, painted or engraved, and sometimes several of these at once. The same basic design could be adapted to hang from the ceiling or on a wall by sitting it in a ring supported by three chains or a bracket. It was easily lifted out when it needed attention. The argument about what constituted 'good design' was applied to lamps with the same rigour as to other manufactured goods.

## Gas

Experiments using gas for lighting were carried out in the 1780s and the first practical systems developed in the 1790s. Gas lighting was subsequently used in shops, factories and public buildings, but not in many private houses. People feared that it created unhealthy fumes and might damage furniture, and the use of gaslight in commercial premises added an unhelpful association with 'trade'.

Various attempts were made to set up commercially viable gas supplies in towns. The National Heat and Light Co., founded in London in 1804 by Frederick Winsor, failed within a couple of years, but by 1810 Winsor was back, using his patented gas-making equipment to provide street lighting in London. In 1818 the Brighton Gas Light and Coke Co. was established in the hope of attracting royal patronage; and indeed in 1821 gas was used on the exterior of the Royal Pavilion to illuminate the stained glass windows at night – an application of the new technology which, in keeping with the spirit of the Pavilion, was more theatrical than practical.

Some country houses had their own private gas works making coal gas. The success of these pioneering installations prompted Loudon to remark that, 'with the progress of improvement, it will be found worth while to adopt [gas] in all country villas'. This was prophetic: Prince Albert had gas installed at Windsor Castle in the 1850s, and by 1864 Kerr assumed that a gas engineer would be consulted about the supply and fittings in a new house as a matter of course. The supply of mains gas to private houses began to be established in major cities in the 1860s.

Early gas lights were naked flames, which burned in 'fishtail' or 'batswing' shapes and were protected and somewhat diffused by tulip-shaped shades of coloured glass. The light they gave was equivalent to a modern 10-watt electric bulb – not at all bright by modern standards, but enough to annoy Mrs Orrinsmith, author of *The Drawing Room* (1878). Gas light, she grudgingly admitted, 'saves much daily labour, is instantly and easily available and confessedly economical', but she found it 'irritating and ineffective'. In low-status parts of the house, shades might be dispensed with altogether.

*Blue glass shade on a gas wall light of the 1870s (subsequently converted for electricity). The pierced brass decoration on the bracket and gas tap is influenced by the designs of Christopher Dresser.*

The incandescent gas mantle, patented by the Austrian chemist Karl Auer von Welsbach in 1885, gave a much brighter light and used less gas than the naked-flame burners. These mantles were little drawstring bags of cotton net that were tied around the gas vent. They were impregnated with thorium and cerium, so that, on first being lit, they puffed up and the cotton burnt away, leaving a brittle bulb of metal oxides that glowed in the heat of the gas flame. Thereafter they had to be lit with great care, as the slightest touch of the match would cause the mantle to crumble.

Gas lights were ideally suited to mass production, as a small number of interchangeable metal tubes, valves, taps, sockets and knuckle joints could be combined to produce infinite numbers of different light fittings. The most common wall light was a swan-neck fitting extending from a round plate screwed to the wall, fitted with a brass key to regulate the gas supply for a high or low light, and terminating in a pretty glass shade. Ceiling lights were adaptations of conventional oil lamps and chandeliers, but with a fixed pipe to carry the gas. Rise-and-fall lights for use over tables incorporated a water slide to stop the gas escaping from the pipe as it telescoped. J. Faraday of London patented a mechanism 'whereby all noxious vapours arising from the gas are carried off... and... the burnt air is discharged into the open air, or an adjoining flue'.

A pair of rococo 'gas chandeliers' exhibited at the Crystal Palace by Cornelius & Baker of Philadelphia showed the degree of elaboration attained in some light fittings: 'They stand about fifteen feet and a half [4.72m] high, by six feet [1.83m] wide, having fifteen burners with plain glass globes, and are of brass lacquered. The design is very rich in ornament... the gas-keys represent bunches of fruit, thus combining beauty with utility.' Eastlake argued that the new technology of gas should be a liberating influence on lighting design, and there was no reason to stick to 'stereotyped forms' or 'the ecclesiastical shapes generally found in the art-metal-worker's catalogue'. He singled out some sinuous gas brackets by Benham & Froud for particular praise.

The American lighting historian Roger W. Moss has pointed out that gas lighting, being a fixed system, 'tended to make the arrangement of furniture more static', and that portable oil lamps were used alongside gas lights to provide task lighting at desks and worktables. Flexible rubber tubes, available from about 1860, made it possible to have gas lamps on tables, but these seem never to have been used with the same freedom as electric lamps would be, at the end of the nineteenth century, and many people continued to use the old forms of lighting alongside the new.

165

*The light fittings designed by Philip Webb for the drawing room at Standen, Sussex, consist of beaten copper wall plates supporting twisted, silk-covered flexes fitted with glass coils to match the shades.*

*A vase fitted with an electric light and glass globe shade in the library at Cragside, Northumberland, where Lord Armstrong pioneered the use of hydro-electricity.*

## Electricity

Gaslight, often thought of as quintessentially Victorian, was in fact the dominant lighting technology in the British home for only about two decades. It was in competition with electricity almost from the beginning, and only Welsbach's invention of the incandescent mantle (which gave a brighter light than the early electric bulbs) and restrictive legislation in 1882 and 1886 (which delayed the expansion of the electricity industry) enabled it to survive as long as it did.

Incandescent carbon-filament lamps were invented almost simultaneously in 1878 by Joseph Swan in Britain and Thomas Edison in the United States. After a court case to determine who owned the rights to the British patent was decided in Swan's favour, the two joined forces in 1883 to sell the new technology in Britain, through the Edison and Swan United Electric Light Company Ltd. Lord Armstrong, a friend of Swan's, installed electric light in his country house, Cragside in Northumberland, in 1880, and in 1886 Lord Kelvin adapted an existing gaslight system in his Glasgow home to electricity. It took rather longer for electricity to be widely adopted in urban and suburban housing. Not until 1896 did the Sambournes install electricity at 18 Stafford Terrace, Kensington, using the rather erratic supply provided by the Notting Hill Company. The following year H.H. Statham remarked that 'electric light is an absolutely new industry, so new that it is in process of modification almost from month to month, and only those who give it their special attention can keep pace with it at present'.

A letter from Armstrong published in *The Engineer* (17 January 1881) shows that, once again, existing lamps were being adapted to the new technology. The electric lamps in the library at Cragside were fitted 'upon vases which were previously used as stands for duplex kerosene lamps'. At Stafford Terrace the gasoliers in the reception rooms were removed, some of the wall fittings were adapted (the gas keys can still be seen on the brackets in the hall, although the pipe now carries electric cable), and several new electric fittings were bought. It was not all plain sailing. Marion Sambourne confided to her diary six weeks after electricity was installed: 'Hate Electric Light – Electric *dark*, does not give as much light as lamps', and noted with grim satisfaction every visit made by the electrician to fix the faltering system.

Another of Marion's bugbears was the number of 'electric globes' broken by the housemaids. Early electric bulbs were available in clear glass only, and had a distinctive peaked tip. In early electric lights no attempt was made to shade the bulb, partly because early filaments made hardly enough light to escape the shade, and partly because nobody yet felt that the bulb should be hidden. In a celebration of the new technology Philip Webb designed elaborate repoussé copper sconces for the wall-lights in the drawing room at Standen in Sussex. The bulbs, which hang from silk-covered flexes, are clearly visible under shallow glass shades.

*The silk shade on the pendant light fitting in the dining room at 18 Stafford Terrace, is a modern replica fitted to the original, wrought iron frame.*

*An adjustable table lamp by W.A.S. Benson with a gathered silk shade. The light cast by green-shaded lamps was considered more restful for the eyes, and was recommended for reading by.*

Alongside adaptations and hesitant reworkings of traditional forms of light fitting, there was some truly innovative design in electric lights. W.A.S. Benson had designed a futuristic oil lamp for Morris & Co. in about 1890, in which a brass reservoir on slender baluster supported a shade of overlapping copper blades arranged like a semi-collapsed propellor. Electricity spurred him to new heights of invention, as Muthesius acknowledged:

> Benson was the leading spirit in electric lighting-appliances in England … He developed not only the most pleasing lines and forms but also many surprising ideas about lighting. Thus he was the first to illumine dining-room tables with light reflected from a shiny metal surface while keeping the actual source of illumination hidden. This eliminates all traces of unpleasant dazzle and lights the table with a soft, gentle, extremely agreeable glow.

Benson particularly favoured tripod stands and arched brass necks with hinge and swivel joints; several lamps designed by him can be seen at Standen.

Once the novelty of the electric bulb wore off, and ways were found to make more powerful bulbs, electric lights began to be shaded as a matter of course. Firms such as James Hinks & Son of Birmingham (whose success was founded on the Duplex burner) crafted complex silk shades, as ruched, pleated and trimmed as any fashionable ball-gown of the period, and sold them in the gilded splendour of their showrooms in Charing Cross Road.

## Lighting the Victorian home today

As Roger Moss has pointed out, 'natural light is the most authentic illumination for historic buildings constructed before the mid-nineteenth century'. It is almost impossible for modern home-owners to imagine just how dark an early nineteenth-century home would have been, and it is unlikely anyone would voluntarily condemn themselves to return to the dark ages. However, a few simple measures will go a long way towards creating a lighting scheme in keeping with the age and style of a Victorian house and yet compatible with modern requirements.

### Light levels

Today we are so accustomed to high overall levels of light in our interiors that it takes real effort to imagine, let alone reproduce, the kind of low, localized light available in most Victorian interiors. For example, a four-light gasolier – perhaps the largest light fitting in the house – would have produced about as much light as a single modern 60-watt bulb. This is not to suggest that house owners today should grope about in such dimly lit rooms, but on the other hand it is not necessary to flood the whole room with light for one person reading in an armchair. With good planning and careful arrangement of light fittings, and the use of modern technology such as concealed lighting and dimmer switches, it is possible to recreate very sympathetic lighting schemes for Victorian houses.

### Safety

Candles, oil lamps and gas jets must all be handled with care because of the risk of fire. Victorians were trained in the careful handling of naked flames from childhood, and must have had an instinctive awareness of fire safety that we, who use candles only as romantic lifestyle accessories, can easily forget. The rules are simple and obvious: always make sure that candles are firmly set in their sockets, do not allow them to drip

An advertisement, dating from the late 1890s, for 'Mediaeval Electric Lighting', a conceit that would have horrified the originators of the Gothic Revival.

and never leave them burning unattended. Do not use candlesticks made of combustible materials such as wood or paper-mâché, and do not allow candles to burn right down in their sockets. Never place a candle near combustible materials. Keep matches out of the reach of children.

Similar rules should be observed when using oil lamps. Move lamps to a safe place before cleaning, adjusting or refilling them. Make sure that fuel spills are cleaned up and fuel containers are sealed and put away before relighting the lamp. Never carry a lighted lamp from room to room.

Many oil and gas lamps have been converted to electricity, and this is certainly the safest way of using them. The conversion should be done by a qualified electrician. The same applies to second-hand light fittings that were converted for electricity some time ago and will probably not meet current regulations. They should be inspected and rewired if necessary by a qualified person.

Always use the correct bulb for the fitting, and remember that light bulbs generate a lot of heat. If you are using antique shades, make sure that they are not in contact with the bulb at any point, and take advice from a textile conservator about flame-retardant treatments for antique fabrics. New shades must be made with fabric treated with a flame retardant.

### Authenticity

Major renovation work that involves taking up floors or redecorating walls gives you the opportunity to plan electrical services for maximum efficiency and minimum obtrusiveness. A minimum of eight sockets installed in each main room will give you plenty of choice in placing lamps. Concealed lighting may be useful for improving overall light levels without introducing a large number of light fittings. Cabling can be chased into plaster or run behind cornices or skirtings, or under floorboards. This requires planning and effort but makes a tremendous different to the final appearance of the interior.

There are several ways to make light switches less obtrusive. So-called 'invisible' switches have a small dolly-type switch set in the centre of a Perspex plate. They are useful in wallpapered rooms, as the wallpaper is carried behind the plate right up to the switch housing, and the continuation of the pattern makes the fitting much less noticeable. Very small, oblong switches, which fit discreetly onto a vertical moulding, such as the side of a doorframe, are also useful in historic interiors where evidence of electrical installations has to be kept to a minimum. Two decorators' tricks to make conventional plastic light switches less noticeable are to place them at waist height and to paint them to match the wall. It is possibly easier and more convincing to recreate the look of an early electrical installation using reproduction dolly switches and metal dome switches. Second-hand switches should not be used, as they may not be compatible or safe to use with modern electrical wiring. Avoid any with eye-catching frosted finishes, rococo borders or rope edging; these have no historical precedent (except perhaps the 'Medieval' light switches offered by Waltham & Co. in the 1890s, which must have been regarded as questionable even in their own day). A simple chrome, brass or white plastic plate is preferable; it may not be authentic but is at least simple, understated and honestly modern.

Reproduction light fittings vary greatly in their authenticity. Details may change because electrical junctions cannot be accommodated in the slender pipework of an original gas lamp, and so the reproduction fitting has fatter tubing and enlarged knuckles, or manufacturers will forget that a gas light originally had a key to turn it on and off. Modern metal finishes are an especially weak point: lacquered brass is often too bright and too yellow, distressed pewter has a machined appearance, and 'bronze' finishes have a grey tinge. It is worth discussing alternative finishes with the supplier, rather than settling for the version on display in the shop if others are available.

It is important to get the detail right, especially when replicating the appearance of the original fuel or power source. White plastic flex strikes a discordant note in a richly coloured Victorian interior, especially when it snakes out from a converted oil lamp, but the same flex with a black plastic covering is much less noticeable. Silk-covered twisted flex is now available for electric lamps; the two- or three-core plastic-insulated cable under the silk covering is fully compatible with modern safety requirements. Gas lights were fed by tubes, so it is illogical to suspend a gasolier (even though it has been converted to electricity) by chain, leaving the flex visible. It will look much more convincing if you run the flex through a metal tube attached to the ceiling rose. The height of gas fixtures is also relevant: they have to be low enough for the key to be reached. Avoid bulbs that flicker to imitate candle flame – they can look very effective in museum and theatre roomsets, but in private houses they are pure kitsch.

# — ❧ 15 ❧ —

# KITCHENS

O F ALL THE ROOMS in the house, the kitchen is the one that appears to have undergone the biggest transformation since the nineteenth century. Whereas even small Victorian houses had separate kitchens, sculleries and larders, today we combine all the functions of these areas into one room. We no longer clean steel knives with emery powder, feed our stoves with coal or polish them with blacklead, so the special storerooms and equipment for these tasks are now redundant. Even our basic understanding of the function of the kitchen, and of processes such as roasting, are quite different.

And yet the modern kitchen may have more in common with the Victorian kitchen than we think. The Victorians were as interested as we are today in rational planning, fuel efficiency, hygiene, labour-saving devices and new technology. They were equally impressed by the pronouncements of celebrity cooks and just as likely to have few cooking skills of their own and to eat ready meals. Many poor families did not possess an oven. Indeed, much of the urban population lived in shared houses without access to a stove, subsisting on a meagre diet dominated by tea and bread. Take-away foods such as oysters, chops or meat pies were readily available, and these could easily be kept warm on a hob grate and supplemented by toast made at the fire – much as today's bedsit-dweller will go to a nearby takeaway and have a microwave oven for heating up snacks.

WRINGING MACHINE.

ABOVE: *a mangle, illustrated in the shilling edition of* Mrs Beeton's Cookery Book, *1890s.*

OPPOSITE: *a reconstruction of a working-class cottage, in which the kitchen was also the main living room. Wet jobs, such as laundry and washing-up, took place in a separate scullery.*

## Plan and layout

Many of the characteristics of Victorian kitchens were derived from the domestic arrangements in aristocratic and high-status buildings. Showpiece kitchens used by famous chefs had been an influence on kitchen design since 1817, when Carême, the Prince Regent's chef, had cooked memorable meals in the spectacular kitchen at Brighton Pavilion. Two decades later, Alexis Soyer's kitchen at the Reform Club in Pall Mall was one of the sights of London. Built in 1841 and incorporating many of Soyer's own innovations, its gadgets included rotating pillars of spice boxes, a steam closet for keeping dishes hot, gas stoves and steam-powered spits.

The real test-beds for new technology and innovative ideas, however, were country-house kitchens, and there was no shortage of advice about how to design and equip them. Architectural writers such as J.J. Stevenson and Robert Kerr took an analytical approach to planning the domestic offices in large houses, but saw no reason to quarrel with the received wisdom that the kitchen should always be sited on one of the cooler sides of the house, facing north or east. All subsequent authorities agreed with the author of *The London Cookery and Complete Domestic Guide* (1827), that 'a kitchen should be light, lofty, and airy – the doors should be so placed as to avoid a draught of air approaching the fire-place'. A roof light ensured good light and ventilation, and a high ceiling helped to keep the room cool (Kerr recommended double-height kitchens 'for important cases'). Where it was not possible to have a top light because of rooms over the kitchen, windows set as high as possible allowed hot air to escape and freed up wall space for cupboards and shelves. The incidental benefit of high windows, from the family's point of view, was that servants could not see out and would therefore not be distracted from their work.

Kitchens in great houses were surrounded by ancillary rooms purpose-built for specific functions. Large households generated huge amounts of washing up, and a big roasting range could consume up to twenty wheelbarrow-loads of coal per day, so it was essential that the scullery and coal store be directly attached to the kitchen. If there was a separate pastry room, it would be sited away from the heat of the kitchen range. The still room, dedicated to preserving and bottling, was part of the housekeeper's domain; her room, the servants' hall and the butler's pantry were located conveniently close to the centre of cooking operations. Crockery, linen, glass and plate were stored in the china closet, linen cupboard and strong room. Food storage areas might include any or all of the following: a wine cellar under the supervision of the butler, a dry goods store to which the housekeeper had the key, a vegetable store conveniently near the garden door, a game larder with racks for hanging kill until it was ready to cook, and a fish larder with marble slabs cooled by running water. There would be a steady traffic of orders and deliveries between the kitchen quarters and the outlying dairy, ice house and laundry. Mid-Victorian mansions could have such large kitchens that a separate service wing was required to house them. At Mentmore in Buckinghamshire (1857), for example,

*The scullery at Cragside, Northumberland. Even in the grandest country houses, these functional areas had no decorative embellishment, just hard wearing, hygienic surfaces, such as glazed brick walls, stone floor and distempered ceiling.*

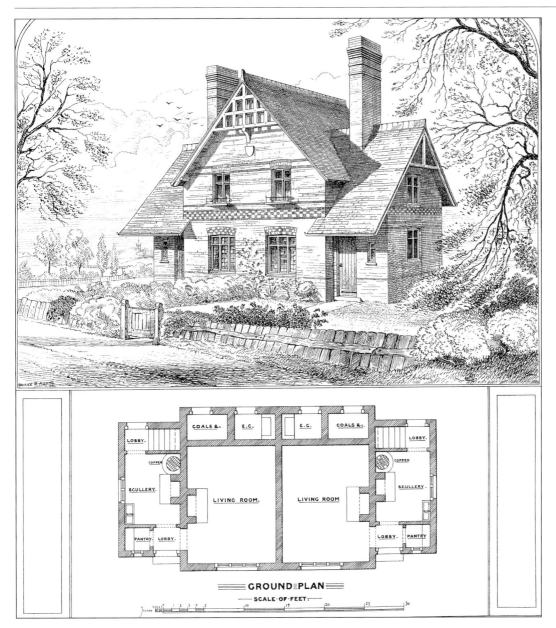

*Design for a pair of model cottages for agricultural workers, by Frederick Chancellor, 1873. The ground-floor plan shows the scullery approaching the modern idea of a kitchen, with cooking, laundry and washing-up all taking place in the same room. Food is stored in a pantry isolated from the heat and steam of the kitchen.*

more than a dozen rooms were built around a large courtyard, the only plan that could get light and ventilation into all parts of the complex. The last country house kitchen to be built on such a scale was the one designed by Lutyens for Castle Drogo, the Devon home of the millionaire grocer Julius Drewe, in 1910. In smaller houses the grand plan of the country house kitchen was necessarily compromised, but as many of its features as possible were preserved. The minimum provision for a respectable middle-class house was a kitchen, scullery, larder and coal store.

The existence of the kitchen was concealed as far as possible. In upper-class housing a baize door marked the inviolable boundary between the domestic and the family territories. Many large country houses had completely separate service wings. In terraced housing the hierarchy could not always be so strictly observed, but kitchens were invariably sited in the basement (the half-landing where the back hall met the service stairs signalling the family/servant boundary) or at the back of the house, entered through a door discreetly placed behind the staircase.

No such reticence was possible in many working-class houses, which had a 'living-kitchen', known in the North of England as the 'house-place'. Although it was used for

*The 'living-kitchen' in this reconstruction of a mid-nineteenth-century Welsh miner's cottage represents a prosperous working-class household. The range, with a kettle on the hob and a roaring fire at its heart, is a domestic altar adorned with a collection of ornaments that convey thrift, piety and a modest level of material comfort.*

cooking, dining and sitting room, this still reflected the kitchen/scullery divide, as Mrs Gaskell's description of a millworker's home in a 'court' or tenement in Manchester in the early years of Victoria's reign makes clear:

> The room was tolerably large, and possessed many conveniences ... On the opposite side to the door and window was the staircase, and two doors: one of which (the nearest to the fire), led into a sort of little back kitchen, where dirty work, such as washing up dishes, might be done, and whose shelves served as larder, and pantry, and store-room, and all. The other door, which was considerably lower, opened into the coal-hole – the slanting closet under the stairs; from which, to the fire-place, there was a gay-coloured piece of oil-cloth laid. The place seemed almost crammed with furniture (sure sign of good times among the mills).

## The scullery

When Kerr listed the essential equipment of the kitchen – 'the cooking-apparatus on whatever scale may be suitable, one or more dressers, a centre table' – he did not mention a sink or water supply. It was universally understood that the kitchen was used only for cooking. Washing-up, scrubbing vegetables and all the messy, low-status activities involving water were done in the scullery. Even the smallest Victorian houses had a separate scullery, and it was rare for sinks to be installed in kitchens before the twentieth century. Indeed, the custom of planning new houses with a 'dry' kitchen and 'wet' scullery persisted until the 1920s.

The scullery had a tiled or flagstone floor with a drain in the centre and a duckboards on the floor in front of the sink (young scullery maids might have had to stand on wooden boxes until they grew tall enough to reach the sink). The sink was placed beneath a window to get the best light and for easy connection to the drain. Sinks were made of stone, or wood lined with lead, copper or zinc sheet. Fireclay sinks were produced in the Midlands from the eighteenth century, and glazed ceramic sinks were widely available by the middle of the nineteenth century. Delicate china and glass were washed in wooden bowls to reduce the risk of chipping. A pump or a single brass tap next to the sink provided cold water only; hot water had to be carried in from the kitchen range.

Few proprietary cleaners were available, and most of the cleaning materials used in the scullery were hard on the hands. A mixture of soda and soft soap was used for washing up. Whiting made a mild, creamy cleaner that would remove grease. Stronger abrasives such as bath brick and emery powder were used for cleaning knives and iron utensils. Rottenstone was mixed with rape oil to make a paste for cleaning brass and tin. When the washing-up was done, the cloths would be boiled in water to which a little vinegar had been added and hung up to dry. Finally, the drain was disinfected with chloride of lime.

In smaller houses the scullery also functioned as a laundry, and contained the 'copper' – a metal tub set into a brick housing with a small fire grate underneath – used for heating water. In many cases the tub was actually made of cast iron, although copper was considered superior, as it would not rust. Sometimes a step was built into the brickwork so the laundress could look down into the tub as she stirred the clothes. Filling and emptying the copper by hand was one of the chores that made washdays so laborious.

Linens were repeatedly rinsed with lye, which dissolved greasy dirt. Dirty clothes were put into a bucket or wooden tub, covered with soap and hot water, and swished about with a 'posser' or washing dolly – a perforated copper dome or a wooden tripod fixed to a broom handle, which kept the clothes moving and thus flushed out the dissolved dirt. The earliest washing machines (which still had to be cranked by hand) appeared in the 1850s; by 1883 Mrs Beeton was recommending Bradford's washing machines.

The wet clothes were pulled out of the hot water with wooden tongs, rinsed, and passed through a mangle to squeeze out the excess water. Early mangles had wooden rollers; after about 1880 rubber rollers became available but were almost as likely as the wooden ones to break buttons and flatten metal hooks – hence the use of stiffened fabric buttons on frequently-washed items such as underwear, nightgowns and pillowcases. Commercial laundries took some of the burden off the middle-class town-dweller; part of Acton, West London, was known as 'Soapsud Island' because of the large number of laundries there.

## The larder

The other essential adjunct to the kitchen was the larder. This had at least one external wall with a small window opposite the door. Instead of glass, the window was fitted with wire gauze or perforated zinc sheet, which admitted a draught while keeping flies out. The cool, dark, dry storage space thus created was surprisingly versatile. A thick slate or marble shelf at waist height provided a surface where cheese, butter and cream could be kept cool. Painted wooden shelves fixed to the whitewashed walls held packets and jars, large bins on the tiled floor contained root vegetables, and a couple of sturdy hooks in the ceiling supported sides of ham or strings of onions. Builders of speculative suburban developments could not always choose the orientation of their houses, but even a south-facing larder would stay acceptably cool, as long as it had thick walls and a shaded roof, and the door was kept closed.

# Furniture

## *The dresser*

The indispensable item of kitchen furniture was the dresser. 'The ordinary kitchen dresser' wrote Kerr, 'stands against the wall, and the space under the drawers is sometimes open and sometimes enclosed with doors; in either case accommodating the cooking utensils, which are placed on a bottom shelf or pot-board raised about 6 or 9 inches [150 or 225mm] from the floor. The wall-space is covered to the height of about 7 feet [2.13m] by the dresser-back, consisting of a surface of boarding which supports several tiers of narrow shelves for the ordinary dinner stoneware, or for the copper articles, the edges being studded with small brass hooks for jugs, &c.' Such a detailed description was necessary because the provision of the dresser was the architect's responsibility. The dresser was usually made of deal and 'seldom painted, it being the pride of good housewives, in most parts of England, to keep the boards of which they are composed as white as snow, by frequently scouring them with fine white sand'. The scoured surface served as an extra worktop. Dressers in the Gothic style, however, were better made in oak, or grained to resemble that wood.

For the upper part of the dresser, open shelves were generally preferred to cupboards, which might harbour dirt or conceal clutter. The crockery and gleaming *batterie de cuisine* made a satisfying display. Copper pans were cleaned with home-made mixtures of brewer's yeast and sand, or half a lemon dipped in common salt; their tin linings were cleaned with lemon or vinegar mixed to a paste with flour, soft soap and silver sand. The pans had to be regularly relined, and the occasion when 'several gentlemen died, and several more were dangerously affected, by partaking of a stew at an inn, which the cook had imprudently suffered to become cold in the copper vessel' was cited as a warning against the danger of verdigris poisoning.

*The kitchen of the Swiss Cottage in the grounds of Victoria and Albert's country estate, Osborne, on the Isle of Wight, where the royal children received practical lessons in domestic economy. The built-in dresser and deal-topped table are scaled-down but fully functional replicas of the kitchen furniture in a middle-class house.*

### The table

A large, sturdy table stood in the centre of the room. It was always made of softwood, since 'nothing bears scouring so well as deal, and kitchen tables require scouring more than once in a day'. The table top was first scoured with fine sand, then scrubbed with soda dissolved in hot water (never soap, which might transmit its smell to the food) and finally rinsed with clear hot water. Under this regime the table top gleamed white, the ridges of the grain eventually standing proud of the surface. Blocks of wood set cross-grain on the floor under the table legs prevented the end-grain of the legs from absorbing water from the frequent floor-cleaning.

Various smaller items completed the furniture of the kitchen. A mortar carved out of marble and set into a wooden stand was used with a large wooden pestle for grinding loaf sugar and other ingredients. A butcher's block had to be sturdy enough to stand up to repeated hackings. Wooden duckboards protected weary feet from wet, cold and hard floors. Two items still found in kitchens today are plate racks made of wooden dowels set in a rectangular frame, and rollers for hand towels.

## Equipment

### The range

The traditional manner of cooking meat was to roast it in front of glowing coals, turning it onto a spit to ensure that it browned evenly. A movable screen with a tin lining stood in front of the hearth; this protected the cook from the heat of the range, while the shiny tin reflected heat back onto the meat, helping to speed up the cooking. Even with the protection of the roasting screen (also known as a 'Dutch oven'), the open fire produced stifling heat, which accounts for the contemporary preoccupation with ventilation. In 1802 Benjamin Rumford had claimed that 'more fuel is frequently consumed in a kitchen-range to boil a tea-kettle, than, with proper management, would be sufficient to cook a good dinner for fifty men', and described a number of improvements that he had incorporated into the Rumford Roasting-Oven, a barrel-shaped closed oven in use from 1799 to about 1840. However, the traditional method of roasting meat had a certain status and cooks were reluctant to change it. Indeed, Victorian cooks would not have considered meat baked in a closed oven to have been properly 'roasted' at all, so stoves continued to have open fires for roasting long after they had begun to incorporate closed ovens.

Several closed ovens predated even Rumford's designs. In 1780 the London ironmonger Thomas Robinson had patented a kitchen grate combined with an iron oven. Three years later Joseph Langmead produced a grate with an oven on one side and a hot water boiler on the other. Ovens attached to one side of the grate suffered from uneven heat, a problem partially solved with the introduction of double-walled ovens, such as that produced in 1797 by Mr Strutt of Derby, and by surrounding the oven with small flues to carry hot air that would otherwise be vented straight up the chimney – the method patented in 1802 by George Bodley of Exeter. Bodley's stove had an iron plate to close off the main chimney flue and direct a stream of hot air into a network of smaller flues surrounding the oven and boiler. The flues were controlled by dampers, hinged iron flaps that were opened and closed by knobs on the front of the range. This was the principle adopted by later manufacturers, whose names were proudly cast into oven doors and hobs: Jeakes & Co. of London; Barnard, Bishop & Barnard of Norwich; the Coalbrookdale Co; the Rotherham Foundry Co; Hattersley Bros. of Sheffield; and the famous Eagle Range and Foundry Co. of London, Bristol and Birmingham. So many stoves made by William Flavel of Leamington were sold in the 1820s that 'Leamington' became for a time synonymous with 'stove'.

*Kitchen appliances and utensils from* Mrs Beeton's Cookery Book. TOP: *patent economic kitchen range, as supplied by Temple & Crook of Belgrave Square, at prices between £18. 10s (£18.50) and £27. 15s (£27.75).*

BOTTOM: *this page of cooking equipment illustrates two types of roasting screen.*

181

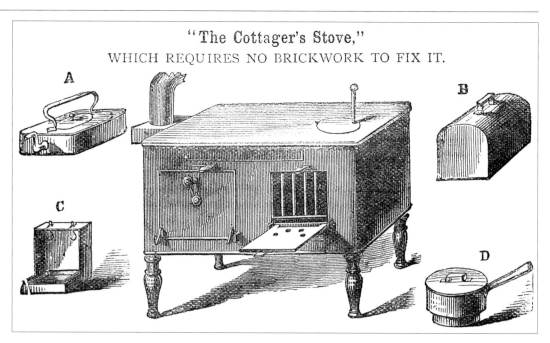

*An 1890s edition of* Warne's Model Cookery and Housekeeping Book *described this stove as 'an economical assistant to the common open range in small kitchens'. The accompanying equipment includes a flat-bottomed kettle (A), which boiled quickly because of the large surface area in contact with the hotplate, and (D) a saucepan with a stepped bottom designed to fit into the hotplate.*

Large country-house ranges were enormous. A 'good standard example' of cooking-apparatus as specified by Kerr consisted of a fireplace with a roasting-range and boiler at the back, an oven (possibly incorporated into the range), a roasting-screen, a smoke-jack (fitted in the main flue), three or four stewing-stoves with charcoal grates, a hot-plate including a broiling-stove, and a hot-closet. He also recommended installing a hot-table 'for keeping the dishes warm during the operation of service', a pair of coppers or a set of three steam-kettles (for boiling vegetables), a bain-marie and a hot-water cistern. The measurements of all the equipment Kerr regarded as indispensable added up to 20 feet (6m) of cast-iron frontage. A range on this scale was installed at Charlecote in Warwickshire in the 1860s; another can be seen in the well-preserved late Victorian kitchen at Gunnersbury Park, West London. If the house had been shut up for the winter, the stove might have to be lit two or three days in advance of a house party's arrival in order to bring it up gradually to a working temperature; too fierce a fire lit in one small part of such a large complex might cause it to crack.

Ranges were made in all sizes for smaller houses. Yorkshire grates were recommended as 'the most convenient and economical … One of the lowest price measures about thirty inches [800mm] in front, and is divided into three equal parts; one side is occupied by an oven, the other by a boiler for water, or an ironing stove – all heated by a very moderate fire in the grate. … All the cooking of a plain family, of seven or eight persons, may be performed with a grate of this size.' So-called 'portable' stoves were also available. These were far too heavy to carry about; their name referred to the fact that they were free-standing and therefore did not need to be built into the brickwork of the chimney breast.

Closed ranges were most readily adopted in the North of England, where coal was cheap, or even (to miners' families) free. Elsewhere, some prejudice against the closed ovens had to be overcome. When open fires were abandoned in favour of closed ranges, the old flues were closed up and cooking smells became more of a problem.

Ranges could be temperamental. A good cook studied her range's eccentricities and became adept at opening and closing the dampers. Flues quickly became blocked with soot and had to be cleaned with a variety of tools: a chain on a stick was used to loosen the soot, which could then be drawn out with long-handled scoops and brushes. Some cooks allowed the soot, which insulated the flue, to build up as a crude method of heat control, creating a 'slow' oven.

Many people, who either had no access to a stove because they lived in shared or subdivided houses, or could not afford enough coal for roasting, would leave their weekly joint and potatoes with the local baker, who would charge a penny for cooking them in the residual heat of the bread ovens once the day's baking had been done. These roasts sometimes shrank alarmingly in the cooking, so that it was said that an honest baker was one who bought his own Sunday dinner.

Gas-fired ranges were exhibited at the Great Exhibition of 1851, and in 1868 Shrewsbury's Portable Gas Oven came onto the market. In *The Young Lady's Book* (1876), Mrs. Mackarness suggested that any girl who wanted to learn to cook (only as a hobby, naturally, and so that she would be better able to instruct her own cook in due course) could use 'one of those gas-rings, which cost but little, will stand on any table, and be supplied with gas by means of a flexible tube fastened to a gas-burner'. However, prejudice, fear of explosions and health scares about eating food impregnated with harmful fumes delayed the widespread introduction of gas ovens, and they did not begin to replace solid fuel ranges in any numbers until the 1890s.

*The kitchen at Wightwick Manor, West Midlands, dates from the 1890s. Clearly visible on the range are the knobs to control the temperature-regulating dampers and the square covers in the backplate that give access to the flues for cleaning.*

### *Refrigeration*

Chilling and freezing without a refrigerator required some ingenuity and forethought. Country houses had ice houses – domed brick structures with tunnel entrances built over deep pits – where ice gathered in winter could be stored, insulated with layers of straw, for use in summer. Suburban and urban households were supplied by ice merchants or fishmongers, who bought ice imported from America and Norway. The first British patent for an ice-making machine was granted in 1834, and in 1857 Harrison patented a machine for making ice in large blocks for commercial purposes. Siebe's ice-making machine 'excited much admiration' at the International Exhibition of 1862. These machines were too big to be installed in private houses, so ice-making remained a centralized service. A retailer would pick up a huge block from the local ice depot and cart it through residential areas on regular rounds. At each customer's request a piece was hacked off using picks and large iron pincers, and carried into the house wrapped in sacking, to be used *en bloc* in an ice cupboard, or crushed to put into an ice-cream churn.

An ice cupboard looked like an ordinary, free-standing wooden cupboard, but at one side it contained a double-walled zinc box insulated with straw or hay, with a drain at the bottom. Once filled with ice, this could chill food on the neighbouring shelves for a couple of days. It was important to remember to empty the tray that caught the melt-water from the drain, or an icy flood would drip onto the floor beneath.

Ice-cream was made using a tub 'large enough to contain about a bushel of ice, pounded small, when brought out of the ice-house, and mixed very carefully with either salt, nitre or soda'. A pewter ice-pot was plunged up to its rim in the salt-and-ice mixture, and into this was poured the flavoured custard. The lid of the ice-pot was fitted with a paddle, which was used to stir the contents as they began to freeze. Once the ice-cream was ready, the pot was covered with more ice and left until the cook was ready to turn it out.

It was possible to manage very well without any ice, however. Fresh milk was available 'straight from the cow', even in cities. The stone floor of an underground cellar was quite cold enough to set creams, blancmanges and jellies, and a well-ventilated larder would keep cheese in perfect condition.

## Decoration

Kitchens usually had stone slab or tiled floors, but these were hard on the feet, so there might be an area of wood flooring or wooden duckboards around the table where the cook stood. Hard floors were also noisy under chairs or where there was lots of coming and going, hence Kerr's observation that 'in small houses ... when the Kitchen serves also as the Servants'-Hall, a wood floor for the whole is sometime preferred'.

The upper walls were of plain plaster regularly whitewashed or distempered. A bag of laundry blue in the paint kettle imparted a faint blue tinge to distemper used on the walls, which imparted a feeling of coolness to the room and was said to repel flies. Lower down, the walls were covered with a high dado of some washable material, such as tongue-and-groove boarding painted with gloss paint, tiles or glazed brick for hard wear and hygiene.

In many mid-Victorian kitchens a motto painted in a conspicuous place on the wall conveyed an improving sentiment, such as 'Do everything in its proper time; put everything in its proper place; keep everything to its proper use' or the immortal 'Waste Not, Want Not'.

# Victorian kitchens today

At the time of writing, clean lines and a sleek steel-and-glass aesthetic predominate in kitchen design, and it is hard to see how this can be reconciled with the scrubbed pine and cast iron of the Victorian kitchen. Fashions change, but the Victorian principles of kitchen design – sensible orientation, good lighting, good ventilation and simple decoration using hygienic, washable surface finishes – will always be relevant. Since the trend throughout the nineteenth century was towards ever more functional kitchens, and the Victorians were enthusiastic users of gadgets and labour-saving devices, it could even be argued that the more modern the kitchen, the better it reflects the spirit of Victorian inventiveness and innovation, and therefore furniture and appliances that are honestly modern are more appropriate than fake-panelled cupboard fronts.

Some elements of the Victorian kitchen can survive any number of decorating fads. A built-in dresser is worth preserving if at all possible, as are original floor plans. While dining-kitchens suit our more informal way of life and tempt us to 'knock through' to ancillary rooms to create the biggest possible single-space kitchen, there is a lot to be said for shutting out some activities. A separate larder keeps food out of the warm and humid atmosphere of the kitchen and provides an intermediate storage temperature for items such as cheese and vegetables, which have a better texture and flavour if they are not chilled in an airtight fridge. If space allows the washing machine to go in a separate utility room, it will ensure that dirty laundry can be hidden and the noise of the machine can be shut out. A lobby just inside the back door, where muddy shoes and wet coats can be removed, will save a great deal of cleaning.

We could also adapt Victorian thrift to suit modern environmental awareness. Peelings and scraps went onto the compost heap. A handful of abrasives and alkalis kept the Victorian kitchen clean, the crockery and glassware sparkling, the floor gleaming and the linen dazzling white – proof that today's constant repackaging of washing powder and cleaning fluids in ever more gimmicky forms is merely a marketing tool to persuade us to buy more (and more expensive) branded products.

≈ 16 ≈

# BATHROOMS

LTHOUGH THE POPULAR IMAGE of the Victorian bathroom is of a temple to hygiene, with tiled surfaces, gleaming pipework and handsome porcelain fittings, the reality is that most people throughout the nineteenth century never dreamed of using such facilities. Few Victorians enjoyed the luxury of a private, indoor, flush toilet, and still fewer had access to a plumbed-in bath in a purpose-built bathroom.

ABOVE: *porcelain 'lavatory basin' on a cast-iron stand with decorative tiled splashback, advertised by Morrison, Ingram & Co. of Manchester in the 1890s.*

OPPOSITE: *bathing in a portable hip bath in one's dressing room, using hot water brought up in brass cans by servants, was a luxury available only to the middle and upper classes.*

## The water closet

Before the advent of indoor plumbing, each bedroom had its chamber pot, kept under the bed, in a bedside cupboard or a 'close stool' (commode). Every morning all the chamber pots in the house were emptied. Sewers, many of them open to the street, carried the effluent into the nearest river. In many cases the chamber pots were emptied into a closed cesspit beneath the house or an open midden nearby, where their contents were mixed with ash. 'Night soil men' (also known as 'scavengers') made regular rounds to collect this waste, which was carried out of town and sold as agricultural fertilizer. Flora Thompson recorded how rural communities coped:

> The only sanitary arrangement known in the hamlet was housed either in a little beehive-shaped building at the bottom of the garden or in a corner of the wood and tool shed known as 'the hovel'. It was not even an earth closet; but merely a deep pit with a seat set over it, the half-yearly emptying of which caused every door and window in the vicinity to be sealed. Unfortunately there was no means of sealing the chimneys!
>
> The 'privies' were as good an index as any to the character of their owners. Some were horrible holes; others were fairly decent, while some, and these not a few, were kept well cleaned, with the seat scrubbed to snow-whiteness and the brick floor raddled.

A refinement of the ash-pit privy was the earth closet, patented versions of which had been around since 1838. A design registered by the Rev. Henry Moule in 1860 consisted of a seat over a bucket and, where one might nowadays expect a water cistern, an 'earth reservoir' containing dry, sieved earth and ashes. A lever handle released sufficient earth to cover the contents of the bucket, which were later used as garden manure. Moule claimed that the earth mixture could be sieved and re-used up to seven times 'without losing any of its deodorising properties'. For several decades in the mid-1900s earth closets were regarded as perfectly viable alternatives to water closets (a view no doubt encouraged by familiarity with the difficulties of disposing of raw sewage). Even Queen Victorian had an earth closet, at Windsor Castle. It was only in the last quarter of the nineteenth century, when reliable water supplies and sewage disposal systems were widely established, that the water closet gained its present unassailable ascendancy.

*The corner of a bedroom with typical bath, washstand and 'toilet set'. 'When a man likes to have his bath regularly, he should think of the labour that half a dozen or more baths entail, and in the evening prepare his can of water for tomorrow's use, place his own bath on his piece of oilcloth, enjoy his tub to his heart's content, pour away the water, put up his tub, and say nothing about it.' (Mrs Caddy, Household Organisation, 1877)*

A series of water closet designs produced in the late eighteenth century prefigured the modern water closet. In 1775 Alexander Cummings patented a design for a closet that had a handle to operate the flush valve and a waste pipe with an 'S' trap to prevent smells from backing up into the room. Three years later Samuel Prosser patented the plunger closet, and in 1778 Joseph Bramah, the London cabinet-maker and industrial entrepreneur, took out a patent on a closet with a hinged valve at the bottom of the bowl. Adam Hart-Davis describes the 'clever refinements' of Bramah's design thus: 'pulling the handle to open the valve and let out the excrement also turned on the water to flush the pan. Pushing it down again closed the valve and activated a neat delaying mechanism in the shape of a brass air cylinder, which kept water running into the pan for about 15 seconds, so as to fill it ready for the next user.' By 1797 Bramah claimed to have sold 6000 of his closets, and they remained in production for a century.

Piecemeal improvements, such as the siphonic flush (patented by Joseph Adamson in 1853) continued to be made, but all these early closets followed the same basic two-piece design, with a toilet bowl perched on top of a second trough, and shared the same problems of mechanical failure or of water, waste or odour leaking at the junction of the two elements. The first truly modern design was the ceramic one-piece pedestal toilet produced by Thomas Twyford in 1885.

Advertising and the cunning deployment of brand names were important to the makers of ceramic closets, who operated in a fiercely competitive market. Names such as 'Niagara' expressed the idea of a torrent of cleansing water; the 'Rock', emblazoned with a picture of a lighthouse lashed by stormy seas, was clearly going to last for ever; the classical 'Triton' lent some much-needed dignity to an essentially humble item. Seats were usually made of wood: scrubbed deal, polished mahogany or fragrant cedar. The pull mechanism for the overhead cistern was worked by a chain with a pendant handle. A galvanized metal chain with a D-shaped pull was basic but serviceable, a polished brass chain with a glazed china or turned wooden pendant handle somewhat smarter. Manufacturers' catalogues illustrated closets with china or mahogany boxes fitted to the back of the seat or clipped onto the downpipe to hold sheets of purpose-made toilet tissue. This, however, was a luxury, and the common practice of recycling newspaper prompted this ominous warning from Mrs Beeton: 'Newspaper, it should be remembered, is apt to stop up the drain and cause much expense, which curling-paper [stiff tissue paper used for hair rollers] does not.' Rolls of perforated paper were first produced in America in the 1870s, necessitating the invention of the modern roll holder. Soft tissue was not available until the 1930s.

Sheer density of population meant that many town-dwellers were forced to use privies shared between dozens of families, or to improvise, and in many cases this continued long after mains water and sewers were installed. The provision of indoor closets in private houses spread erratically, according to geography and social status. Thus at the end of the nineteenth century, when no middle-class family would tolerate having to share a toilet, local building regulations still permitted one outside closet per pair of workers' houses in Leeds.

## Washing

Water for washing was kept in a large jug and poured as needed into a large shallow basin that stood on a washstand. As ever, wealth determined how elaborate these arrangements were. The mistress of a country house had a 'toilet service' of fine china decorated with hand-painted flowers and gold leaf, with matching accessories such as soap dish, brush tray and sponge bowl, all arranged on a marble-topped mahogany washstand with a tiled splashback, which stood in her bedroom or dressing room. The farmhand's wife managed with an enamel jug and basin on a deal table, or washed at the scullery sink.

*Tip-up ceramic basin surrounded by mahogany and marble in the downstairs cloakroom at 18 Stafford Terrace, Kensington.*

Early plumbed-in basins, or 'lavatories' as they were always called in the nineteenth century, were straightforward adaptations of the traditional wash-stand, with a fixed basin set into a timber cabinet. The plughole basin soon rendered other types obsolete, although a tip-up type of basin, which had no plughole and swung on a pivot to drain, was unaccountably persistent; an example dating from the 1870s survives in the ground-floor cloakroom of 18 Stafford Terrace in Kensington.

Manufacturers' catalogues illustrated a wide range of lavatories. At the top of the range were floral-patterned basins set into elaborate cabinets with marble tops, tiled splashbacks, turned legs, mirrors, cupboards and shelves. The decoration of the wash-basin itself could be as elaborate as that on any dinner service. The ceramic body of the basin could easily be cast to incorporate a moulded lip or scallop-shaped soap dish, while the glazed surface could be adorned with any picture or design likely to appeal to the design-conscious householder – flowers, classical motifs and even aquatic animals such as dolphins, goldfish or kingfishers. Most basins were of blank white porcelain supported on plain metal brackets, but even these had elaborate crests and makers' marks next to the overflow.

## Bathing

Bathing required a portable bath, which had to be laboriously filled and emptied by hand. The privileged bathed in front of their bedroom fires in hot water brought up from the kitchen in polished brass cans by servants. Middle-class housewives who followed Mrs Beeton's advice ensured that 'in the master's room the bath [was] dry and spotless, the water-cans filled, and standing on a Kamptulicon mat'. Less privileged families took turns in a tin tub in front of the kitchen range, where the relative convenience of being close to the source of hot water compensated for lack of privacy.

Plumbed-in baths began to appear in the 1850s. Early baths were press-moulded from sheets of tin, zinc or copper, and galvanized or given a painted finish to mimic woodgrain or marble. Cast iron baths were available from around 1880, when the technical problems of casting such a large item in one piece were finally solved. The interiors of cast iron baths were enamelled white, while the exterior – if it was not hidden with wooden panelling – was painted, often with stencilled patterns of acanthus leaves or scrolling waves. Cast iron brackets or ball-and-claw feet were bolted onto lugs cast into the underside of the bath, and the top edge of the bath was finished with a roll, or with lugs to which a shelf of marble or timber could be attached, to finish off the side panelling.

Not all baths were cast iron: the Marquess of Bute could easily afford the extravagance of his silver-inlaid, solid Roman marble bath at Cardiff Castle, but there was also a cheaper version made from sheets of white marble installed by Edward Linley Sambourne in the relatively modest, middle-class terraced house in Kensington that he and his family occupied in the 1870s.

Freestanding shower baths had been available since the Regency period. These consisted of a cistern supported over the bather's head by a tripod, one leg of which was a hollow tube, up which water from the bath could be sent using a hand-operated stirrup pump at the side of the bath. Once full, the cistern was emptied by a sharp tug on a chain attached to a valve. Showers of various types were on display in the Great Exhibition of 1851, and the advent of the plumbed-in cast iron bath opened up all kinds of possibilities. The 'improved spray bath' of 1882 was housed in a hooded shower compartment at one end of the bath and fitted with ten controls, offering hot or cold showers from an overhead rose, side jets from a network of pipes at various heights, a

*Old and new (plumbed-in) washstands in the bathroom at Lanhydrock, Cornwall. The warm cork floor and magnificent polished mahogany roll top to the cast iron bath show an exceptional consideration for comfort.*

'Domestic Sanitary Regulations', a cartoon of about 1851 by John Leech, vividly conveys the effort and upheaval of 'bath night' before the era of the plumbed-in bathroom.

douche, and flattened streams of water that created waves or ripples in the bath. Shanks's 'Independent' plunge, spray and shower bath had a double-walled, semi-cylindrical enclosure of sheet zinc, perforated inside to give a fine spray all over the body.

Gwen Raverat remembered one such shower bath in the 'alarming' bathroom at her uncle's house in Egerton Place, London, in the 1890s: 'The enormous mahogany-sided bath was approached by two steps, and had a sort of grotto containing a shower-bath at one end; this was lined with as many different stops as the organ in King's Chapel. And it was as difficult to control as it would be for an amateur to play that organ. Piercing jets of boiling, or ice-cold, water came roaring at one from the most unexpected angles, and hit one in the tenderest spots.'

## Plumbed-in bathrooms

'No house of any pretensions will be devoid of a general Bath-room', wrote Robert Kerr in *The Gentlemen's House*. At Osborne on the Isle of Wight, the country seat built for the royal family in 1848, Victoria and Albert had a bath and shower in their respective dressing rooms; the Queen's bath was in an alcove that could be artfully concealed behind panelled doors when not in use. Others were swift to follow the royal example, and in the 1850s and 1860s increasing numbers of houses were provided with bathrooms as a matter of course. Kerr was writing for architects designing houses from scratch, who were in the happy position of being able to incorporate plumbing into their plans from the beginning.

In older and smaller houses, bedrooms were converted into bathrooms, or bathrooms were 'built on' in a back extension on the ground floor or projecting off the landing at the

*The Patent Oriental Spray Bath came in a choice of mahogany or walnut panelled cabinet with tiled inset.*

*OPPOSITE: The Marquess of Bute's bathroom at Cardiff Castle, designed by the architect William Burges in 1872, was more splendid than comfortable, since hot water cooled quickly on contact with the marble, while the silver sea creatures set into the sides of the bath were painfully hot against naked skin.*

turn of the stairs. Any redundant space would do at a pinch: a tip-up bath, which was stored vertically after use, could be fitted into a cupboard under the stairs, and it was not unusual to fit a bath into the kitchen under a hinged table-top that provided a work surface when the bath was not in use. The architectural historian Stefan Muthesius tracked the spread of bathrooms in London: 'by the 1880s most new houses in inner London of a rental of £100 or more, and in the suburbs of £50 or more, had bathrooms installed'.

No 'superior' house, claimed Kerr, would have a water closet installed in the same room as the bath. Separating the two avoided not only 'unpleasant associations of ideas' but also the 'awkward and inconvenient consequences' of not being able to use the water closet while someone else was in the bath. The siting of bathrooms and water-closets 'so as to be convenient for access and yet not prominent' was an art in itself, at a time when people were acutely embarrassed to be seen entering or leaving them. However, Statham's suggestion that all the baths and closets for a large country house should be 'grouped in a tower partially disconnected from the house, such as is required in workhouses, asylums, etc.', with separate entrances on different floors for women, men and servants, did not catch on.

Hot water was fed from the back boiler on the kitchen range up to the bathroom, where a high-level tank insulated with felt and encased wood stored it ready for use. From 1868 the tank system was supplemented by gas-fired geysers, such as the optimistically-named 'Instantaneous', which intercepted a flow of cold water and heated it just before it entered the bath. In 1904 Hermann Muthesius reported that, 'With the disappearance of the geyser we have seen the last of a piece of bathroom furniture that was difficult to use, sometimes dangerous and always unwelcome and the bathroom will become more hygienic, spacious and pleasanter in general appearance.' Clearly, whichever method was favoured, timing one's bath to ensure a good supply of hot water in a busy household required good judgement. In any case, not everyone was persuaded of the benefits of hot water on tap. Marion Sambourne was convinced that piped water was a health hazard, and had water for her bath brought up from the kitchen, despite having a plumbed-in 'lavatory' in the bedroom and a bathroom on the nearby landing; the latter was used more by her husband, as a photography darkroom.

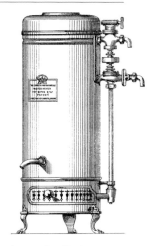

ABOVE: *Doulton's 'Lambeth' Instantaneous Water Heater in polished copper promised 'a hot bath in 10 minutes'.*

## Decoration of bathrooms

The incorporation of bathrooms into private houses created a demand for sanitary appliances and accessories. Numerous manufacturers made fortunes from serving this new market, and some, such as Shanks of Barrhead near Glasgow, Twyford of Cliffe Vale, Hanley, and Doulton of Lambeth, became household names. They produced handsome catalogues with colour illustrations of their wares, including many pictures of bathrooms completely fitted out with tiles, stained-glass windows, mirrors and towel rails.

Bathroom cabinetwork of the 1880s was as elaborate as any drawing-room furniture. Walls were tiled in horizontal bands of contrasting colour and pattern that echoed Aesthetic wallpaper schemes, or covered with varnished wallpaper or gloss paint that

could resist a steamy atmosphere. By the end of the nineteenth century a more functional look was preferred: dirt-harbouring mahogany casings were abandoned in favour of freestanding baths and washbasins on nickel-plated tubular metal stands. Hermann Muthesius saw no merit in the spartan style of bathroom decoration, believing that, 'The bathroom ... is a room that should be as agreeably appointed as possible, for bathing is pleasurable and not a necessary evil.'

## The Victorian bathroom today

The bathroom is perhaps the easiest room in the house in which to recreate an authentic Victorian appearance. Every manufacturer of sanitary ware has at least one range of products in plain white porcelain and cast iron that will suit a Victorian bathroom, and many of the patterned wares are direct reproductions of Victorian originals. Taps with 'hot' and 'cold' enamelled buttons, shower roses and 'telephone-style' combination fittings can be bought in chrome, nickel and brass finishes.

Original nineteenth-century baths, basins, lavatories and cisterns can be found in architectural salvage yards, although they should be carefully examined for chips, cracks and flaws before buying. The enamel finish on cast-iron baths can be re-coated by specialist companies, some of whom will visit your house to carry out the work *in situ*.

To be convincing, the decoration of a Victorian bathroom or toilet should tend towards simplicity and solidity, with an emphasis on hygiene clearly conveyed by hard, washable surfaces. Bathrooms were never fitted with carpets or curtains in the nineteenth century. The Victorians would have regarded soft furnishings in the bathroom as unhygienic, and would have feared the effects of steam on the textiles. The windows should be left bare and the floor covered with cork tiles or linoleum (now sold under the trade name of 'Marmoleum'). Walls can be decorated with tiles, gloss or eggshell paint, or washable wallpaper. 'Themed' decoration, and 'dressing the room' with pictures, ornaments and accessories should be avoided: the Victorians simply would not have understood why a bathroom should look 'nautical' or 'Mediterranean', and would have found such themes bizarre and pretentious in what were regarded as essentially functional rooms.

OPPOSITE: *A modern recreation of a Victorian bathroom using reproduction fittings, this scheme depends for its success on simplicity and lack of frills.*

# PART IV
## *Interior Decoration*

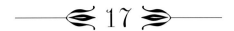
# Plain and Decorative Plaster

P LASTER NOT ONLY GIVES a neat finish to walls and ceilings, but is also used for architectural mouldings fundamental to the character of Victorian interiors. Elements such as cornices, ceiling bands and ceiling roses enhance the proportions of a room and underline their respective importance. Whereas timber mouldings largely developed out of a need to disguise the crude structural elements of the building, some of them even playing an important structural role, plaster mouldings are on the whole more purely decorative.

Almost anything that can be planed or carved in timber or stone can be imitated in plaster, and a great many plaster mouldings are copied directly from prototypes in the 'nobler' materials. Occasionally skirting boards of plaster are found (they were thought to be effective in controlling the spread of fire), but in most Victorian houses the use of plaster ornament is confined to the upper part of the walls, the cornice and the ceiling. Decorative plasterwork is particularly vulnerable to changes in taste, and much was lost during the fashion for 'modernisation' that prevailed in the mid-twentieth century. Fortunately, it is a relatively simple matter to reinstate it.

## History

Before the nineteenth century, most internal plastering was carried out with lime plaster. However, by 1800 gypsum (plaster of Paris) was becoming more common. New formulations seeking to improve plaster of Paris by making it stronger whilst preserving its fine texture included Martin's cement, patented in 1834; Keene's cement (1838 – a variant of this is now available as 'Class D' plaster); and Parian cement, patented in 1846 by J. Keating.

Plaster was applied straight onto the brick or stonework of masonry walls, and over laths on stud walls and ceilings. Laths are narrow strips of timber (about 1 inch x ¼ inch, or 25mm wide x 6mm thick). They were usually made of oak or chestnut, and were riven by hand until the introduction of steam-powered woodworking machinery in the 1840s, after which sawn laths became more common. Laths were nailed to the underside of the ceiling joists with small gaps (usually ½ inch or 10mm) between them, until the ceiling area was completely covered. Plaster was typically applied in three coats, of increasingly fine finish. Wet plaster, stiffened with animal hair or other fibres, was pressed upwards against the

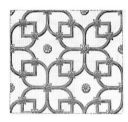

ABOVE: *design for a plaster ceiling with ribbed compartments in the Jacobean style from* Picturesque Designs for Houses, Villas, Cottages, Lodges Etc. *by C. J. Richardson, 1870. The intersections of the ribs were ornaments with pendants, and a fleur-de-lys was offered as an alternative to the rose motif shown here.*

OPPOSITE: *in an interior of 1895 a very similar effect is achieved at much less cost using Lincrusta ceiling panels.*

199

*Design for a ceiling from* The Mason's, Bricklayer's, Plasterer's and Decorator's Practical Guide, *edited by Robert Robson and published in 1862. Robson suggested painting the ceiling plane salmon pink and the mouldings in bands of pale pink, leaf green and white. The centre rose, leaves and flowers in the guilloche were painted green.*

laths, and some of it oozed through the gaps and spread out over the tops of the laths, forming a hook of plaster called a 'nib', which held the ceiling in place. A second coat, known as the floating coat, was spread over the first. Finally, the ceiling was skimmed with pure lime putty or plaster of Paris to give a smooth finish. In 1797 Edmund Cartwright had patented a system of wire netting to support ceiling plaster, and the first expanded metal laths appeared in about 1890, but plaster applied directly to masonry or laths is by far the most common kind of internal plastering encountered in Victorian houses.

The earliest plaster mouldings were created *in situ* by the simplest means – running fingers along the edge of wet plaster, or chamfering the edges of a window opening to make them less vulnerable to damage. Seventeenth-century plasterwork ceilings were divided by plaster ribs into compartments containing heraldic or naturalistic images. Repetitive motifs such as rosettes were separately cast and applied later. In the eighteenth century a tradition of freehand plaster decoration was imported by Italian *stuccadores*, who created the exquisite fantasies of Rococo decoration.

During the eighteenth century the number of profiles and types of plaster ornaments, many of them copied from Antique examples, increased enormously, and a complex set of rules was developed to govern their use in 'polite' architecture. The nineteenth-century inheritors of this tradition interpreted the rules with considerable freedom and less emphasis on classical 'correctness'. Even so, the ability to choose and use mouldings in an appropriate manner remained an important aspect of the builder's art and of the marketing of houses.

Developers matched the mouldings they chose to their intended market. It would have been a waste of money to provide elaborate decoration in artisan housing, because the price of the lease would not cover the cost of the work. On the other hand, an expensive suburban villa would not sell if the mouldings were too skimpy to appeal to the middle-class taste for elaborate detail. Within the house, too, decorative plaster-work was used to emphasize the social hierarchy. Rooms intended to be seen by visitors had the largest and most elaborate mouldings. Bedrooms used by the adults in the family had simpler decoration, perhaps just a straight-run cornice.

Mouldings were matched to the use of each room. Ceiling bands cast with the shapes of fruit, vine leaves, grapes and shells were considered suitable for dining rooms, and floral swags lent feminine elegance to the drawing room. Plaster enrichments were also used to provide architectural accents where a particularly impressive effect was desired, such as in entrance halls and around fireplaces. Modillions and rosettes derived from grand classical prototypes adorned porch ceilings, to impress visitors as they arrived, and an arch supported on scrolled brackets is a common feature in the halls of terraced houses.

During the first decades of the nineteenth century the prevailing taste was for light, delicate, flattened mouldings: fluting, reeding and incised lines predominated in Regency interiors. Later mouldings, whether of timber or plaster, projected more and became bulkier, with heavier detail. As the formal eighteenth-century habit of lining up chairs against the wall when they were not in use was abandoned, the dado rail (which had kept chairbacks from rubbing against valuable wall hangings) became redundant. By the 1830s it was abandoned, but old habits of dividing the wall surface according to the rules formulated for the proportions of classical columns remained. Skirting boards were made taller and cornices deeper in order to balance the blankness of a wall without a dado.

There was a move towards heavier and more elaborate decoration in the 1840s. The tendency throughout the mid-Victorian period was for the decoration at the top of the wall (the frieze) to become narrower, and for the plaster ornament to creep upwards onto the ceiling. As the frieze shrank, ceiling bands became wider and more elaborate. Straight-run cornices were made on site by running a zinc template cut to the desired profile through wet plaster. Three-dimensional enrichments, such as rosettes or modillions, were cast separately in moulds and applied to the flat parts of a cornice that had been run *in situ*, for a more elaborate effect. Papier-mâché and a similar paper-based compound called 'carton-pierre' were also used for cast enrichments and ceiling roses.

Two inventions of the 1850s made elaborate plaster decoration available to a much wider market. Gelatine moulds were shown at the Great Exhibition of 1851. These flexible moulds made it possible to produce repeated projecting and undercut enrichments, which previously had to be cast in several pieces or modelled by hand. Fibrous plaster, invented in 1856, was stronger and lighter than solid plaster and could be cast into lengths of cornice, incorporating raised decoration, which could be fixed into place in a single operation on site. Designs consequently became more densely elaborate.

Ceiling decoration centred on the rose from which the light fitting was suspended. Early Victorian ceiling roses were sometimes made by applying separately-cast ornaments to the centre of the ceiling, From about 1840 roses were increasingly cast in one piece; this required less skill of the on-site plasterer but led to heavier and less detailed designs. The relief decoration of the rose acted as a 'smut-catcher' for the smoke rising from chandeliers and gasoliers, and some rose designs incorporated grills allowing 'vitiated air' (stale air containing fumes from gas lights) to escape into a duct in the space between the ceiling and the floor above.

*Designs for plaster ceiling roses in Loudon's* Encyclopaedia *(1833).*

*Design for plaster cornice, from* The Mason's, Bricklayer's, Plasterer's and Decorator's Practical Guide, *1862. Decoration crept onto the ceiling as the depth of the cornice was reduced. In large rooms of the 1860s the ceiling bands might be as wide as 900mm (36 inches).*

In the 1860s grander houses might have whole ceilings decorated with floriated panels between the cornice and the central rose. Architects and builders studied books of architectural details, and adapted Gothic or Renaissance designs to suit houses built in historical revival styles. In many Gothic Revival houses plaster ribs or vaulting were applied across whole ceilings in designs copied from the ceilings of seventeenth-century houses. The separate compartments created by such schemes might also be adorned with bosses, pendants or heraldic motifs such as Tudor roses or fleurs-de-lys. Plaster mouldings were also introduced to define areas of panelling on walls as a cheap alternative to real wooden wainscot.

The taste for massive and elaborate mouldings prevailed until about 1880, by which time new fashions in interior decoration encouraged a simpler approach. The decorative interest of the wall became concentrated in the suites of wallpaper designed to work in harmony on the dado, filling and frieze. Plaster mouldings were reduced to a narrow, straight-run cornice. The heavy cornices and ceiling decoration that had characterized mid-century interiors were now despised by authorities on decoration like Lucy Crane, who dismissed them as 'ugly and meaningless ... looking like the ornaments of a wedding cake'. It was a question not only of good taste, but also of hygiene: enriched plaster mouldings were regarded as dust traps – although builders and householders who were more concerned about respectability than fashion continued to regard a ceiling rose and a modest cornice as essential elements in the decoration of a drawing room.

In an inevitable reaction to Aesthetic austerity, and perhaps also to the introduction of electricity, which threw glaring light onto flat ceilings, architects of the 1900s reintroduced ceiling decoration. They continued to ignore the ceiling rose, however, preferring flattened all-over designs in the Adam revival style or reworkings of French Renaissance or Rococo ornament (referred to dismissively as 'tous les Louis'). There was also a revival of hand-modelled decoration; ceilings adorned with simple ribs, flowers and animals in the seventeenth-century tradition are sometimes found in better-quality Arts and Crafts houses at the end of the century.

## Reinstatement and repair

If you need to get access to ceilings or high walls above stairwells, make sure that any ladders or scaffolding are sturdy and properly fixed. Disconnect the power supply and remove light fittings before carrying out work on ceiling roses.

### Repairing plaster ceilings

Signs of trouble in plaster ceilings include cracks, damp patches, and plaster crumbling or dropping off. You will need to take up floorboards or go into the roof space to inspect the condition of the plaster. When moving about in unfloored roof spaces, take care to step only on joists. Clear away accumulated dirt and dust so that you can see the laths and plaster properly. You can use a vacuum cleaner but proceed with care; if you hear chunks of plaster rattling up the hose, stop immediately – you may be breaking off pieces of the 'squeeze', which keys the plaster to the laths and is vital for holding the ceiling up. Watch out for electric cables, which can be hard to see in poorly-lit ceiling voids, and be especially careful if you are testing the soundness of laths by poking them with a screwdriver.

The most common kind of ceiling is a single ceiling plastered onto laths fixed directly to the floor joists. Double ceilings are fixed on their own, separate set of joists suspended with hangers from the floor joists. Laths can fail through damp, decay or beetle attack. It is more common for the plaster to fail, either because it was mixed with insufficient hair to reinforce it or because the laths were originally fixed too close together, leaving too

202

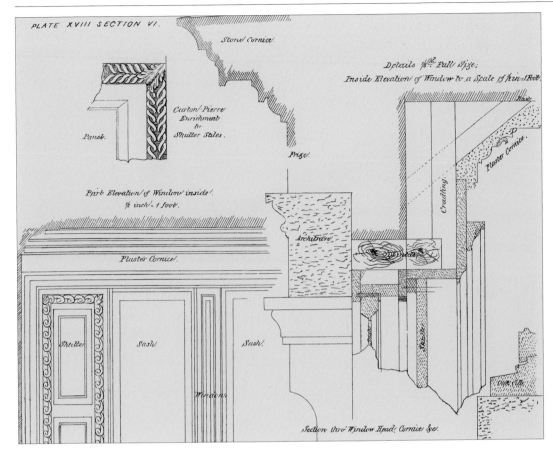

*PLATE XVIII SECTION VI.*

*Construction details for
a window (1855),
showing how the plaster
cornice overlaps the
timber window frame to
make a seamless join.
The enrichments on the
shutter panels are
made of carton-pierre.*

narrow a gap for the plaster to squeeze through and form adequate nibs.

A simple procedure for a small area sagging because the nibs have broken is to prop and patch the plaster. Prop the plaster from below with a sheet of plywood and length of timber so that the sag is pushed back into position. The rest of the repair is carried out from above. Clean the ceiling and remove the broken nibs, then lightly spray the laths and plaster with water (this prevents the dry material from sucking too much water out of the new plaster mix). Pour rapid-setting plaster along the line of the gaps between the laths, to form new nibs. Wait for the plaster to set and remove the prop from below.

Even large areas of sagging ceiling plaster can be screwed back into the joists. Working from below, use long stainless steel screws and large washers, and place them at frequent intervals along each joist. The washers and screw heads can be sunk into the thickness of the plaster and patched with new plaster or filler before repainting. The same method can be used to refix a cornice that is sagging along with the ceiling. If the damaged area is too large to be dealt with in this way, ask your plasterer to repair with lath-and-plaster the minimum area necessary to ensure a sound ceiling. Fine, hand-made decorative plasterwork ceilings should always be repaired by experts.

Crumbling or falling plaster must be removed and replaced. Take down all loose material. When you reach sound plaster, undercut the edges to help support the new material. Clean away the broken nibs from above. Repair, replace or respace the laths as necessary, using galvanized clout nails to fix them to the joists. Any new laths should be made from rough-sawn softwood. Reapply backing, floating and skim coats, and wait for it all to dry out properly before redecorating. Plasterers will often suggest that the whole ceiling be taken down and replaced with sheets of plasterboard and a skim coat. This should only be considered as a last resort, as it means losing a lot of original material and abandoning a traditional building method, resulting in a very flat, characterless ceiling.

203

*Cornice repaired as part of the restoration of a house that had been poorly converted into flats.*

ABOVE: *a length of the fibrous plaster cornice in the plasterer's workshop.*

RIGHT: *the cornice reinstated. The seams where the new work joins the old are filled with wet plaster, which is then smoothed over the join by hand. A new length of picture rail has been specially cut to match the original.*

Not every room of a Victorian house was originally provided with a cornice, nor did every reception room have a ceiling rose. Careful consideration of the age and style of the house, its original status and the function and importance of each room within it, as well as comparison with similar houses, will help you to decide what level of architectural decoration is appropriate in each case.

Before undertaking any work on decorative 'plaster', it is important to discover exactly what you are dealing with. Compounds such as 'compo', papier-mâché and carton-pierre may need specialist handling by a qualified conservator, and can be damaged by chemical stripper or water that would leave true plaster unharmed.

Old paint that has clogged the fine detail of plaster ornament can be removed with relative ease, but is physical evidence of earlier colour schemes, so consider whether you need to record the layers you find. Proprietary chemical strippers work on most kinds of paint. Liquid strippers can be dabbed onto vertical surfaces but are impractical for use on ceilings. Paste-type strippers can be applied to all types of mouldings and left to work under a layer of foil or polythene to prevent the stripper from drying out. The stripper is scraped away and the moulding washed clean before redecoration. Sharpened sticks, dental picks and old toothbrushes are handy for picking out fine detail.

The traditional distemper used for painting ceilings in the nineteenth century was water-soluble and meant to be washed off before every redecoration. However, the temptation to just slap a new layer on over the old must have been great, and stubborn layers of distemper which will not respond to chemical strippers will often be found underneath the more recent layers of paint. Washing down with warm water may help to loosen these. As a last resort, a steam machine may be used, but this is a job for an experienced contractor; the process generates a large amount of condensation, which can damage other decorations or lead to problems with mould growth.

Minor damage to plaster mouldings can be repaired by filling in the broken parts with fresh plaster or filler. Missing parts can be replaced by taking a latex mould from sound plaster and casting new elements to match. Where large repairs are envisaged, it is important to use plaster of the same type as the old, otherwise cracks will appear as the new and old plasters respond to changes in temperature and moisture by expanding and shrinking at different rates.

Where one rosette in a row of enrichments is broken or missing, it can be replaced by taking a copy from one of its undamaged counterparts. The undamaged rosette is carefully removed, thoroughly cleaned, and used to make a mould from which new rosettes can be cast. Rosettes and other relief details were usually fixed in place with a dab of plaster of Paris. It may be necessary to replace a damaged cornice altogether. A skilled plasterer can run a plain cornice *in situ*: an armature of laths, corresponding roughly to the intended shape of the cornice, is fixed to the corner between wall and ceiling. A first coat of plaster is applied and scored to provide a key for the floating coat. The floating coat is built up to a close approximation of the finished cornice before a metal template or 'horse' cut to the desired profile is run along the wet plaster to refine the shape and remove excess plaster. Finally the 'horse' is dragged over a thin finishing coat of plaster to give a smooth and finely detailed surface to which applied ornament can be added.

Several companies cast fibrous plaster cornices to nineteenth-century patterns. Plaster is poured into moulds made of rigid GRP (Glass Reinforced Plastic) or, for more complex or undercut designs, flexible silicone rubber. The plaster is strengthened with hessian. Non-standard designs can be copied from existing mouldings for an extra charge. Fibrous plaster cornices are brought to site in lengths of up to 12 feet (3.66m), ready to be measured, cut and mitred, and fixed into place using plaster of Paris or special PVA adhesive. Long, rust-proof screws fixed into wallplugs and ceiling joists at regular intervals will help to secure heavy cornices. Plastic or fibreglass products are cheaper, but rarely match the quality of the original plaster designs. Shallow ceiling roses made out of pressed sheet plastic will not have a convincingly robust nineteenth-century character or texture.

Where a ceiling rose is to be reinstated, the new rose should, if possible, be positioned so that the light fitting hanging from it is aligned with the centre of the chimneypiece (which may not correspond to the geometrical centre of the ceiling, since chimney breasts are often slightly off-centre). This ensures that the room's most elaborate light fitting is squarely reflected in the centre of the overmantel mirror that adorned every middle-class reception room in the mid-nineteenth century.

The modern fashion for painting ceilings and cornices brilliant white does not do justice to elaborate ornamental plasterwork. Whites were used, particularly towards the end of the nineteenth-century and in the Edwardian period, but they were softer shades than the bleached 'brilliant white' so often chosen today. Victorian decorators often devised elaborate paint schemes, in which mouldings might be picked out in several colours, or even gilded. The current revival of interest in historic colour has made traditional paints such as distemper widely available today. It would be good to see this matched by a return to the adventurous colour combinations that enlivened plaster mouldings in many nineteenth-century interiors.

# DECORATIVE TILES

**H**AND-PAINTED GLAZED TILES were imported from Holland in the eighteenth century and a few English tile works were set up to imitate this fashionable Delft ware. In 1756 a patent was granted for a transfer-printing process that increased production of decorated glazed tiles, but it was not until the 1830s, when the porcelain manufacturer Herbert Minton began to invest in tile production, that the astonishing growth of the industry began. Minton started the revival of encaustic tile-making and was one of the first to see the potential of the dust-pressing process by which most modern tiles are made.

Victorian tile manufacturers found that the market for mass-produced tiles was insatiable. Cheap to obtain and easy to install, tiles offered the speculative builder the chance to incorporate cheerful, hygienic and fashionable decoration into all kinds of houses. By the mid-century tiled decoration of some kind was to be expected in all but the cheapest new housing.

## Encaustic and geometric tiles

In 1830 Minton bought a share in a patent for making encaustic tiles by machine and began to develop the process. Encaustic (literally, 'burnt-in') decoration is achieved by stamping a design into the body of a plain clay tile before firing while it is still damp, and filling the stamped impression with liquid clay of a contrasting colour. The tile is then fired to fuse the two clays together. Originally developed in medieval monasteries, the technique was the monastic legacy of complex inlaid pavements, such as the thirteenth-century floor of the Chapter House in Westminster Abbey, which inspired many Victorian tile makers and designers, notably Minton and Pugin. Monastic tile-making came to an end when the monasteries were dissolved in 1538, and the encaustic technique was lost. In most English domestic interiors the use of tiles was unknown until the seventeenth century, when plain clay tiles began to be used for floors – but only in the better houses.

The first encaustic tiles produced by Minton bore ecclesiastical motifs in a limited range of red and buff colours, and were intended for the rapidly growing market created by the need to furnish new churches. Within a few years, however, his catalogue included designs suitable for civic buildings and private houses in a wider range of colours, and several rival manufacturers, including Maw & Co., had entered the market. Encaustics might be wholly or partly glazed, but the majority were unglazed. The more elaborate tiles might incorporate as many as six different colours – a remarkable technological achievement considering the number of firings required, during which each

*ABOVE: catalogue page showing tiles incorporated into window boxes, to 'impart a cheerful aspect to Residences in all styles of Architecture'.*

*OPPOSITE: Minton tiles lining the walls of a converted dairy in Holyhead. A rich decorative effect is achieved by imaginative combinations of plain tiles enriched with a handful of conventionalized floral motifs from designs by Pugin. The insets in the dresser are late-nineteenth century reproductions of traditional Delft designs*

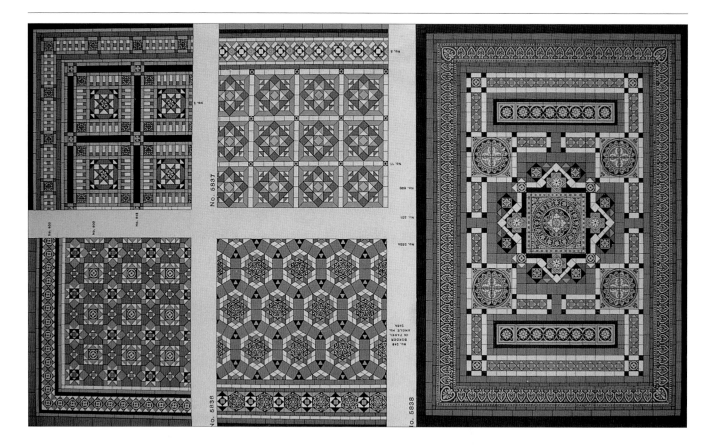

*Suggestions for geometric tile pavements incorporating encaustic tiles, from a catalogue produced in the 1890s by Craven Dunnill & Co. of Jackfield, Shropshire.*

clay might shrink or warp at a different rate in the kiln. It took Minton several years of trial and error to perfect the industrial production of encaustic tiles.

Minton's encaustics were used for the tiled floors at Osborne, Victoria and Albert's new house on the Isle of Wight, in 1848. The publicity given to the floors Minton supplied to royalty and the aristocracy in the 1840s helped to establish these as *the* fashionable floors to have. However, encaustic tiles were relatively expensive, so they were often combined with quarries (plain square tiles) and geometric tiles in order to cover large areas at less cost. Sometimes erroneously referred to as 'mosaic' tiles, geometrics are small, usually unglazed, tiles in straight-edged shapes such as triangles and lozenges, which can be combined in a variety of patterns to make floors. Dozens of shapes and sizes were available, all based on subdivisions of a 6-inch (150mm) square tile, and the catalogues of all the major manufacturers contained several pages of suggested arrangements for 'geometric pavements'. Most geometrics were of natural clay colours, ranging from off-white through red and brown to blue-black. Hall floors made entirely of geometric tiles quickly became commonplace in middle-class houses. They were composed of common clay colours – red, buff and brown – enlivened with the occasional, more costly, blue, white or green tile.

Geometric pavements were restricted to those areas that might be seen by visitors: garden paths, porch floors, entrance halls and conservatories. Kitchens, sculleries and passages used only by the servants had floors made up more cheaply of 6-inch (150mm) quarry tiles, in plain red clay or red alternating with blue-black.

## Tiles on walls

Walls of plain glazed tiles or glazed brick were installed in areas that received the most wear and tear. Eastlake thought that 'an inlay of encaustic tiles to a height, say, of three or four feet from the ground, would form an excellent lining for a hall or ground-floor

passage'. This would particularly protect against the ladies' dresses brushing the wall as they walked through these narrow rooms. In fact most wall tiling was carried out in glazed plain, embossed or printed tiles. One of the commonest forms was the white glazed earthenware used in kitchens, dairies and other functional rooms. The cheapest kind was composed of 6-inch (150mm) square tiles, although slightly dearer 6½-inch and 4½-inch (165mm and 115mm) hexagons and small octagons were also often used. Plain tiles were available in ivory, cream, buff, celadon, turquoise and olive – pale colours that would reflect light and show the dirt, and were therefore ideal for areas where hygiene was important. The relative grandeur of tiling schemes in different parts of the house was closely related to the status of different rooms. Present-day manufacturers offer expensive and elaborate tiles for use in kitchens, but the Victorian householder would have considered these inappropriately extravagant.

*Cheap tiles in plain clay colours are combined with encaustic motifs for a superior effect in a hall floor of the late 1880s.*

*The staircase walls at Cragside are decorated with relief-patterned tiles made by the Medmenham Pottery in about 1895.*

211

In better-class houses the provision of bathrooms and toilets gave more scope for tiling the walls. An extremely elaborate tiled scheme for Gledhow Hall, Leeds, was devised by the Burmantofts company in 1885, in which every inch of the room – the coffered ceiling, pedimented chimneypiece, arcaded walls and elaborate dado – was clad in glazed ceramic. This was exceptional, but in the bathrooms of many lesser houses a tiled dado with a moulded ceramic top rail was installed, a hygienic innovation reflecting the modern attitude to sanitation.

In the public parts of the house, tiles were used to draw attention to noteworthy features of the architecture. From about 1870 tiled dados began to appear in porches, sometimes extended into an entrance lobby, giving visitors landscapes or floral panels to admire as they waited for admittance.

## Fireplaces and special features

Fireplaces were the natural home for decorative tiles in every class of house. Entire chimneypieces of glazed ceramic were on offer for wealthy customers, but in most cases the tile decoration was restricted to a pair of framed panels in the reveals or 'cheeks' flanking cast iron fire surrounds of the 1870s and after, which could be filled with any standard 6-inch tiles. Fireplace tiles were accurate mirrors of contemporary taste: all developments in fashionable interior decoration were studied by tile manufacturers, who rushed out appropriate designs to complement them, often buying them from artists who were also producing patterns for textiles or wallpapers. Floral bouquets were perennial favourites, sunflowers in blue and white pots adorned the fireplaces of Aesthetic interiors in the 1870s and 1880s, and various historical revival styles all had their day. Designs would be matched to the rooms in which they were used: perhaps flowers in the drawing room, scenes from Shakespeare in the study, Aesop's *Fables* in the schoolroom and children's games in the nursery.

The decorative hierarchy was as strictly observed in fireplace tiles as in other elements of the Victorian interior. Reception rooms had the smartest tiles, often in panels. Bedroom fireplaces were more likely to have sets of identical tiles. In lesser bedrooms the fireplaces had plain glazed tiles.

*Tile panels designed in the 1890s for use in hearths. The slabs incorporate mottled background tiles (the better to conceal dust and cinders) and a moulded ceramic 'fender'.*

Tiles were also incorporated into furniture, appearing as splashbacks in washstands, waterproof tops on tables for conservatories and in framed panels on hallstands, chairs and sideboards.

Many millions of tiles were produced, most of them to conventional designs by anonymous artists. The industry also employed some well-known designers, and tiles

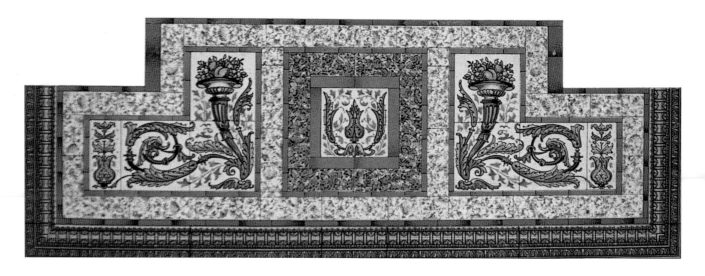

by Pugin, John Moyr Smith, Kate Greenaway, Walter Crane and Voysey have become sought after by collectors.

Most tiles used in Victorian houses were mass-produced, but the high value that the Arts and Craft movement placed on making things by hand led (in better-off households) to a rejection of the standardized designs of many transfer-printed tiles and a revival of hand-painting techniques. William Morris designed simple decorations of stylized flowers, painted by hand in the traditional blue and white of old Delft tiles. He produced his first lustre tiles in about 1870. William de Morgan was an extremely gifted tile designer particularly interested in reproducing the brilliant turquoise blue and lustre glazes of ancient Persian pottery. His animal and flower designs, and panels featuring Viking ships and classical figures are among the most outstanding products of the Arts and Crafts movement, and are now very sought-after. Inevitably, mass-produced tiles were adapted to cater for this change in taste, and firms such as Minton's were soon producing printed tiles in imitation of the hand-painted variety.

Tiles can be simply categorized according to the way in which they are decorated:

*Transfer-printed tile showing 'Potato Lifting' from a series of 'Village Life' designs produced by William Wise for Minton & Co., and first introduced in 1882.*

## Glazed tiles

Glaze is the hard, shiny finish applied to the surface of a tile to make it durable. The final appearance of the tile can be altered by adjusting the opacity of the glaze or by adding chemicals to colour it. Slight variations in the density of coloured glaze occur as a result of the glaze pooling on one side of the tile when dipped by hand. This creates a pleasing 'moiré' effect when plain glazed tiles are combined across large areas of wall, and should not be regarded as a defect.

## Relief decoration

Damp clay or clay dust can be pressed into a mould to produce raised or incised areas on the tile surface. Damp clay was used for the more expensive high relief tiles, dust-pressing for lower relief designs. During firing the liquid glaze runs into the depressions, creating pools of darker colour that enhance the three-dimensional effect of the design.

## Transfer-printing

Most decorated tiles produced before about 1850 were decorated with outline designs printed from engraved copper plates onto tissue paper, with any colour added by hand. The development of lithographic block printing in 1848 made it possible to print both line and flat colour directly onto the tile surface in one go, which meant many more tiles could be produced at much greater speed and less cost. One of the first to produce designs for this new block-printing process was Pugin, who ordered Gothic tiles for the smoking room of the House of Commons. The new process led to 'every possible variety of design – floral, geometrical, mythological, historical and otherwise', and several manufacturers produced themed series of tiles. Moyr Smith specialized in literary themes, depicting scenes from Shakespeare, Tennyson and Aesop's *Fables*.

## Tube lined tiles

Tube lining involves outlining a simple design on a plain tile using soft clay or slip squeezed through a nozzle – exactly like icing a cake. The spaces within the lines are filled with coloured glazes and the tile is fired. The technique lends itself particularly well to large panel pictures, since the strong lines carry the design well from one tile to

the next, and to the sinuous lines of Art Nouveau designs. The effect of tube lining can be mimicked by dust-pressing, and many tiles with simple coloured motifs were produced by this method at the end of the nineteenth century.

## Restoration and maintenance

### Cleaning floor tiles

Ordinary household surface cleaners, used according to the instructions on the label, will take care of day-to-day cleaning. To remove stubborn dirt use a specially formulated product such as BAL Ceramic floor cleaner or HG Systems Extra Cleaner. Scouring powder, metal scourers or wire brushes should never be used on tiles. Although cleaning products will help to shift a great deal of built-up dirt and old wax, be prepared to contribute a lot of elbow grease.

Tiled floors covered with sheet flooring are often disfigured by the remains of mastic adhesive. This can be removed with a solvent such as HG Tarol. Surface dirt can be scraped off using a Stanley blade-type scraper, keeping the blade at an acute angle to the surface of the tile so as to avoid scoring or gouging it. Nylon scourers and white scouring pads of the kind designed for non-stick saucepans can be used with a gentle circular action to clean unglazed tiles.

Where fitted carpet has been removed from tiled floors, the holes where gripper strips were screwed to the floor will remain around the edges. These can be filled with a filler such as Polyfilla, and coloured or painted with acrylic colours to blend into the surrounding tile. Mix the colour slightly darker than the tile, as the mix will lighten a little as it dries and a slightly darker final colour will stand out less than a slightly paler one.

### Repairing tiled floors

The tiles in geometric pavements are usually so closely packed together that they are impossible to loosen unless they start to lift up of their own accord. Since the small unit size of these tiles often causes these pavements to fail in sections, only patch repairs, carefully matched to blend into the surrounding tiles, may be required. In halls the central strip suffers most from heavy traffic; in garden paths it is frequently the edges, vulnerable to rainwater run-off and encroaching grass, which fail. If many of the small tiles have broken or been lost, it may be possible to retain the remaining tiles and reduce the cost of the repair by redesigning the pavement, using the remaining original tiles in a border around a central panel of new plain quarries, or vice versa.

*Damage to the tiled walls of this converted dairy has been repaired with plain white filler. The Minton tile panel depicting a dairymaid was hand-painted by W.P. Simpson, an artist who specialized in rural scenes for shop interiors, in the 1890s.*

Geometric tiles are still being made and the art of laying elaborate geometric pavements is enjoying a revival. However, for patch repairs to an existing pavement it is sometimes best to look for plain, 6-inch square tiles of the right colours, which can be carefully cut to the shapes and sizes required. This is because many modern geometrics are made to slightly different sizes and have cushioned (i.e. slightly rounded) edges that do not align well with the Victorian originals. Patience will be required in the search for a good colour match; a meticulously cleaned sample of the original tile should be used as a guide, and the old and new tiles should be compared under both natural and artificial light. Differences in the surface texture of unglazed tiles are just as noticeable as differences in colour, since they affect the way the tiles reflect the light. Many modern tiles are thinner than Victorian ones, so it may be necessary to build up the substrate below the patched-in tiles with cement to bring them up to the right level. Where tiles have lifted themselves, the cement left behind bears the imprint of the tile backs. This should be gently chipped away in order to give a good key and enough room for the new cement.

In recent years the fashion has been for wide bands of grouting, but in Victorian floors the tiles were set very closely together. Geometric tile pavements in particular rely for their effect on close-butted tiles. In floors of one colour the quarry tiles were often laid in staggered courses like brickwork, or diagonally, rather than in the square grid pattern favoured today.

### Finishes for tiled floors

The traditional treatment for a tiled floor after cleaning was to apply warmed linseed oil. This was wiped sparingly over the floor and left to absorb into the tiles, followed by a coat of wax polish. This gave a stunning, lustrous finish to the floor, but it is so labour-intensive to apply and maintain that it is inappropriate in most modern situations. Linseed oil tends to yellow on exposure to light, and unless the wax seal is rigorously maintained, the oil also attracts dirt. Modern cold wax polishes, for example Johnson's Traffic Wax, are perfectly adequate.

On no account should tiled floors be sealed or varnished with any kind of resin-based or polyurethane finish. Besides giving an inauthentic plasticky appearance, these may cause long-term problems by sealing in damp under the floor.

### Cleaning glazed tiles

Since glaze prevents dirt from penetrating the body of the tile, most glazed tiles are easy to clean, but care must be taken not to damage the glaze. Loose dirt can be washed off with warm soapy water and the tile polished to a shine with a clean, soft cloth. Never pour boiling water over a tile, as this can cause the tile or its glaze to crack. Diluted household bleach can be used to remove dirt that has worked its way into fine cracks or crazing, but only after soaking the tile in plain water. This prevents the dry clay from absorbing the dirt once it has dissolved into the bleach solution. Iron stains appear as rust-coloured patches on the tile surface. They can be removed with a rust remover such as Jelonite (sold for car maintenance). Painted-over tiles can be cleaned with a proprietary paint stripper such as Nitromors.

White scouring pads are ideal for use on stubborn dirt. Use a soft scrubbing brush or an old toothbrush to work away built-up dirt from relief or tube-lined tiles. Take particular care when cleaning tube-lined tiles, as it is all too easy to chip or break the fine lines of clay that stand proud of the surface. On-glaze decoration and gilding, which can be recognized by their matt appearance when the tile is tilted against the light, require expert cleaning.

Removing old cement from the back of a tile is difficult and should never be attempted on a valuable tile; the chipping action of a chisel can easily shatter the tile. This risk can be reduced by laying the tile face down on a tray filled with sand to a depth of at least 2 inches; the sand will absorb most of the shock. A heavy build-up of cement can be removed using an angle grinder held at an acute angle to the tile surface. The tile must be firmly clamped face down in a vice before any work with power tools begins. A mask and goggles should be worn to protect against cement dust.

## Repairing glazed tiles

The degree of damage found on glazed tiles depends greatly on where they were used. Porch dados may suffer frost damage; hearth tiles were often cracked when fire irons were dropped on them; any kind of relief tile – mouldings, edges, corners – is particularly vulnerable. Tiled walls tend to escape accidental damage but may have been deliberately scarred for the installation of new wiring or plumbing.

Damage such as drill holes and chipped edges to mouldings can be made good with a filler such as Polyfilla, smoothed to finish flush with the surface of the surrounding tiles. Left white, this is a neat and honest finish, but it can also be painted to blend into the surrounding area using acrylic paints and glazes. Where deep mouldings (e.g. on ceramic chimneypieces and architraves) are damaged beyond repair, it may be possible to remove the damaged unit and replace it with a short length of wooden moulding cut and painted to match.

As with floor tiles, it is important to copy Victorian styles of layout and grouting. Plain tiles were usually offset like brickwork or laid diagonally, but rarely in a squared grid. Grouting was generally applied in the thinnest possible line. New grouting can be coloured to match old by mixing it with universal stainer (an oil pigment sold in tubes and available from paint suppliers). These stains become lighter in colour as they dry, so do a test patch first to check the colour match before grouting a large area.

In most cases the glaze itself is the only finish required. However, to enhance the shine and further protect the surface of glazed tiles in a vulnerable area such as a porch or hearth, a microcrystalline wax such as Renaissance Wax may be used.

## Buying tiles

Architectural salvage yards can be a useful source of original tiles, provided that you buy with care. Look for clean tiles with no cement adhering to the back, clean edges and no chips. Crazing of the surface need not impair the practical functioning of the glaze; unless it is so bad as to distort the colour or the pattern, it gives character to the tile. Tiles that have been stacked in a shed or in the open air are often very dirty; insist on seeing them washed or wiped so you can assess any damage before buying.

Some manufacturers will make new tiles to order, to match Victorian originals, and most manufacturers produce reproduction tiles for the Victorian house market. Some of these are precise replicas of nineteenth-century tiles, while others are disappointing pastiches. Do not rely on photographs in glossy catalogues but ask to see samples of the tiles themselves before buying. Remember the hierarchy of decoration in Victorian houses: grand effects should be reserved for entrances and reception rooms, so resist the temptation to create a more elaborate tile scheme than is appropriate for the room, or for the size of the house.

# PAINT COLOURS AND FINISHES

T HE CONFIDENCE AND VERVE with which the Victorians used bright, strong colour in domestic interiors was undermined in the twentieth century by Modernism, and many nineteenth-century paint schemes were obliterated by brilliant white or magnolia paint. The fashion for stripped pine also caused the loss of much original paintwork. Happily, however, much of the consequent damage to the historical integrity of old houses can be repaired by repainting with appropriate colours and finishes.

In a few cases it will be appropriate to undertake historical research and analyze the paint layers with a view to uncovering, conserving or recreating a Victorian decorative scheme, but in most cases a careful choice of modern paints in appropriate textures and matched to matured Victorian colours will enable you to decorate your house in a sympathetic style.

## Recipes and applications

Painting and decorating was usually undertaken by professional house-painters, who mixed their paints on site following recipes published in builders' handbooks or handed down as trade secrets. The paints were usually either oil- or water-based. Oil-based paints, which dried to a more or less glossy finish, were used on woodwork and some plaster surfaces. Water-based paints were generally used only on plaster. Resin-based varnishes were also used on timber and to protect imitative finishes, such as marbling or woodgrain, and embossed wallcoverings.

Oil paint was essentially white lead mixed with linseed oil and modified with turpentine and thinners. The finish, or degree of surface sheen, depended upon the ratio of oil to turpentine. Driers and other ingredients were added, depending on the nature of the paint required, and the paint was coloured by the addition of pigments ground in oil. These were chosen both on the basis of taste and according to what could be afforded, as pigments varied in price. Common earth colours, such as ochre, were cheaper than those made from minerals, such as the rich blue of lapis lazuli.

Oil paints' glossy finish tended to dull over time. The linseed oil content caused it to yellow, especially in areas deprived of light. This was most obvious in white paint, but colours would also change, blues taking on a greenish tinge. The tendency to yellow could be corrected by adding a little blue or black, but often this problem was avoided altogether by the deliberate use of a stone colour. Certain pigments tended to work better in one medium than the other. Blue verditer, for example, was generally reserved

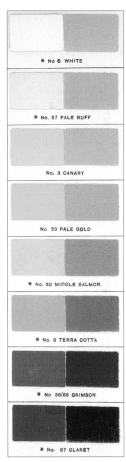

| |
|---|
| ✳ No 6 WHITE |
| ✳ No. 57 PALE BUFF |
| No. 3 CANARY |
| No 23 PALE GOLD |
| ✳ No. 30 MIDDLE SALMON |
| ✳ No. 8 TERRA COTTA |
| ✳ No 36/65 CRIMSON |
| ✳ No. 67 CLARET |

ABOVE: *detail of colour card for Hall's Sanitary Washable distemper, showing the effect of varnish on flat colour.*

OPPOSITE: *the palette is modern but these strong colours and striking contrasts capture the bold spirit of Victorian colour schemes and work well in a late nineteenth-century setting.*

for use in distemper, being liable to darken and go green in oil. Chalk worked well in water but became translucent and rather grey in oil.

An inexpensive matt finish, widely used on plaster walls and ceilings, was soft distemper, or 'size colour', made with whiting (ground chalk) bound with an animal glue size and then tinted with the required pigment. Cheap and easy to make, soft distemper dried quickly, could be made in a wide range of tints and washed off before each redecoration. It did not trap moisture within the wall but allowed the structure to 'breathe', making it especially appropriate for newly built houses. New plaster needed to dry out for a year or so before it could be painted with oil-based paint, so it was common practice to decorate a new house throughout in soft distemper or 'builder's finish'.

*Frontispiece to* The Painter's and Colourman's Complete Guide *by P.F. Tingry, 1830. A sunny day has been chosen for painting the exterior of the house: one painter grains the front door while his colleagues paint the stucco. In the foreground are oil cans and paint kettles, which remained essential equipment for house painters before the introduction of ready-mixed paints at the end of the nineteenth century.*

220

Soft distemper had to be applied quickly or there would be a visible line where the leading edge dried. It was not particularly durable (lasting two or three years on walls), and was neither washable nor suitable for areas of heavy traffic. Proprietary, oil-bound distempers such as Duresco became available in the late Victorian period.

The idea of all colours being equally available in all finishes is a relatively new one. Indeed, until the 1870s ready-mixed paint was hardly sold in shops, although made-up colour in a thick paste form was available. Pigments were ground in small portable mills or by hand, which could result in uneven colour, and it was very difficult to mix a new batch to match an existing colour exactly. Victorian paint surfaces accordingly looked more lively than those produced with today's highly refined and consistent paints.

## Colours for Interiors

The choice of appropriate colours was more than a matter of personal taste. Apart from protecting vulnerable surfaces, painted decoration was designed to enhance architectural features, to complement the functions of individual rooms, and to express the relative status of different parts of the house.

By 1830 colours derived from archaeological discoveries, such as lilac, terracotta and 'Pompeian red', were frequently found in fashionable interiors. Brownish reds or brighter crimsons were particularly used in principal rooms, where they were considered the most suitable background for gilt-framed pictures.

In the 1840s the use of restrained, secondary tints like beige, lilac and pink was common. These were often used in combination with stronger versions of their complementaries: buff and blue, lilac and green and so on. Whatever the strength of a Victorian colour as it appeared on a colour card, it could always be softened by being made paler. Pale tints were common in the nineteenth century and quite appropriate in recreated schemes today – Victorian interiors were by no means always the dark and gloomy rooms of popular caricature.

The appearance of the first aniline dye (mauve) in 1856 made little difference to the very conservative house-painting trade, which was slow to take up the new chemical dyes: they tended to fade quickly and there was little demand for bright colours. Indeed, during the late nineteenth century paint colours used for interior decoration were if anything even more subdued than those of previous years, despite the colour possibilities the new technology offered.

Dark greens were used widely on ironwork and woodwork. The yellower 'bronze greens' were also popular, sometimes being dusted with bronze powder to give an impression of weathered bronze. 'Drab' olive greens were also very common. From the 1870s onwards, rich Brunswick greens were often used to decorate both external joinery – having been much in favour for windows and external doors since the 1830s – and internal woodwork. Browns were also used on ironwork; purple browns and cherry browns have been identified on Victorian railings. Browns generally were frequently used during the Victorian period, partly because of their resemblance to the traditional wood colours and their use in graining, and partly because they were very cheap. Olive browns and purple browns were also popular for interior joinery. Alternatively, softwoods used for internal woodwork were occasionally stained to resemble more expensive and exotic woods. Staining on its own was not, however, considered sufficient protection for external joinery, which would normally be covered with varnish.

Very few blues are evident in the Victorian colour cards that survive, which suggests that blue was not extensively used in the average Victorian house.

*George Scharf's drawing of his study at 29 Great George Street, London, (1869) contains detailed annotations concerning the colours and finishes of the decoration, including a 'yellow oak' woodgrain effect used on the window reveals, and a combination of green and white on the egg-and-dart moulding of the cornice.*

Whites were often used for ceilings. Nonetheless, during the 1830s ceilings were also painted with colours, or even *trompe-l'oeil* sky and clouds. Victorian decorators often 'picked in' individual elements of the cornice in different – and surprisingly strong – colours. From the mid-century richly coloured ceilings, with individual elements of plasterwork, papier mâché or embossed wallpaper picked out in vibrant tones, became increasingly common, even in relatively modest middle-class homes. George Scharf's drawing of the study in his house at 29 Great George Street, dated 1869, contains pencilled notes about the colours used: sage green walls, flat white ceiling and yellow on the window reveals and shutters (although the window sill is 'br. oak'). The cornice is pale green, with a band of egg-and-dart moulding picked out in pale green and white, and the join where the cornice meets the wall is masked with a gold bead (i.e. a line of thin gilt moulding). What can be seen of the walls above the crowded bookshelves in Scharf's library, drawn in the same year, is dark crimson, under a cornice and ceiling painted plain white.

Colour theory influenced many of the rules laid down for the decoration of interiors by writers in the middle of the century. In *The Grammar of Ornament* (1856) the influential designer Owen Jones explained that 'colour is used to assist light and shade, helping the undulations of form by the proper distribution of the several colours'. This gave a systematic basis for choosing certain colours for particular elements of architectural decoration, thus, 'in using the primary colours on moulded surfaces, we should place blue, which retires, on the concave surfaces; yellow, which advances, on the convex; and red, the intermediate colour, on the undersides; separating the colours by white on the vertical planes'.

The point was repeated by Christopher Dresser in *Studies in Design* (1874–6), which emphasized the 'harmonious' combinations of colours preferred in Aesthetic circles. Dresser's approach was detailed and prescriptive: 'if the ceiling decoration presents various pure colours so arranged that its general hue is olive, and the wall ornaments are formed of bright colour so disposed that they yield a citrine tint, and the dado is made up of such an admixture of colours that the general tone is russet, the three will together produce a harmony'. As this suggests, the 1870s saw a shift in taste away from bright colour, but achieving the desirable 'artistic' colour scheme was not easy. Decorators in search of fashionably muted effects could get it disastrously wrong.

The Queen Anne style of the 1870s and 1880s set a trend for white-painted joinery that continues to this day. The bright, clean effect of these whites was enhanced by the introduction of electricity. As paint surfaces were no longer made dingy by smoke from gas and oil lights, it became possible to choose more delicate colour schemes. At the end of the century the interest in healthy homes also encouraged lighter and brighter interiors; dark paint surfaces, it was feared, might conceal dirt. Covering up Victorian colour schemes became easier, too, as various proprietary brands of paint in ready-mixed colours came onto the market. The popularity of ivory white enamel (gloss paint) in the period 1900–1910 foreshadowed the end of the complex, intensely coloured rooms of the Victorian age.

## Colours for Exteriors

Early nineteenth-century leases typically specified that external wood and ironwork had to be painted 'twice over with good and proper oil colours'. White lead-based paint tended to 'chalk' when exposed to the elements, but its protective properties were not affected. Eight years was the average repainting cycle on railings in Bath. Front doors were repainted at least once every six or seven years and windows about once every six years.

Stucco façades were painted with a limewater and copperas solution that gave a Bath stone effect in a permeable coating. This was maintained by being 're-coloured and re-jointed in imitation of Bath stone', as Benjamin Wyatt specified in 1860. The colour of the stucco was 'always to be kept in imitation of blocks of stone' and, according to Peter Nicholson in 1823, 'promiscuously touched with rich tints of umber'. The effect of lichen or weather staining was occasionally created using the technique of splashing with blood, milk or oil. According to Loudon in 1846, 'The kinds of colours most suitable for exterior walls should generally be such as belong to the stones or bricks of the county in which the dwelling stands.'

By 1860 painted stucco was becoming less popular. Those stuccoed houses still being constructed were finished in more pollution-resistant oil paint. Although the intention was no longer to deceive the eye by suggesting blocks of unevenly coloured stone, the stucco façades of townhouses tended still to be jointed, whilst painted in a uniform stone colour. The appearance of Portland cement in the mid-nineteenth century led to the introduction of cooler grey, Portland stone-coloured paint.

Sanding – flicking sand or powdered stone onto a wet paint surface to imitate stone – was occasionally used on wall surfaces, but more common for external woodwork. Besides its attractive appearance, sanding offered extra protection. By the mid-nineteenth century proprietary paints were fulfilling this function. 'Anti-corrosion' or 'lithic' paints were prepared from ground glass, the slag from lead works or even burnt oyster shells, and mixed with pigment and linseed oil. Road dust (grandly called 'crotia') was used to make a variety of greens, chocolate, black, lead colour, stone colour and a browny red. Such was the durability of these products that, when applied to iron, well-seasoned timber or masonry, they rarely required renewal during one lifetime.

During the first half of the nineteenth century certain colours were considered more appropriate than others for painting iron. 'Invisible' greens (so called because they would blend into a background of foliage) were used for fences, gates, railings and

*Edward Linley Sambourne painted his own Aesthetic decorations in the panels of the dining room door at 18 Stafford Terrace, Kensington.*

223

garden furniture. In 1840 Humphrey Repton decried the use of lead colour because it resembled an inferior metal: 'If we wish it to resemble metal, and not appear of an inferior kind, a powdering of copper or gold dust on a green ground, makes a bronze, and perhaps it is the best colour of all for ornamental rails of iron.' This bronze colour was achieved using a number of different recipes, some producing a bluer patinated form, some rather greener, which could be dusted with bronze powder. It was also found on external doors and shutters.

Olive or purple-brown was widely used for exterior joinery, and can still be detected on old window frames and doors. Windows were also painted red-brown; a striking russet colour was discovered on some of the windows at Osborne House. Brunswick green was widely used for external window frames and doors. Another popular finish, both inside and outside the house, was graining. P.F. Robinson, writing in 1836, thought that the external paintwork of 'humble dwellings' 'should be made to resemble oak, and no other colour used', in the hope of suggesting that the inhabitants themselves had hewn the joinery from local trees. A more conventional style of deception was practiced in middle-class housing, where grained varnishes were used to give cheap deal the appearance of oak or mahogany.

## Choosing paints today

*Sample of black and gold marbled paint finish 'in great use for superior chimneypieces' from* The Decorative Painters and Glaziers' Guide *by Nathaniel Whittock (1827).*

A great deal of publicity has been given to authentic paints made to traditional recipes, marketed as the most appropriate for old houses. At the same time mass-market paint makers have responded to the interest in historic decoration by promoting colours from their standard ranges that might be particularly appropriate for Victorian or Edwardian houses. Each approach has its advantages. Traditional paints can be made to order in small or large amounts to match samples of historic paint, whereas a colour card for a ready-made range may offer only an approximation of the original colour. The surface finish of traditional paints has a liveliness and subtlety hard to replicate; the texture and quality of, say, soft distemper has yet to be matched by any mass-produced modern paint. On the other hand, traditional paints cannot always meet the modern demand for a consistent and reliable product, specialist skill may be required to apply them properly and they may be relatively expensive. There are also legal constraints that make it difficult to replicate once common paints: for example, the supply and use of lead sulphate and carbonate in paint (except in some special cases) has been banned since 1992 (for information on the safe removal or preparation of old paint containing lead, see Useful Addresses, p.266). It is up to the house owner to decide between the merits of the traditional 'tailor-made' and the modern 'off-the-peg' approach, and to seek appropriate advice regarding the preparation of surfaces and the compatibility of products to be used.

There is still much to learn about the Victorian use of colour. As most interiors have been routinely overpainted and very few historic interiors survive unaltered, research to establish historic schemes includes the study of contemporary watercolours, paintings and photographs, specifications and accounts, contemporary descriptions and painting manuals, as well as archaeological investigation of surviving paint layers.

A full archaeological investigation can only be carried out by a professional conservator. It is very expensive and only appropriate for buildings of particular historic or architectural interest. In some cases, particularly where a house has been unmodernized for many years, an original or very old scheme may have been retained and it may be appropriate to conserve this finish; the local conservation officer can be consulted for advice. Alternatively, it may be possible to uncover parts of the original scheme (usually areas of stencilling or marbling which would be difficult to recreate authentically) by removing later layers of paint.

It is impossible for any decorator, however knowledgeable, entirely to escape the tastes and prejudices of the age in which they live; Victorian rooms restored in the 1970s now tell us as much about the taste of thirty years ago as they do about that of the nineteenth century. With all this in mind, therefore, it may be as well to adopt a few well-established principles, and then to trust one's own taste and judgement. The fear of choosing the 'wrong' colours should not prevent house owners from attempting their own versions of period colour schemes. After all, unlike many other things done to old houses in the name of restoration, the application of paint is, in most cases, reversible.

There are, however, a few conventions that all Victorian decorators followed, and which should be adhered to by anyone attempting to decorate in a historically appropriate style.

While exterior stucco was painted with oil-based and textured paints, plain brick or stone walls were seldom painted with either of these finishes. Covering good Victorian brickwork, terracotta details or even stonework with a layer of paint not only robs the house of much of its character, but can also do structural damage by trapping damp.

No surface in the Victorian or Edwardian house was left unprotected by a coat of paint, varnish or at the very least staining. Only expensive woods such as mahogany or oak would be exposed to view, and then they would be limed, stained or waxed as appropriate. The fashion for stripped pine is a modern fetish that has no historical precedent and which has done tremendous damage, not only leaving vulnerable softwood unprotected, but also destroying the record of previous decoration.

*Painter's combs used to create woodgrain effects.*

Imitative finishes such as marbling and graining were widely used but always in a logical way, on surfaces and in locations where the material being imitated could actually have been used. Thus a skirting board might be marbled, but not a cupboard door. On a staircase the banisters might be 'bronzed' to suggest metal, but a stone colour might be considered more appropriate for the treads.

The status and use of each room within the house also influenced the choice of paint. The 'masculine' dining room, library, billiard room and study were decorated in darker colours than the 'feminine' drawing room or morning room. Elaborate paint effects and combinations of colours used to 'pick in' moulded decoration would only be used where they could be appreciated by visitors, such as in the hall and reception rooms.

The relative durability of different paint surfaces was important for practical reasons. The odd chip or scratch shows less on a 'broken' finish such as graining, and so a coarse form of graining was often used in service quarters. Dados were frequently painted with dark colours and then varnished to protect them from dirt and signs of wear and tear. Oil-based paint, although expensive, was extremely durable and preferred for good quality work, especially on walls where distemper might be rubbed off. Water-soluble distemper, which could be washed off before each redecoration, thus preventing delicate mouldings from becoming clogged with a build-up of paint, was chosen for elaborate plasterwork. And because it was easily removed, distemper could also be used to advantage on ceilings, which quickly became dirty in rooms with coal fires and oil or gas lighting.

*Details show the difference between high-quality* trompe-l'oeil *graining in a drawing room (middle) and a hastily-sketched 'oak' designed to provide a conventional, broken finish that would not show knocks and scuffs on a kitchen door (bottom).*

Whether through the fading of pigments or discoloration due to atmospheric pollution, bright white and high gloss paints eventually became dull. Semi-gloss finishes and creamy or greyish whites (rather than 'brilliant white') may therefore help to give a more authentic 'period' appearance in old houses.

# Dr Dresser's Patterns

| | | | | |
|---|---|---|---|---|
| Rack 336 | D Ind Fueze | | | 0 |
| Rondell | | | | |
| 4 Block | 8 | 0 | 0 |
| + cures wog | | | |
| Rack 338 | D Ind | | | |
| 5 Block | 8 | 10 | 0 |
| + oney + cures wog | | | |
| H — | 7 | 10 | 0 |
| Rack 338 | D Daff | | | |
| 4 Block | 6 | 10 | 0 |
| Rack 336 | D Daff Border | | | |
| Rack 328 | D Flame Fueze | | | |
| 4 Block | 9 | 10 | 0 |
| Rack 328 | D Flame | | | |
| 3 Block | 6 | 15 | 0 |
| 2222 | | | |
| 4 — | 4 | 10 | 0 |
| Rack 336 | D Fire Border | | | |
| 2 Block | 5 | 0 | 0 |
| Rack 328 | D Fire Dado | | | |
| D Nemo | | | |
| Rack 338 | | | | |
| 3 Block | 6 | 0 | 0 |

Dr DRESSER

# WALLCOVERINGS

ABOVE: *the traditional method of printing wallpapers from wood blocks.*

OPPOSITE: *Page of designs by Christopher Dresser, from a logbook of the wallpaper manufacturers Jeffrey & Co., around 1874.*

T HE NINETEENTH CENTURY was the Golden Age of wallpaper. Thanks to mass-production techniques and the repeal in 1836 of the 124-year-old wallpaper tax, the industry grew considerably, bringing the price of wallpaper within the reach of most householders. The number and variety of papers produced to serve this voracious market was enormous, ranging from sophisticated designs printed by hand onto heavy rag paper, to mass-produced floral patterns roller-printed onto cheap wood-pulp paper. Thus the wallcovering became perhaps the single most important element in the decoration of a Victorian room.

The earliest surviving printed wallpapers in England date from the sixteenth century. These were block-printed with designs in black, sometimes with patches of stencilled colour. The designs were heraldic or derived from textiles such as damasks and brocades. Some papers carried scenes similar to those appearing in tapestries or woodcuts. In the eighteenth century formal designs of acanthus, pineapples or other motifs derived from classical architecture were used to complement Palladian interiors, and wealthy house-holders bought hand-painted scenic wallpapers imported from China. Novelty designs featuring fantasy architecture, Gothick ruins or Chinoiserie designs were popular during the Regency period.

Block printing remained the principal method of printing wallpapers until well into the nineteenth century, and an extremely high standard of design was achieved, notably in the large-scale formal papers of the eighteenth century. The size of the pattern repeat was determined by the width of the paper and the maximum weight of wood block that could be managed by the printer. Single sheets of hand-made paper were pasted together in order to make strips long enough to cover the wall. Twelve sheets made a single drop or ‘piece’ of approximately 11½ feet x 21 inches (350cm x 53.5cm). The wooden printing blocks were slightly narrower than the paper, so that a blank margin or ‘selvedge’ was left along both edges of the piece: this was necessary for accurate registration during print-ing, and protected the printed area from damage during transport. The paper-hanger would trim the selvedge by hand immediately before pasting the paper.

Two technological developments led to the astonishing growth of the wallpaper industry in the nineteenth century. One was the mechanical production of paper in continuous rolls instead of single, hand-made sheets. This provided the impetus for the development of the second innovation, the rotary printing press, which did away with the laborious – and therefore expensive – process of hand-printing.

A Frenchman, Louis Robert, managed to produce continuous roll paper in 1798. His invention was developed in England by Fourdrinier, who patented a paper-making

*A mid-nineteenth century 'print room' wallpaper combines illusionistic frames and landscape scenes with a flat background of repeating fleurs-de-lys.*

machine in 1801, and another, 'for manufacturing paper of an indefinite length', in 1807. But these innovations could not be properly exploited by the wallpaper industry until 1830, when the Excise Office lifted its prohibition on the use of continuous paper for printing wallpaper. The tax on all kinds of paper imposed since 1695 was repealed in 1861. By the late 1840s successful companies such as Woollams were using good quality machine-made paper for their hand-printed wallcoverings, although a few smaller firms unable to raise the capital to set up a continuous paper mill kept on using the old-fashioned pasted-together pieces until the 1870s.

In 1839 Harold Potter, the owner of a wallpaper mill in Darwen, Lancashire, patented a roller-printing machine for wallpaper. An employee of his, Walmesley Preston, had modified a copper roller used in the textile industry for printing chintz. By giving it a raised rather than an engraved pattern, he produced a cylindrical equivalent of the traditional wooden printing block. The distemper-based colours used in hand-printing were too thick to work successfully in a roller-printing press, so new, oil-based inks were developed that would flow smoothly onto the roller and coat the paper more thinly. The new process also had an influence on pattern design: because the early copper rollers were rarely more than 6 inches (150mm) in diameter, they could not print patterns with repeats of more than about 18 inches (450mm). Early machine-printed papers therefore tend to have small-scale designs, which might sometimes be overprinted by hand-blocking larger designs onto the patterned background. Production in the newly mechanized wallpaper mills increased enormously.

William Perkin's discovery of aniline (coal tar-derived) dyes in 1856 led to an increase in the number – and a reduction in cost – of colours available for wallpapers. Consequently, the price of wallpaper fell steadily throughout the century, but many of those involved in the industry paid dearly: the arsenic and white lead used in many Victorian papers were responsible for widespread health problems among workers. By the 1870s the major firms were responding to the public's awareness of these health risks by advertising arsenic-free papers.

Wallpaper designers took inspiration from many sources, including textiles, architecture, and landscape and flower paintings. Motifs were made to look as realistic as possible using a wide range of colours and shading to create a three-dimensional appearance. The blowsy roses on the popular floral papers were 'rendered with the full force of their natural colours and light and shade', while the emphatic perspective of the architectural papers drew the eye irresistibly into the design. These papers sold well but offended the educated taste of the critics, who condemned them as 'dishonest' because they attempted to deny the two-dimensional reality of a flat wall surface. Pugin was scornful of 'Gothic pattern paperhangings where a wretched caricature of a pointed building is repeated from skirting to cornice in glorious confusion – door over pinnacle and pinnacle over door'. His own wallpaper designs for the new Palace of Westminster, produced in the 1830s and 1840s, are patterns rather than pictures, and use conventionalized motifs with no attempt to render shadows or natural gradations of colour.

Another criticism of wallpaper designs at this time was that their combinations of Rococo scrolls and overblown flowers were merely inferior copies of French papers. Matters came to a head over the Great Exhibition of 1851. This was supposed to show the very best of British manufactured products, but despite some outstanding technical achievements (one of the hand-printed British papers required over sixty separate blocks), the designs were disappointing and the top prizes went to a French company.

*Gothic wallpaper of about 1840. This fragment was removed from a house in Acton, West London, and is now in the English Heritage architectural study collection.*

*Two mid-nineteenth century block print borders, probably made by William Woollams & Co., show the influence of French design in their Rococo architectural 'mouldings'.*

Pugin and other artistic reformers campaigned to raise the standard of art and design by publications, education and example. One of the most influential campaigners was Owen Jones, who in 1856 published *The Grammar of Ornament*, a catalogue of motifs and styles used in decoration through the ages, which swiftly became every designer's bible. Jones's wallpaper designs, which featured flat, repeating motifs, diaper patterns and geometric shapes in strong colour combinations, were hugely influential.

As a result of the artistic reformer's efforts, the role of wallpaper was redefined, and many mid-century papers were designed to work as understated backdrops to pictures and furniture rather than as strong decorative statements in their own right. Sombre colours were felt to be particularly appropriate for this purpose, and since gas lighting was widespread by the 1850s, it was no longer so important to make the most of daylight by covering the walls with a pale paper. Dark papers also had the advantage of not showing the dirt created by airborne pollution in the industrialized cities.

*A block print wallpaper designed by Owen Jones in about 1870, is typical of the flat, stylized patterns recommended by reform designers.*

*Wallpaper depicting the Crystal Palace, produced to commemorate the Great Exhibition of 1851. This topical variant of the 'pillar and arch' wallpapers despised by reformist designers was displayed at the Museum of Ornamental Art to illustrate the 'False Principle' of repeated, distorted perspective.*

The work of William Morris has dominated the popular perception of Victorian wallpaper. His extraordinary gift for pattern design, and his ability to articulate and publicize his design theories, have overshadowed the work of his contemporaries and placed a misleading emphasis on his work at the expense of other designers'. Morris's first wallpaper designs were the 'Trellis', 'Daisy' and 'Fruit' patterns, published in 1864. In all, he designed forty-one wallpapers and six ceiling papers. Machine-printed adaptations of Morris papers are now so readily available it is easy to forget that when his papers first appeared they were an expensive luxury. Only wealthy customers could possible afford them, and only the minority whose taste was sufficiently avant-garde actually bought them.

In *Hints on Household Taste*, Eastlake gave detailed advice on choosing wallpapers:

> The choice of a wallpaper should be guided in every respect by the destination of the room in which it will be used. The most important question will always be whether it is to form a decoration in itself, or whether it is to become a mere background for pictures. In the latter case the paper can hardly be too subdued in tone. Very light stone colour or green (not emerald), and silver-grey will be found suitable for this purpose, and two shades of the same colour are generally sufficient for one paper. In drawing-rooms, embossed white or cream colour, with a very small diapered pattern, will not be amiss, where water-colour drawings are hung. As a rule, the simplest patterns are the best for every situation; but where the eye has to rest upon the surface of the wall alone a greater play of line in the ornament may become advisable. It is obvious that delicate tints admit of more linear complexity than those which are rich or dark. Intricate forms should be accompanied by quiet colour, and variety of hue should be chastened by the plainest possible outlines. In colour, wall-papers should relieve without violently opposing that of the furniture and hangings by which they are surrounded.

Eastlake also, somewhat grudgingly, suggested that wallpaper printed in imitation of marble could be used in entrance halls. He mentioned the improvements made since Pugin had started to design wallpapers, but still felt it necessary to warn householders that 'many wretched specimens continue to be displayed', and to condemn the 'gaudy and extravagant trash' on offer in the wallpaper showrooms. He may have been thinking not only of the cheap, overblown florals, but also of the commemorative papers that celebrated current events. These were produced throughout the Victorian period to mark occasions such as the Queen's Jubilees or military campaigns, or to celebrate more generalized achievements, such as the building of railways.

The Aesthetic movement was a major influence on wallpaper design from the 1870s onwards. The use of dado and picture rails to divide the wall into dado, filling and frieze became a hallmark of 'artistic' taste, and British manufacturers produced wallpapers in sets of three – one for each compartment of the wall. While designers such as Godwin and Christopher Dresser produced adaptations of Japanese motifs, it was also possible

*Anglo-Japanese room decoration by Arthur Silver, about 1885, featuring a co-ordinating dado, filling and frieze.*

*Advertisement for Anaglypta, 1890s. Relief wallcoverings that offered a cheap alternative to decorative plasterwork, carved wood or stamped leather have in many cases proved more durable than the real thing.*

# ANAGLYPTA
## THE CHEAPEST SUBSTANTIAL WALL DECORATION IN RELIEF.
### Sanitary, Durable and Beautiful.

ELIZABETHAN FRIEZE, No. 295. 1/6 PER PANEL. 36 INCHES x 9 INCHES.

*Works:* Darwen, Lancashire.

232

to buy the real thing, imported from the Orient. The most committed devotees of the Japanese style used rush matting to cover the dado.

Those who could not afford Japanese embossed papers had the option of using the new relief papers that imitated stucco, embossed leather or wood panels, including two that are still in production: Lincrusta (introduced in 1877) or Anaglypta (1887). The first of these was produced by Frederick Walton, under the trade name 'Lincrusta-Walton'. Walton used the same ingredients that went into his previous invention, linoleum – linseed oil, gums, resins and wax – but mixed them with wood pulp instead of cork dust. The mixture was then pressed between heavy metal rollers, one of which bore the engraved pattern to create the embossed effect of the finished wallcovering.

The new wallcovering could imitate any kind of relief decoration: moulded plaster, wainscot (including linenfold panelling), carved wood or stone, stamped leather or ceramic tile. Although the material was available in a range of natural colours from white to chocolate brown, it would also accept all kinds of paints, glazes, gilding and varnish. It was extremely practical: it could cover up uneven walls, provide good thermal insulation, resist water and stand up to any amount of wear and tear.

Having failed to register linoleum as a trademark and thereby losing the right to the exclusive use of the name, Walton took care to ensure his name was securely attached to Lincrusta and properly registered. Even so, his business acumen failed him again when one of his employees, Thomas J. Palmer, approached him with an idea for a lighter, more flexible wallcovering made of wood pulp. He showed no interest in the idea, so Palmer took out his own patent for the wallcovering, called Anaglypta, in 1886. Two years later it was made available to the public, and by 1897 the *Journal of Decorative Art* was raving that 'so quickly did the new material "catch on" that within two years of that time it had slipped into its place as one of the necessaries of a modern decorator's establishment ... It seized the taste – and the pocket – of the public and literally jumped into vogue.'

Other manufacturers produced relief wallcoverings from various ingredients, including rubber and cork, and under a variety of trade names: Tynecastle Tapestries (which imitated gilded and embossed Spanish leathers), Cordelova, Subercorium, Calcorian and Cortecine. The 'Salamander' brand was made of pure asbestos and promoted for its fire-resistance.

*Designers whose wallpaper patterns were featured in the architectural press included W. Jones (top), Pugin (centre) and Bruce Talbert (above). These examples were redrawn for* The Builder *by Maurice B. Adams.*

Manufacturers made a point of hiring well-know designers and mentioning them in promotional literature. The names of George Haité, Lewis F. Day, Dresser and Voysey had a certain glamour that rubbed off onto the more run-of-the-mill products by anonymous designers that accounted for the bulk of the companies' sales. The luxury imported goods market was catered to by Alexander Rottmann, who began importing high-quality, gilded 'leather' papers from Japan in 1884.

Relief wallcoverings were thought particularly suitable for the dado, as they could stand up to the wear and tear inflicted on this area, particularly in narrow hallways and on staircase walls. Dados were usually painted a dark colour, which might be enriched with gilding, or grained to resemble a dark wood, following the established convention of using progressively lighter colours from the bottom to the top of the wall divisions. Anaglypta had great success from the start as a ceiling paper. The company specialized in imitation Jacobean and Elizabethan ceilings with deep coffering and pendant drops. Special designs were also produced for the frieze along the top of the wall, where embossed wallcoverings could mimic the look of fancy plasterwork at a fraction of the price of the real thing.

Dados remained immensely popular during the 1880s, and builders continued to install them in the halls and stairwells of new suburban houses as a matter of course until World War I. Horizontal scenic papers were specially designed for friezes, with borders that could

*A Silver Studio design for a floral wallcovering, 1892.*

be left on or trimmed to fit any depth of frieze. Lincrusta in imitation of plasterwork was another popular option for the frieze. At the end of the century the simplest treatment was often adopted: the frieze was painted white as a continuation of the ceiling and to offset the bold swirls of an Art Nouveau paper designed by Voysey or one of his followers.

In 1871 single-colour washable papers, printed with water-resistant ink and known as 'sanitaries', were introduced, and in 1884 it became possible to buy multi-coloured washables. For obvious reasons these were promoted for use in nurseries and bathrooms. Also in 1884 Walter Crane designed 'The Queen of Hearts' paper, heralding the arrival of a new category of wallcovering: nursery papers by children's book illustrators. In 1893 Kate Greenaway produced a washable paper, 'The Months', which featured children in eighteenth-century costume.

Designs by famous names are convenient waysigns in the history of wallpaper design, but it should be remembered that they do not always represent the taste of the average householder. The middle market was catered to by lesser-known designers such as Arthur Silver, whose family company supplied designs to wallpaper manufacturers from 1880 until the 1960s. Firms like the Silver Studio were skilled at adapting the work of the 'name' designers whose innovative work led the market. They produced high-quality patterns in similar but comfortably diluted styles – patterns that would have a long life in the middle-class market before they were finally discontinued.

# Cleaning and conservation

'To Clean Paper Hanging. First blow off the dust with the bellows. Divide a white loaf of eight days old into eight parts. Take the crust into your hand, and beginning at the top of the paper, wipe it downwards in the lightest manner with the crumb. Do not cross nor go upwards. The dirt of the paper and the crumbs will fall together. Observe, you must not wipe above half a yard at a stroke, and after doing all the upper part, go round again, beginning a little above where you left off. If you do not do it extremely lightly, you will make the dirt adhere to the paper. It will look like new if properly done.' This advice, quoted from *The New London Cookery and Complete Domestic Guide* of 1827, was paraphrased in mid-century editions of Mrs Beeton and repeated word-for-word in *Warne's Model Cookery and Housekeeping Book* at the end of the century. The bread rolls up into pellets, picking up dirt as it goes. The method is still valid, but immense patience (and a lot of bread!) is required for cleaning a large area, so curators nowadays prefer to use low-suction vacuum cleaners with filter nozzles. A domestic vacuum cleaner on a low setting with muslin fixed taut across the nozzle by a rubber band will do the job equally well. Any more invasive cleaning methods should only be undertaken by a qualified conservator.

The original crisp detail of relief wallcoverings is often blurred by successive layers of paint, but it is difficult to remove the paint without damaging the surface of the wallcovering. Even though a paste-type proprietary stripper might peel away, bringing the paint with it, the problem remains of how to clean off the residue and neutralize the surface of the wallcovering without softening or scraping off the relief decoration. The professional conservation approach would be either to use industrial alcohol to soften the paint and then to peel it off with masking tape, or to pick off the paint with a scalpel. The former requires considerable technical expertise and fine timing, and both are very time-con-

*Old wallpapers are often discovered during renovation work. A room on the top floor of 18 Stafford Terrace was papered in the 1870s, first with William Morris' 'Diaper', and then with a nursery paper based on designs by Walter Crane. When the children had grown up, the room received a more dignified and luxurious decoration with embossed and gilded wallpaper better suited to its new use as an artist's studio.*

suming. The cost of such work would probably only be justified in a museum-quality interior, and it may be better to paint another coat onto the existing paint and accept the inevitable blurring, or touch up the existing paint if it is in good condition.

It is not unusual to come across Victorian wallpapers during renovation work, or in undisturbed corners of the house such as cupboards and behind built-in furniture. These can often be dated by comparing them with illustrations in books about wallpaper design. Local museums and the Wallpaper History Society (see Useful Addresses, p.266) can sometimes identify papers from photographs, and will be able to advise whether the paper is worth preserving. Photographs will also be useful for reference if you need to look through wallpaper sample books to find something similar in current ranges, and will serve as a record of what was found once the redecoration is complete.

The removal, cleaning and conservation of valuable old wallpapers should always be entrusted to a professional conservator, since it can be difficult to remove large pieces of paper without damaging them. Wood pulp paper, which replaced rag paper in the nineteenth century, contains lignin. This produces acid as it decays, rendering the paper yellow and brittle. Where several papers have been pasted on top of one another it can be impossible to separate the layers of the resulting 'sandwich' without shredding them in the process unless specialized equipment is used.

## Choosing papers for Victorian houses

*Faithful modern reproduction of a wallpaper of about 1840 used at Uppark, Hampshire.*

Wallpaper was not used in every room in the house. Kitchens and bathrooms were sometimes papered with varnished 'sanitaries', but more often had tiled or painted walls. Lesser bedrooms and servants' quarters, especially in the early Victorian period, are likely to have been painted rather than papered. Numberless designs of wallpaper

are on offer, and very few suppliers can give accurate information about the origins of their designs. The so-called 'Victorian' collection of one manufacturer may not contain a single paper taken from a nineteenth-century original, while accurate reproductions of Victorian papers may pass unnoticed in other manufacturers' sample books.

Wallpapers suitable for old houses fall into two categories: 'document' papers that replicate nineteenth-century originals, and adaptations or new designs 'in the manner of' old papers. The aristocracy of wallpapers is undoubtedly those printed from the original wood blocks. Some Pugin and Morris papers, for example, are still made in this way. They are printed to order, the colours specially mixed for each batch and hand-printed on high-quality paper. They have a selvedge that must be cut off before they are hung. Similarly authentic – but not so expensive – are the traditional Anaglypta and Lincrusta reliefs, made using identical materials and moulds to those first employed in the 1880s.

A few specialist companies will reproduce historic papers from surviving examples. This is expensive, because the design has to be redrawn, or perhaps reconstructed from a few small fragments; the screens for printing have to be specially made, and trial print runs conducted so that the colour of the replica paper can be compared with that of the original. Such work is usually commissioned by museum curators for reconstructions of historic interiors, and the replica papers are sometimes sold to the general public under a licensing agreement between the museum and the manufacturer. In order to ensure the broadest possible commercial appeal, the manufacturer will often produce the same design in several different colourways, even though the original document only exists in one combination of colours. Close cousins to these replica papers are the screen-printed versions of historic papers produced from photographs of the hand-printed originals.

The advantage of choosing the papers described above is that they are known to be closely related, if not identical, to papers actually used in Victorian rooms. However, adaptations of Victorian designs can be very good. Pattern designers have always reworked the motifs of previous ages, so there is no reason to despise such designs as inferior to their Victorian ancestors. Changes may include altering the scale to make an old pattern fit standard modern paper sizes, or reducing the number of colours to keep down production costs.

Lastly, there are entirely new designs in Victorian style. These vary tremendously in quality. Some capture the designs, colours and texture of Victorian wallpaper admirably, while others are abject failures. A little preparatory research in historic houses and museums or the expert advice of a historic wallpaper specialist can be a great help.

## Hanging papers

Most DIY manuals have comprehensive chapters on how to hang wallpaper. However, hand-printed or embossed papers require special handling and should be hung by professional decorators, using traditional flour paste or a paste recommended by the manufacturer. Lincrusta comes in flat sheets that need to be soaked before use and hung with special paste, following the manufacturer's instructions. Both Lincrusta and Anaglypta are supplied with a uniform pale cream surface and require painting, glazing or gilding once they have been hung.

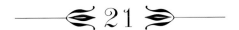

# 21

# CURTAINS AND BLINDS

O NE ASPECT OF VICTORIAN INTERIOR DECORATION puzzling to modern observers is the treatment of windows. The introduction of plate glass made larger panes possible, the repeal of the window tax in 1851 encouraged the provision of more windows, and the single-pane sash admitted more light than ever before. Yet Victorian decorators seemed intent on cancelling out these advantages by dressing windows – at least in the principal rooms – with large quantities of fabric in several layers of curtains. In fact, they had several good reasons for this apparently perverse behaviour. Light and views were less important than privacy and the ability to exclude the outside world from the cosy domestic space. Precious possessions had to be protected from the damaging effects of sunlight. Above all, curtains provided unrivalled opportunities for the display of wealth and taste through the colour, pattern, texture and surface finish of the textiles chosen and the skill with which they were arranged.

Principal windows were dressed in several layers of blinds and curtains. Working from the glass inwards, the first layer was a blind. Venetian blinds – slats of painted timber slotted into linen tapes – were introduced during the eighteenth century and widely used in the Regency and early Victorian periods. They were less fashionable by the middle of the century, although Isabella Beeton still preferred them to roller blinds.

Roller blinds were more common. Early versions were operated with a continuous loop of cord at one side. Spring mechanisms gradually became universal, but opinions were divided as to their efficacy. The authors of the *Encyclopaedia of Domestic Economy* (1844) were unimpressed, complaining that they cost more than unsprung blinds, and were more likely to break. Mrs Beeton thought the kind 'that go up with a gentle spring, and come down with a gentle click-click are best'. By the end of the century Hermann Muthesius was confidently asserting that 'the mechanism is so well designed that it never goes wrong'. The pull cord on a sprung blind was finished with an acorn of stained and polished wood, a tassel or a 'Turk's head' knot dyed to match the blind.

Fabrics of various weights and thicknesses were used for roller blinds, from heavy canvas and coarse calico to lawn or gauze made of linen or cotton. White holland (linen similar to that used today for glass cloths) was a conventional choice, but dyed or printed cloth was also used. Blinds could even be painted with 'landscape, interiors of buildings, or arabesques', which glowed vividly when sunlight shone through them. This illuminated effect worked particularly well on fabrics printed to imitate stained glass windows in Gothic architectural frames. Webster opined that painted blinds were particularly useful

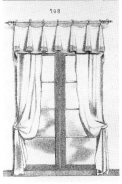

ABOVE: *simple, early Victorian window treatments from Loudon's* Encyclopaedia *(1833).*

OPPOSITE: *design for a printed textile by Arthur Silver, 1891.*

239

for concealing unattractive views. The concealment worked both ways, of course, and blinds were used to preserve privacy, especially in towns. Their chief purpose, however, was to protect the contents of the room from direct light. A rather specialized arrangement of roller blinds was found in artists' studios in the last quarter of the nineteenth century. Luke Fildes' studio in Melbury Road, Kensington, built in 1876, had blinds of 'dense moleskin stuff, hung on a double series of cords and pulleys, so that they may either be drawn up from the bottom or lowered from the top of the windows, and by this simple contrivance a high, middle or low light can at once be arranged'.

The 'sad work' of cleaning roller blinds, as itemized by the partisan Mrs Beeton, was 'first, to get the blinds from the rollers, then to wash them and iron them straight, then to replace them, and then to find that no one in the house can pull them up straight.' She evidently felt that laundering blinds was hardly worth the effort, recommending instead that the old fabric be turned into glass cloths and the rollers fitted with new fabric.

A basketwork blind was a flat sheet of woven wicker that could be propped or fastened against the lower part of a window to ensure privacy in the manner of a Regency 'snob screen'. Few have survived, but contemporary catalogue illustrations show that they were very decorative. Woven wire blinds were associated with business rooms and offices, and were just about acceptable in situations, such as doctor's surgeries, where a brass plate proclaimed the professional status of the occupier, but would otherwise carry unfortunate overtones of 'trade'.

In front of the blinds it was customary in the best houses to provide up to three separate sets of curtains in the principal rooms: sub-curtains of lace or sheer fabric, a middle set of lined curtains in cretonne, chintz, velvet or damask, and perhaps a top pair of some heavy fabric such as tapestry or brocatelle. Pelmets or lambrequins were used to dress the top of the window, and overlong curtains were looped up over large

*The drawing room at Bryn Glas, Newport, Monmouthshire, depicted in watercolour by Julia Mackworth, 1871. The layered dressings of the floor-length sash windows consist of Venetian blinds, sub-curtains of white muslin and top curtains surmounted by a pleated pelmet.*

FAR LEFT: *Loudon's recommended treatment for the drawing room windows of a villa: a carved wooden pelmet supports a lambrequin of gathered fabric with tasselled tails. The muslin subcurtains are carefully looped back so as to frame the damask top curtains.*

LEFT: *Arthur Silver specialized in designs for Nottingham lace curtains; this panel dates from 1898.*

hooks, one on each side of the window, with enough length left to 'puddle' on the floor, making an impressive frame for the whole composition.

Various combinations and permutations were possible, according to the money available, the architecture of the room or the whim of the householder. A window overlooking a shady garden might not need a blind, a set of box shutters might make the middle curtains redundant, or the top curtains might be omitted, leaving only an ornamental pelmet. Charlotte Bosanquet's watercolour of the drawing room at White Barns, Hertfordshire, painted in 1843, depicts a grand treatment given to the widely-spaced windows in the long wall of the room: a continuous pelmet of deep blue fabric fringed with gold runs across all the windows, hanging from an ebonized pole with gilded finials and ending in a fringed swag and tail on an invisible support. There are no outer curtains to match this pelmet; inner curtains of yellow silk are looped back over cloak pins, and there are sub-curtains of printed muslin, also looped back. The effect is dramatic and studiedly symmetrical.

Sub-curtains were also indispensable for catching dirt coming in from outside and thus protecting the top curtains, which were less easy to clean or replace. The finest were made of Brussels lace, but this was so costly that machine-made Nottingham lace was an almost universal substitute. It was sold in panels available in numerous standard widths between 36 and 86 inches (90cm and 220cm), and varied in length between 2 yards and 4 yards (183cm and 366cm). This choice of sizes enabled the customer to buy panels fitting the window very closely, so that the lace could hang flat and the pattern could be appreciated.

Most lace curtains had a central motif or 'filling', with borders all round, the bottom border often being deeper than the others. The edges were sometimes plain but more usually scalloped, so no hemming was required before they were hung. Nottingham lace was ubiquitous: as the designer Arthur Silver put it, 'These are fabrics which supply decorations for the cottager's home and the millionaire's mansion ... As the majority of houses have these curtains in their front windows, you will not have far to go to see the various styles in vogue.'

There were alternatives. Lang & Co. of Ingram Street, Glasgow, were major manufacturers of Madras muslin, woven in patterns that gave 'a lace effect more flexible and soft in texture than "lace" itself'. Madras muslin was available in small- and large-scale

*Charlotte Bosanquet's watercolour of the drawing room at White Barns, Hertfordshire, (1843) depicts a late Regency window treatment with deep and dramatic fringed pelmet, and curtains draped back over large cloak pins.*

designs and might incorporate up to three colours. Another semi-transparent curtain fabric was 'Swiss lace', a fabric of net squares based on sixteenth-century lace patterns. This was coarser and less complex than Nottingham lace.

Plain silk muslin was used for sub-curtains in the 1840s, and its use continued in the less important rooms of middle-class homes throughout the Victorian period. Loudon in 1833 recommended 'inner curtains of figured muslin edged with silk ball fringe to match the outer curtains' for the drawing room and plain muslin for the library. Cheap cotton muslin always had its place in poorer or less fashion-conscious households, and fine muslin returned to the drawing room towards the end of the century as part of the reaction against mid-Victorian ostentation. Bleached white or dyed in a variety of 'art' shades, it was used in lightly gathered curtains that hung straight, without any looping or flouncing.

In many cases only the middle curtains would be functional in the sense that they would be regularly opened and closed. They were made of medium-weight or heavy fabrics in silk, wool or cotton. At all price levels there was a bewildering array of pure or blended fibres, weaves, patterns and colours to choose from.

The Regency taste for woven patterns, prompted by the development of new looms and weaving techniques, persisted into the early years of Victoria's reign. Although it was invented in 1801, the Jacquard loom was not introduced into England until 1821, and its use did not become widespread until the 1840s. The dobby loom, which produced small repeating woven patterns, was invented in 1818 and adapted for use on powered looms in 1824. Such inventions made it possible to weave fabrics of high quality and detail at a much lower cost. Densely-packed flowers and leaves, subtly shaded scrollwork and strapwork, fine outlines and delicate background details were woven in silk, in designs influenced by (or blatantly copied from) French fabrics. English silks were cheaper than imported ones, but the more refined French designs had a snob appeal that justified the price difference and intensified competition between the two countries. The repeal in 1860 of the duty on imported silk caused great hardship in the English silk-weaving industry, as the market was flooded with French fabrics. No imports, however, could rival English wool fabrics, such as merino damask and moreen (stamped with a damask surface pattern), which were recommended because they draped beautifully, were very warm and could be used without lining. They were also cheaper than silk and took dyes better than cotton.

Advances in weaving were matched by innovations in dyeing and printing. At the beginning of the nineteenth century manufacturers relied on dyes derived from plants, such as indigo (blue), madder (red), weld (yellow) and quercitron (gold and brown). These were used with animal substances such as cochineal (a beetle, dried and crushed to produce red dye) and mineral mordants that caused dyes to react in different ways. Madder, for example, could be persuaded to make many shades when fixed with different mordants, from bright 'Turkey' red to deep purple-brown. Although a wide range of colours and many subtle gradations were possible, dyeing was a hit-and-miss affair relying on the skill and experience of the dyer; natural dyes were hard to replicate consistently, and they offered the printer a very 'soft' palette. More assertive shades were introduced following William Perkin's discovery of the first aniline dye, mauve, in 1856. Thereafter the race was on to find new synthetic dyes. Magenta (1866) supplanted mauveine, red azo (1877) challenged madder and cochineal, and several new blues joined the dyer's repertoire in the 1880s.

Traditional wood block and copper plate printing were supplemented by new mechanical processes such as roller printing. From the mid-1820s the use of engraved wooden or copper rollers, much faster than the painstaking reapplication of blocks or plates, began to dominate the cloth-printing industry. Transferring a small background pattern from a small 'mill' roller to a larger one, which would then print several repeats of the design with each revolution, enabled printers to apply 'fancy grounds' over the entire surface of the cloth before printing a bolder pattern on top, thus creating extra depth and texture in their prints.

The demand for new designs was insatiable, and designers turned for inspiration to books of ornamental designs, the most influential of which were Owen Jones's two volumes of *Plans, Elevations, Sections and Details of the Alhambra*, published 1842–5, and *The Grammar of Ornament*, which followed in 1856. The latter quickly became the designer's bible, and a copy was found in every commercial design studio. Designers also looked to the past for patterns to complement revivalist architecture and furniture. Particular textures, motifs, colours and ways of making-up were associated with different 'looks'. The use of novel woven fabrics in simple vertical pleats was favoured for Greek revival interiors at the start of the nineteenth century but gave way to more complex draperies in the 1840s. *The Workwoman's Guide*, published by 'A Lady' in 1838, illustrated not only the neoclassical designs that were the established fashion, but also swags and festoons which hinted at extravagance to come. Heraldic motifs or diaper patterns were used in Gothic revival rooms, where the curtains would be hung from plain wooden or brass poles with large rings – a style of hanging that was fashionable in the 1840s and returned to favour in the 1870s. Cut velvet or damasks in formal classical designs were considered appropriate for 'masculine' apartments; 'Louis XV' patterns gave elegance to drawing rooms in the 1850s. Neo-Renaissance interiors of the 1860s were furnished with tapestry or lampas in colour combinations of red, black and brown, with curtains and upholstery 'paned' – that is, made up of strips of fabric joined together with the seams outlined in braid to create a grid effect.

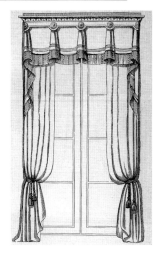

*Gilt cornice with 'handsome drapery' of damask or chintz with bullion fringe, illustrated by Loudon (1833), who felt the need to explain in detail the workings of the cord tiebacks, which were a departure from the more familiar cloak pins.*

In many cases the historical character of the ensemble could only be gauged by what was going on above the window. Pelmets of carved timber, moulded plaster, 'compo' or stamped metal hid the curtain pole and any mechanical parts, such as tracks or pulleys. Strictly moulded according to architectural rules (neoclassical), fatly scalloped and scrolled (rococo), or pierced with ogee lancets (Gothic), pelmets would be gilded or painted to match the woodwork of the room. Lambrequins were frames of fabric, which might be draped, gathered or pleated, or else stiffened with buckram and used flat, with a shaped border hanging down at either side of the window and emphasized with tassels or fringe. A pelmet or lambrequin gave a good 'finish' to the top of the window; the latter were particularly useful for imparting a neo-renaissance flavour to a room.

The excesses of the mid-nineteenth century upholsterer were scorned by Eastlake, who regretted the evolution of simple curtains hung from rings on metal rods into 'extravagant and cumbrous shapes'. His description gives an idea of curtain accessories in mid-century schemes:

> The useful and convenient little rod has grown into a huge lumbering pole as thick as a man's arm, but not a whit stronger than its predecessor; for the pole is not only hollow, but constructed of metal far too thin in proportion to its diameter. Then, in place of the little finials which used to be fixed at each end of the rod to prevent the rings from slipping off, our modern upholsterer has substituted gigantic fuchsias, or other flowers, made of brass, gilt bronze, and even china, sprawling downwards in a design of execrable taste. Sometimes this pole, being too weak for actual use, is fixed up simply for ornament – or rather for pretentious show – while the curtain really slides on an iron rod *behind* it.

The design reform movement promoted formalized patterns inspired by, but not directly imitating, nature. A curtain fabric should not pretend to be something – a bunch of flowers, perhaps, in realistic colours with three-dimensional shading – that it was not. Reformed design demanded that the method of supporting and drawing the curtains should be visible and decipherable: rings on rods could not be bettered. Muted, 'natural' colours were preferred: barely a decade after the first synthetic dyes came on the market, William Morris and Thomas Wardle were 'reviving' natural pigments, experimenting with vats of weld and madder. Morris, Marshall, Faulkner & Co. began to sell printed textiles using these pigments in the late 1860s.

Other designers who produced flat, formalized patterns for furnishing fabrics were Lewis F. Day, Bruce Talbert and Voysey. Liberty and other stores selling imported Indian and oriental fabrics also promoted fabrics for 'artistic' interiors. These efforts at improving the taste of the buying public had little impact, however, on the taste of the average consumer, who continued to prefer lavish use of colour.

Concern for hygiene and a lightening of colour schemes in the last two decades of the nineteenth century made lightweight, washable cotton and linen fabrics popular once again. Cretonne, a cotton fabric with a thick warp that gave it a slightly ribbed surface, was particularly popular. Chintz was more troublesome, as washing removed the glaze, which could only be restored professionally. In *Warne's Model Cookery and Housekeeping Book,* Mary Jewry offered an alternative method of cleaning:

> Shake off the loose dust, then lightly brush with a small long-haired furniture brush; after which wipe it closely with clean flannels, and rub it with dry bread. If properly done, the curtains will look nearly as well as at first, and if the colour be not light they will not require washing for years. Fold in large parcels and put carefully by.

*A design for a printed textile by John Illingworth Kay, 1894, reflects the influence of continental Art Nouveau.*

While the furniture [i.e. curtains] remains up it should be preserved from the sun and air as much as possible, which injure delicate colours; and the dust may be blown off by bellows. By the above method, curtains may be kept sufficiently clean to make up again with new linings.

Curtains were often changed according to the season, a light chintz being substituted for a thick velvet in the warmer months, or, as Mrs Beeton recommended, 'white curtains hung up in place of the damask or chintz'. This was an opportunity to complete the spring cleaning by taking down the curtain poles, washing them with vinegar and polishing them with furniture polish.

## Choosing curtains for Victorian houses today

Today's home decorator is in the happy position of being able to choose from a range of fabrics as large as that which bewildered the Victorian housewife. Although some fabrics, notably cretonne, are no longer being made, most of those mentioned in contemporary accounts are easy to buy today. Synthetic fibres were unknown to the Victorians, so it is a good rule to stick to the four historic natural fibres: wool, cotton, linen and silk, or blends of these. As with wallpapers, 'document' and reproduction designs are readily available.

Copying the many layers and dense fabrics of Victorian window treatments would certainly do our possessions no harm. We habitually expose them to levels of light that would horrify our Victorian counterparts. Our familiarity with furnishings made from light-resistant materials such as glass, steel, polymers, plastics and synthetic pigments has made us complacent about the dangers of sunlight (although that complacency is not justified: even plastics will eventually deteriorate if exposed to ultraviolet light for a long time). We may not want to imitate the more elaborate nineteenth-century window treatments, but simple layering of blinds, sheers and curtains will help to preserve fine furniture, carpets, upholstery and watercolours.

Extravagant effects should be confined to the principal rooms. Most of the information in this chapter applies only to these rooms because they illustrate the full range of fashions and tend to be better documented than other rooms. Bedrooms had simpler curtains and sub-curtains, usually in washable fabrics. Nurseries or servants' rooms were likely to have cast-offs too worn or faded to continue in use downstairs. 'It is desirable to have as little window drapery as possible to family or secondary rooms, particularly nurseries or servants' rooms, on account of their liability to catch fire, especially as toilet tables are so often situated within the window', wrote one authority, happily justifying a widely-practised economy.

Too close adherence to the styles in fashion at one particular time will not necessarily produce a historically accurate result. Contemporary pattern books can give a misleading impression that new styles were followed to the last stitch, whereas they were often adopted half-heartedly. The 1850s and 1860s have the worst reputation for excess, but as early as 1833 Loudon had pleaded for simplicity.

There is ample evidence that, just as today we may adopt some elements of new fashions but cling stubbornly to old furnishings out of custom, sentiment or financial necessity, Victorian decorators often ended up with a mélange of half-baked decorative themes.

Compromises were and are inevitable, but there are some that will positively undermine the authenticity of your recreated Victorian window dressing. Polyester or nylon net curtains, puffy festoon blinds and white plastic or nylon fittings in any visible form – tracks, beaded chain for roller blinds or blind pull finials – should not form any part of a historic window treatment.

TRELOAR'S
MATS

An Illustrated
Catalogue of all

the Best Floor Coverings
Sent Free on application to
TRELOAR & SONS,
LUDGATE HILL

# FLOORCOVERINGS

I N FITTING OUT the Victorian house the balance between practical need and decorative preference, and between economy and status, was nowhere more carefully considered than in the treatment of floors. Servants stepped on bare boards and thin drugget in their garrets, and on hard tiles and cold flagstones in the domestic offices. Even quite well-off families were accustomed to the hygienic chill of linoleum in bedrooms and bathrooms, and to stair carpet that changed abruptly to coarse matting at the landing, where it could no longer be seen by a visitor standing in the hall. In most houses only the reception rooms had carpets of any quality, and even these were rarely seen in all their glory, since a variety of protective covers was almost permanently in place to prevent dirt, wear and fading.

Entrances, lobbies and halls were provided with hard-wearing floors that could be washed and polished. In the early Victorian period, especially in the country, limestone or slate pavements were favoured for the better class of housing, while the gentry remained faithful to inlaid marble. At the bottom of the social scale, cottages had handmade, plain clay tiles or beaten earth floors. Most terraced housing in towns and new suburbs had raised floors of timber of sufficiently good quality to be exposed to view, or of plain boards that supplied a sound substrate on which a smarter finish could be laid. (For information on tiled and wooden floors, see Chapter 18, Decorative Tiles, and Chapter 8, Carpentry and Joinery).

ABOVE: *design for a floorcloth imitating geometric tile floor with encaustic inlays, from Michael Nairn & Co., late 1880s.*

OPPOSITE: *advertisement for floorcoverings retailer, 1894.*

## Floorcloths

Hard-wearing, decorative and waterproof, floorcloths made from heavy, painted canvas were widely used in British homes from the early eighteenth century. By the early nineteenth century there were more than twenty factories in England making floorcloths. It was a laborious process: heavy canvas in widths of up to 24 feet (7.3m) was stretched on upright frames and both sides were thoroughly covered with size, allowed to dry and then rubbed with pumice to give a key for the next coat. Another layer of size and several coats of thick paint later, the cloth resembled 'a flexible, well-tanned hide'. This was then painted or printed with a surface pattern using wooden blocks and left to 'season' for up to six months before being sold. Floorcloth made by this method was sold in large quantities throughout the nineteenth century, alongside new formulations such

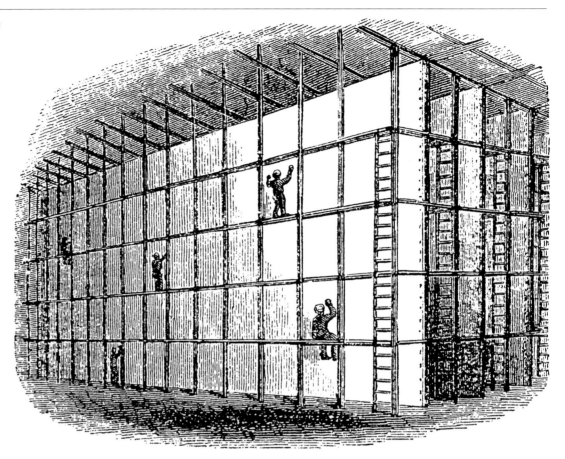

*The laborious task of applying size to a stretched canvas in Smith & Baber's floorcloth factory, Knightsbridge, 1842.*

as Kamptulicon, a waterproof mixture of india rubber, gutta-percha, linseed oil and powdered cork invented by Elijah Galloway in 1843 and manufactured from 1851 by Tayler, Harvey & Co. Kamptulicon was 'guaranteed to last for 20 years' and recommended by Mrs Beeton. However, it was a later invention, linoleum, which eventually dominated the floorcloth market.

Linoleum was invented by Frederick Walton around 1860 and in commercial production by 1864. It consists of cork dust and wood flour (very fine sawdust) bound with a mixture of linseed oil, gums, resins and wax and pressed through heavy metal rollers onto a coarse canvas backing. Walton neglected to register the name 'linoleum' (an amalgam of the Latin words for 'flax' and 'oil') in time to prevent its being adopted as a generic name by other manufacturers, and shortly afterwards it was being produced by several companies in England and Scotland. Some manufacturers, such as Nairn of Kircaldy, were already making floorcloths, and eventually switched production to the more profitable linoleum. At first linoleum was only available in plain colours, but it was soon being printed with patterns. The printed surface was quickly worn away in areas of heavy traffic, so in 1882 Walton brought out an 'inlaid' linoleum, in which the colours were solid right through the material.

Eighteenth-century floorcloths had been painted in imitation of inlaid marble floors, tiles or oriental carpets, and this convention of mimicking more expensive flooring materials was maintained into the nineteenth century on both floorcloths and linoleums. The repertoire expanded considerably, however, to include such delights as illusionistic trellis, rococo scrolls, flowers or even leopardskin spots. Reformist designers were, naturally, appalled at the false taste these patterns represented, and by the 1880s Eastlake happily reported that such 'conceits ... are now being gradually abandoned'. He felt that two colours ought to be considered sufficient for floorcloth designs, a view that may have been influenced by what he perceived to be the humble nature of the material.

Encapsulating as it did the virtues of hygiene, cleanliness and durability, linoleum quickly became acceptable for use in middle-class homes, especially in bedrooms, bathrooms, lavatories and nurseries. It could also appear in the 'polite' parts of the house. An inventory made in 1882 of the contents of Down House, Charles Darwin's home in Kent, shows that the entrance hall and inner hall floors were covered with 'floorcloth'. By 1899 the entrance hall is described as having 'a quantity of linoleum'. Emma Darwin no doubt considered this the only practical course, as she and Charles had several children and by contemporary standards were indulgent parents who accepted the need for decoration that would stand up to rough treatment (rubbing with fresh milk, or polishing with a mix of beeswax and turpentine was recommended to restore a tired-looking floorcloth). Several manufacturers offered designs that imitated geometric tiles, clearly intended for use in halls. A linoleum dating from the 1870s or 1880s, patterned with imitation mosaic in a Greek key pattern, survives at Linley Sambourne House, where it was used on the staircase and landings.

The general feeling by the 1890s, however, was that floorcloths and linoleum were no more than useful and economical substitutes for 'the real thing'. According to Muthesius, floorcloth was found in 'workmen's cottages and in the cheaper suburban houses of the lower middle-classes as a floor-covering for landings, staircases, kitchens and sometimes even reception-rooms'. That 'even' suggests that such coverings were used only as a last resort; and it should be remembered that Muthesius was writing in

*A finished floorcloth, printed in imitation of mosaic, hangs up to dry, while workmen on the factory floor put the finishing touches to a marble-effect floorcloth and roll up the finished products.*

249

*Cork flooring for a children's room, printed with nursery rhyme illustrations.*

1904, by which time the image of 'lino' was suffering from an indelible association with institutions and the smell of boiled cabbage. Another cheap and hard-wearing floorcovering that would not be seen in the 'best' parts of the house was 'coconut matting', nowadays known as coir matting.

## The British carpet industry

Carpet-weaving was well established in a handful of key locations by the time Victoria came to the throne. Carpet-manufacturing towns like Kidderminster, Axminster and Wilton gave their names to the different weaves said to have originated there – although, confusingly, neither the place of manufacture nor the precise definition of each term remained constant for each type of carpet.

Axminster in Devon was famous for hand-knotted (pile) carpets, first made there in 1755. In 1835 production moved to Wilton, but the Axminster name stuck. Many of these heavy, hard-wearing carpets imitated oriental designs; hence Loudon's suggestion that, when furnishing a library, the householder might choose either 'a large Turkey carpet or an Axminster carpet'. Admired for their quality and durability, Axminsters were regarded as the equivalent of the luxurious carpets imported from France and the Middle East, and were correspondingly expensive. Even in the last quarter of the nineteenth century, by which time hand-knotted Axminsters had to be called 'Real Axminsters' to prevent confusion with the many varieties woven on powered looms, they remained the most expensive English machine-made floorcovering. The machine-made 'Turkey' or 'Old English' designs imitating hand-knotted carpets remained very popular, and were acceptable even in those artistic homes where mass-produced decoration was normally despised. Liberty stocked Axminsters woven in Glasgow by James Templeton and in Kidderminster by Tomkinson and Adam. A method of making chenille carpet, sometimes referred to as 'patent Chenille Axminsters', was patented in 1832 by Templeton as a cheaper alternative to true Axminster carpet.

Less expensive than Axminster, but equally durable, Brussels carpets had a looped pile, which upon close inspection had the appearance of tiny cobbles set in distinctive rows. The Wilton factory was set up in about 1740 with Brussels looms. The carpet that became known as 'Wilton', however, had a cut pile, made by slicing through the loops of the Brussels weave to produce a 'velvet' nap.

Flatweave carpets were rather cheaper. Kidderminster carpet, also known as 'ingrain' or 'Scotch' carpet, was produced at Kidderminster and various other locations, including the Scottish towns of Alloa and Kilmarnock. The double-weave technique used to make these carpets resulted in a pattern that was equally clear on the underside of the carpet, although the colours were reversed.

Carpet weaving was slower to mechanize than other branches of the textile industry. In the early nineteenth century most carpets were still knotted or woven by hand on unpowered looms, as they had been a century earlier, but from about 1825 Jacquard looms began to replace the old hand looms. New types of loom, powered by steam and able to produce continuous rolls of carpet in broader widths, followed in the 1830s and 1840s. The initial cost of the machinery was high, but entrepreneurs who were prepared

*Detail of a Brussels weave fitted carpet used at Audley End, Essex. This reproduction of a Victorian pattern was commissioned in the 1980s to replace the worn original.*

to seize new opportunities were handsomely rewarded. One particularly innovative company was that founded by John Crossley in Halifax in 1803. While exhibiting his carpets at the Great Exhibition, Crossley was struck by the steam-powered Brussels looms exhibited by the American, Erasmus Bigelow. He bought the British rights to Bigelow's invention and installed the machines in his ever-expanding factory. Between 1840 and 1860 Dean Clough grew into one of the largest carpet mills in the world, dominating the town of Halifax as powerfully as the Crossley company dominated the regional economy. In 1852 William Grosvenor opened a purpose-built factory equipped with power looms in Kidderminster.

Another exhibitor at the Crystal Palace was Richard Whytock of Edinburgh, whose patent for looped pile 'tapestry carpet' had been registered in 1832 (and purchased by Crossley the following year). Whytock's carpets were 'woven from one continuous length [of yarn], which, by exact calculation of the quantity of each tint that is required to complete the pattern, is dyed of various colours before it is woven' – a method which yielded a 'rich effect' at low cost.

*Tropical plant foliage in an unlikely combination with Rococo scrollwork in a Brussels velvet carpet by Brinton & Sons of Kidderminster, exhibited at the Great Exhibition of 1851.*

The display of French carpets at the 1851 Exhibition prompted admiration, and not a little envy, from British manufacturers. The *Art Journal Catalogue* acknowledged the superiority of the French exhibits, and especially their mastery of colour. Eventually the adoption of better looms in England made it possible to produce carpets in a much wider range of colours: as one designer remarked, 'thirty to forty shades should be ample for all ordinary purposes'.

*The morning room at 18 Stafford Terrace, Kensington, was furnished with an array of hand-knotted oriental carpets over oak woodblock flooring.*

## Hand-made carpets revived

Despite the popularity of machine-made carpets, owning a hand-made floorcovering retained an undeniable allure. Reviewing nineteenth-century fashions in floorcoverings, Muthesius asserted that oriental carpets had never fallen out of favour, and that 'genuine French Aubussons were still the thing for the drawing-rooms of good houses'. The use of oriental rugs and carpets became fashionable once more in the 1870s as part of the Aesthetic movement's reaction against the florid designs of machine-made carpets. It went hand in hand with the revival of polished boards and parquet floors, which were thought to be healthier than fitted carpet.

In the 1860s and 1870s, as Britain's trade with the East increased, oriental carpets began to be imported in quantity, although they remained luxury items. In the 1870s Arthur Liberty began to import oriental textiles, including carpets, to supply his shop on Regent Street. Besides stocking machine-made carpets, Liberty supported attempts to produce hand-knotted carpets on a commercial basis in Europe, by importing carpets from Bohemia and Ireland. The Irish carpets came from Alexander Morton & Co., who had started a factory in Killybegs, County Donegal, in 1896, partly motivated by a desire to relieve poverty and unemployment in a 'congested district'. Morton's commissioned designs from Voysey and Archibald Knox, among others, and from 1901 they specialized in 'Celtic' designs featuring interlace and knot patterns inspired by sources such as the *Book of Kells*.

William Morris registered his first carpet designs in 1875, and set up a factory for making hand-knotted carpets in Hammersmith in 1878. Unfortunately, this aspect of Morris's crusade to return dignity to the working man by replacing mere mechanical labour with craftsmanship was not compatible with the demands of the market: Hammersmith carpets cost over twice as much as the equivalent Donegal or oriental carpet.

## Animal skins

Both Jean-Jacques Tissot's *Hide and Seek* (1880–2) and Thomas Armstrong's *The Test* (1865) depict the use of animal skins in Victorian housing. Indeed, it was not unheard of to find a large animal skin hearthrug, lying on an oriental rug, which was placed in turn over the fitted carpet. Big game trophies such as leopard, tiger and lion skins – sometimes complete with stuffed head and glass eyes – bore witness to the riches of the Empire. Bear skins, and the less exotic sheep or goat skin, were also used as hearthrugs.

## Home-made floorcoverings

Needlepoint, a form of tent-stitch embroidery on open-weave canvas, was used for making all kinds of furnishings for the Victorian home, including hearth rugs and other, larger, carpets. This traditional type of embroidery was revived in the early nineteenth century when Frau Wittich of Berlin persuaded her husband, a book and print seller, to produce coloured embroidery designs on squared paper. Each square represented a single stitch, enabling the amateur needlewoman to reproduce the design on canvas by counting the squares and copying the colours. From 1831 imported Berlin charts were sold at Wilks' haberdashers in Regent Street, and a craze for 'worsted work' was born.

*A modern reworking of a conventional Berlin woolwork design showing a seated spaniel. By 1850 the use of such designs on home-made hearthrugs was a cliché – albeit a charming one.*

Strips of needlepoint were used to edge larger carpets, the stitched surface sitting particularly well alongside the closely looped surface of Brussels weave. Needlepoint borders on staircase carpets were particularly effective. The technique also lent itself particularly well to small pictorial designs suitable for hearthrugs. The mechanical nature of the work, and the lack of original creativity involved, meant that needlepoint was heartily despised by design critics. The hackneyed nature of most Berlin charts further provoked their scorn, Eastlake complaining that 'if people will prefer a bouquet of flowers or a group of spaniels worked upon their hearthrug ... it is difficult to convince them of their error'.

A humbler style of home-made floorcovering was the variety of rugs that could be made from scraps and strips of old cloth. Some rag rugs were made by weaving strips of torn fabric on a cotton warp; other varieties used rags knitted or plaited into long 'sausages' that were stitched into coils to make oval or circular mats. Since the remnants arranged themselves randomly during the making-up, these rugs relied for their decorative effect on carefully combined colours. Formal patterns or pictures could be achieved in hand-tufted rugs, in which strips of fabric were knotted onto coarse sacking, and some of the crouching cats and bouquets of flowers thus produced had a great deal of naive charm. Rag rugs were products of peasant thrift and tended to be used to destruction in farmhouses and cottages, so very few have survived. In the very poorest houses, wrote Flora Thompson, 'there was but one room downstairs ... with only a table and a few chairs and stools for furniture and a superannuated potato-sack thrown down by way of a hearthrug'.

## Carpet designs

Early carpets were made in long strips, typically 26 inches (68cm) wide, which were sewn together and edged with borders to make larger carpets. Stripes, dots and small diapers were easy to match and worked well in carpets of all sizes, and consequently were much used in carpet designs of the 1830s and 1840s. Heraldic motifs such as fleurs-de-lys, or medievalizing patterns such as quatrefoils or interlacing tracery reflected the influence of antiquarian taste in early Victorian interiors, and were given a new lease of life by the Gothic Revival.

Tartan carpet enjoyed a certain vogue in the middle of the century. Queen Victoria first visited Scotland in 1842, and was instantly smitten with the Highlands. She and

Albert went on to create a model estate around Balmoral Castle, which was remodelled between 1853 and 1856 to provide the royal family with a rural retreat. A watercolour painted by J. Roberts in 1854 shows the Queen's Bedroom at Balmoral in all the freshness of its new decoration, with a very striking fitted carpet in blue and green tartan.

Elaborate 'Rococo' and 'Renaissance' designs, as well as 'all-over' floral patterns were also popular. Templeton's chenilles were produced in widths of up to 33 feet (10m), and his broadlooms were the first to achieve carpets of such size without the need for piecing-together. The widespread introduction of broadlooms made it possible to produce machine-made carpets with larger and more complex designs. The patterns and colours favoured in the mid-nineteenth century can be inferred from the scornful descriptions of the critics who railed against them. The problem was one of lack of 'honesty' and 'appropriateness', summed up by Ralph Wornum when he complained that the British carpets in the Great Exhibition, although 'distinguished' by the quality of their manufacture, ignored 'the most essential feature, aesthetically ... namely that a carpet is made to be trodden upon'.

It was a subject that provoked splendid outrage from Eastlake: 'When Materfamilias enters an ordinary upholsterer's warehouse, how can she possibly decide on the pattern of her new carpet, when bale after bale of Brussels is unrolled by the indefatigable youth, who is equal in his praises of every piece in turn? Shall it be the "House of Lords" diaper, of a yellow spot upon a blue ground; or the "imitation Turkey," with its multifarious colours; or the beautiful new *moiré* design; or yonder exquisite invention of green fern-leaves, tied up with knots of white satin ribbon?' The last 'preposterous pattern', Eastlake complained, 'has not only been employed for carpets, but was once very popular, and may be noticed as an instance of the degradation to which the arts of design can descend'.

ABOVE: *Design for a carpet with fern leaf pattern of about 1870, from the archive of Woodward Grosvenor.*

BELOW: *English Heritage's reconstruction of the decoration in the drawing room at Down House, Kent, the home of Charles Darwin, includes a machine-made imitation oriental carpet laid over dark red felt borders.*

Popular taste was robust enough to withstand such criticism. Indeed, there is something perversely attractive about the catalogue of 'horrors' cited with such disdain by the critics: rose wreaths, malachite marble, moiré, shaded vine-leaves, water-lilies, 'overhanging branches, with pleasant little peeps of blue sky', baskets of fruit, Rococo scrolls, and 'a spread of hippopotamus tusks' – especially as all that an authority like Eastlake could suggest by way of 'approved' design was the safe option of diaper patterns in colours that contrasted with the colour of the wallpaper.

Taking a more pragmatic line, the commercial designer Alexander Millar agreed that light and shade had 'nothing whatever' to do with carpet design, but felt that it was 'useless to shut one's eyes to the fact that the average householder and his wife have by no means arrived at this point. Many manufacturers find themselves constantly obliged to violate their own ideas of what is right in design, in order to provide what the public will buy.' Millar believed that French carpet designers had an advantage because they were trained to indicate light and shade by 'a few broad and simple touches which, when viewed at a proper distance, have all the effect of elaborate gradation. They have the power of representing, for instance, by a few blotches of colour, a perfectly modelled flower or scroll with lights, shadows, and reflected lights.' British designers were losing out because the design training in British schools of art failed to teach students how to indicate light and shade, encouraging them to rely instead on outline to define form.

Millar's remarks suggest that it would be hard to make a living designing carpets solely according to the tenets of the design reform movement. The strongly outlined, formalized designs of Morris, Voysey and their followers are popular today, but they were a minority taste when they were first offered to the public.

## Carpets in interiors

Carpets were extensively used in the 1830s and 1840s, and 'close-carpeting' (fitted carpet) was popular for reception rooms. If a carpet did not cover the entire floor, drugget or felt could be used to cover the edges up to the skirting board. Large carpets were often supplied with matching hearth rugs. Loudon recommended using a large Axminster carpet laid on polished oak boards, 'and a hearth rug to match', the idea being that the hearth rug would not disrupt the visual unity of the floorcovering and could easily be replaced when it had worn out. Certainly by 1850 no fashionable interior was without a small rug – *en suite* with the main carpet or not – to catch soot, smuts and sparks from the fire.

Carpets with central roundels or medallions posed certain problems. Mrs Merrifield described an Axminster carpet in the 1851 Exhibition with 'a centre variously ornamented, surrounded with a border of a rich design', which was not suitable for use where the furniture was informally arranged around the room.

Besides providing a convenient place to park the furniture, the edges of the room were more easily cleaned if they were not carpeted. It was more hygienic to leave a frame of up to 39 inches (1m) around the carpet, and by 1870 fitted carpets were entirely out of fashion. The exposed floorboards were stained or painted a dark colour and then polished or varnished; alternatively, they were covered with parquet, felt or linoleum. Matting was another popular choice for borders, as it was easy to clean. Parquet borders might be tailored to frame a particular carpet and stand a little proud of the underlying boards, so that the carpet appeared to be sunk into the floor.

The opulent taste of the mid-century had decreed that bedroom floors should be carpeted all over, but Eastlake argued for a return to the 'old custom' of having bare boards or floorcloth with a rug at the side of the bed, considering it, 'a healthier and

COMPLETE · BED ≈ ROOM FURNISHERS. HEAL&SON Nos 195·196·197·198 TOTTENHAM·COURT·Rd

THE "St IVES" SET OF PLAIN OAK FURNITURE WITH DULL STEEL HINGES AND HANDLES: SOUND CONSTRUCTION ☒ INEXPENSIVE.

*A bedroom scheme proposed by the furniture retailer Heal's in 1897 shows bare oak floorboards with hand-knotted rugs in fashionable Celtic designs.*

more cleanly, as well as a more picturesque, fashion than that now in vogue'. Mrs Beeton believed that children's rooms should be carpeted in winter, 'but this should be removed at spring-cleaning'. Bedroom floorboards, which did not require the same decorative finish as those in the principal rooms, should be regularly scoured, and neglected floorboards could be whitened with lime and washing soda mixed in boiling water and left to settle. In accordance with their lowly status, servants' rooms and the domestic offices had bare floors, drugget or linoleum, or hand-me-down carpets too shabby for use in the best rooms.

Carpets were cleaned with great care. Mrs Beeton famously recommended sprinkling them with damp tea leaves before sweeping: dust and dirt would stick to the leaves and be swept up with them. The first carpet sweeper was patented by James Hume as early as 1811, but it was not until the 1870s, when the more efficient design of the American, Melville Bissell, came onto the market, that they were adopted with any enthusiasm. Small rugs and carpets were regularly taken outdoors and beaten, and spring cleaning was an opportunity to take up large carpets, beat them, mend them, and even turn strips to even out areas of wear. The thrifty housewife was reminded to take care to match the pattern when reassembling the strips.

Protective covers were used to ensure that carpets stayed clean, did not become worn in areas of heavy traffic and kept their original brightness. A watercolour of the sitting room at No.7 Owen's Row, Islington, by Richard Parminter Cuff and dated August 1855, shows a carpet patterned with pink and red flowers and green foliage, which covers the whole floor and is fitted into the recesses of the bay window and the chimney-breast alcoves. On top of this lies the hearthrug, probably of Berlin woolwork, patterned with rococo scrolls of flowers within a green border. In front of the window there is a white damask crumb cloth, used under the table at mealtimes to prevent dropped food from being trodden into the carpet, and whisked away when the table is cleared and moved aside after the meal. A crumb cloth also appears in a drawing made by George Scharf in 1868 of his mother's sitting-room, the front room on the top floor of No.29 Great George Street, London. Scharf's pencilled annotations show that this floor was layered with floorcloth (visible round the edges of the room), carpet, hearthrug and crumb cloth.

This was not just a bourgeois shibboleth; the habit of covering-up carpets was ingrained in the most bohemian and design-conscious households. At The Grange, the London home of Edward Burne-Jones, drugget covered the hall and stair carpets; it was clipped into place with the stair-rods as permanently as the 'proper' carpet.

## Choosing floorcoverings today

Fortunately for present-day owners of Victorian houses, all the floorcoverings and finishes described in this chapter are easily obtained or recreated today. Machine-made carpets in the traditional Wilton, Axminster and Brussels weaves are all widely available in many of the patterns used in the nineteenth century. Some companies specialize in recreating archive designs in authentic colourways.

After decades when it was ignored in favour of vinyl flooring, linoleum has become fashionable once more. It is now sold under the trade name 'Marmoleum' and is made in Scotland by a descendant company of the Nairn Company that was one of the first to set up in competition with Frederick Walton in the 1870s. Inlaid linoleum is no longer made, but borders and designs can be cut and laid to order by specialist fitters. Linoleum requires no special cleaning or finishes, although a liquid wax finish can be applied if a surface sheen is required.

Layering floorcoverings is one of the most effective ways to give an authentic Victorian look to an interior: leave a border of stained and polished floorboards around a large oriental carpet or 'Turkey' Axminster, with a hearth rug in front of the fire and perhaps another mat in the doorway to protect the 'best' carpet.

Hand-made and valuable carpets should be protected from light as far as possible, and all carpets should be laid on an appropriate underlay. Unfitted rugs and carpets on hard floors should each have their own piece of underlay cut to size; non-slip underlay will stop smaller carpets from skidding dangerously underfoot. Hand-knotted carpets should be cleaned by specialists, and repairs to valuable historic carpets should be entrusted to textile conservators, who will also be able to advise on the best way to protect carpets in use.

Regular vacuuming will prevent dirt from becoming ingrained and remove grit that might otherwise slice through the fibres of the carpet as it gets trodden in. The best all-round protection for all floor surfaces, hard or soft, is to ensure that dirt and grit do not come into the house in the first place. A rubber 'honeycomb' mat outside the door and a large, thick fibre mat just inside it will go a long way towards preventing damage.

# *Further Reading*

## Part 1: The Victorian House
### *History: general*

Susan Beattie, *A Revolution in London Housing. LCC housing architects and their work 1893–1914*, London: GLC/Architectural Press, 1980

Roy Bigden, *Victorian Farms*, Ramsbury: Crowood, 1986

Asa Briggs, *Victorian Cities*, London: Pelican, 1968

John Burnett, *A Social History of Housing 1815–1970*, London: Methuen, 1980

Annette Carruthers (ed), *The Scottish Home*, Edinburgh: National Museums of Scotland, 1996

Roger Dixon and Stefan Muthesius, *Victorian Architecture*, London: Thames & Hudson, 1985

Mark Girouard, *The Victorian Country House*, 2nd edn, London and New Haven: Yale University Press, 1979

Mark Girouard, *Sweetness and Light: The Queen Anne Movement 1860–1900*, (paperback edn), London and New Haven: Yale University Press, 1984

Wendy Hitchmough, *C.F.A. Voysey*, London: Phaidon, 1995

Helen Long, *The Edwardian House*, Manchester: Manchester University Press, 1993

Stefan Muthesius, *The English Terraced House*, London and New Haven: Yale University Press, 1982

Margaret Richardson, *Architects of the Arts and Crafts Movement*, London: Trefoil Books, 1983

Andrew Saint et al, *London Suburbs*, London: Merrell Holberton, 1999

Isobel Watson, *Gentlemen in the Building Line. The development of South Hackney*, London: Padfield Publications, 1989

### *Nineteenth-century pattern books and reprints*

Matthew Holbeche Bloxam, *The Principles of Gothic Ecclesiastical Architecture*, 8th edn, London: David Bogue, 1846

Charles Locke Eastlake, *History of the Gothic Revival* (reprint of 1st edn, 1872), Leicester NY: Leicester University Press, 1970

Francis Goodwin, *Rural Architecture: Designs for rustic, peasants' and ornamental cottages, lodges and villas, in various styles of architecture*, 2nd edn, 1835

Robert Kerr, *The Gentleman's House; or, How to plan English residences, from the parsonage to the palace* (reprint of 3rd edn, 1871), New York and London: Johnson Reprint Co., 1972

John Claudius Loudon, *The Encyclopaedia of Cottage, Farm and Villa Architecture and Furniture* (reprint of 1st edn, 1833), London, Shaftesbury: Donhead, 2000

Hermann Muthesius, *The English House* (reprint of 1904 edn), Oxford: BSP Professional Books, 1987

Ernest Newton, *A Book of Houses*, London: Sprague & Co, 1891

A.W.N. Pugin, *Contrasts*, London: 1836

A.W.N. Pugin, *The True Principles of Pointed or Christian Architecture*, London: 1841

P.F. Robinson, *Rural Architecture, or, A Series of Designs for Ornamental Cottages*, 1836

P.F. Robinson, *Designs for Gate Cottages, Lodges and Park Entrances*, 1837

P.F. Robinson, *Village Architecture*, 1837

John Ruskin, *The Seven Lamps of Architecture*, London: Smith, Elder & Co., 1849

John Ruskin, *The Stones of Venice*, London: Smith, Elder & Co., 1851–53

H. Heathcote Statham, *Modern Architecture*, London: Chapman & Hall, 1897

E.L. Tarbuck, *The Builder's Practical Director*, London: 1855

Young & Marten, *The Victorian House Catalogue* (reprint of 1897 catalogue), London: Sidgwick & Jackson/The Victorian Society, 1990

### *Care for Victorian houses: general*

John Ashurst and Nicola Ashurst, *Practical Building Conservation*, 5 vols, Aldershot: English Heritage/Gower Technical Press, 1988

Albert Jackson and David Day, *Collins Complete Home Restoration Manual*, London: HarperCollins, 1992

Alan Johnson, *How to Restore and Improve Your Victorian House*, 2nd edn, Newton Abbot: David & Charles, 1992

Victorian Society, *Coming Unstuck. The removal of fixtures from listed buildings*, London: Victorian Society, London: 1993

## Part 2: Structure and materials
### *Chapter 4: Brick and terracotta*

John and Nicola Ashurst, *Practical Building Conservation: Volume 2: Brick, Terracotta and Earth*, Aldershot: English Heritage/Gower Technical Press, 1988

Nicola Ashurst, *Cleaning Historic Buildings*, 2 vols, London: Donhead, 1994

Tim Birdwell, *The Conservation of Brick Buildings*, London: Brick Development Association, 1977

British Standards Institution, *BS8221: 2000. Cleaning and Surface Repair of Buildings*, London: BSI, 2000

Ronald Brunskill, *Brick Building in Britain*, London: Gollancz, 1990

Ronald Brunskill and Alec Clifton-Taylor, *English Brickwork*, London: Ward Lock, 1977

Society for the Protection of Ancient Buildings, *Information Sheet No. 8: Tuck Pointing in Practice*, London: SPAB

Society for the Protection of Ancient Buildings, *Information Sheet No. 9: An Introduction to Building Limes*, London: SPAB

Michael Stratton, *The Terracotta Revival*, London: Gollancz, 1993

Andrew Thomas, *Technical Pamphlet No. 8: The Treatment of Damp in Old Buildings*, London: SPAB, 1986

John Warren, *Conservation of Brick*, Oxford: Butterworth/Heinemann, 1998

Gilbert Williams, *Technical Pamphlet No. 5: Pointing Stone and Brick Walling*, London: SPAB, 1986

Gilbert Williams and Nicola Ashurst, *Information Sheet No. 6: An Introduction to the Treatment of Damp*, London: SPAB, 1987

English Heritage has produced a 30-minute video, *Making the Point* (Product ref. XV 10707), which explains the importance of correct pointing and demonstrates pointing techniques. For information on how to order, contact English Heritage Customer Services, PO Box 569, Swindon SN2 2YR. Tel: 0870 333 1181 Fax: 01793 414926 E-mail: customers@english-heritage.org.uk. Website: www.english-heritage.org.uk.

## Chapter 5: Stone

John and Nicola Ashurst, *Practical Building Conservation Volume 1: Stone Masonry*, Aldershot: English Heritage/Gower Technical Press, 1988

Building Research Establishment, *BRE Digest 420 Selecting Natural Building Stones*, London: CRC, 1997

Alec Clifton-Taylor, *The Pattern of English Building*, London: Faber & Faber, 1987

Pamela Cunnington, *Care for Old Houses*, 2nd edn, London: A & C Black, 1991

Francis G. Dimes and John Ashurst, *Conservation of Building and Decorative Stone* (2 vols.), Oxford: Butterworth/Heinemann, 1998

Elaine Leary, *The Building Limestones of the British Isles*, London: HMSO, 1983

Elaine Leary, *The Building Sandstones of the British Isles*, London: HMSO, 1986

## Chapter 6: Render, stucco and tile-hanging

John and Nicola Ashurst, *Practical Building Conservation Volume 3: Mortars, Plasters and Renders*, Aldershot: English Heritage/Gower Technical Press, 1988

Philip Hughes, *Information Sheet No. 4: The Need for Old Buildings to Breathe*, London: SPAB

## Chapter 7: Roofs

Peter Brocket and Adela Wright, *Technical Pamphlet No. 10: The Care and Repair of Thatched Roofs*, London: SPAB

Building Research Establishment, *Defect Action Sheet No. 94: Masonry Chimneys: DPCs and Flashing – Location*, Garston, Watford: BRE/DOE/HMSO, 1987

C.E. Dobson, *Notes on Slating and Tiling* (reprint of 1945 edn), London: Langley, 1983

English Heritage, *Mansard Roofs*, (Guidance leaflet), London: English Heritage, 1990

Valentine Fletcher, *Chimney Pots and Stacks*, Fontwell: Centaur, 1968

Brian Ridout, *Timber Decay in Buildings: The conservation approach to treatment*, London: E. & F.N. Spon/English Heritage, 2000

Adela Wright, *Craft Techniques for Traditional Buildings*, London: B.T. Batsford, 1991

## Chapter 8: Carpentry and joinery

English Heritage, *Office Floor Loading in Historic Buildings*, Guidance Leaflet, London: English Heritage, 1994

Philip Hughes, *Information Sheet No. 10: Patching Old Floorboards*, London: SPAB, 1988

John Macgregor, *Technical Pamphlet No. 2: Strengthening Timber Floors*, London: SPAB, 1985

Peter Nicholson, *Treatise on the Construction of Staircases and Hand-rails*, London: J. Taylor, 1820

Peter Nicholson, *The New Practical Builder, and Workman's Companion*, London: 1861

## Chapter 9: Windows

R.W. Douglas and S. Frank, *A History of Glassmaking*, Henley-on-Thames: Foulis, 1972

John Fidler et al, *Sash Windows*, Traditional Homes Technical Information Leaflet, London: n.d.

Historic Scotland, *Technical Advice Note 3: Performance Standards for Timber Sash and Case Windows*, Edinburgh: Historic Scotland, 1994

Hentie Louw, 'The Mechanisation of Architectural Woodwork in Britain from the late Eighteenth to the Early Twentieth Century ... Part IV: The End of an Era', *Construction History*, Vol.12, 1996, pp.19–40

Raymond Osborne, *Cast Iron Window Frames c. 1790–1914 and the Question of Obtaining Replacements*, unpublished thesis, London: Architectural Association, 1989

Steven Parissien, *The Framing Opinions Campaign*, London: English Heritage, 1994

Andrew Townsend and Martyn Clarke, *The Repair of Wood Windows*, London: SPAB, 1991

John Wright, "One Very Convenient Thing". A case for the preservation of vertically sliding timber sash windows by careful repair and maintenance, unpublished thesis, London: Architectural Association, 1993

## Chapter 10: Doors

Charles Viney, *London Doors*, Harpenden: Oldcastle, 1989

## Chapter 11: Ironwork

John and Nicola Ashurst, *Practical Building Conservation: Volume 4: Metals*, Aldershot: English Heritage/Gower Technical Press, 1988

Marian Campbell, *Ironwork*, London: Victoria and Albert Museum/HMSO, 1985

Jacqueline Fearn, *Cast Iron*, Princes Risborough: Shire, 1990

John Gay, *Cast Iron. Architecture and ornament, function and fantasy*, London: Murray, 1985

# Part 3: Services
### Chapter 12: Conservatories and extensions
English Heritage, *The London Terraced House 1660–1860. A guide to alterations and extensions*, London: English Heritage, 1996

John Hix, *The Glass House*, London: Phaidon, 1974

James Shirley Hibberd, *Rustic Adornments for Homes of Taste* (reprint of 1856 edn), London: National Trust, 1987

Georg Kolmaier and Barna von Sartory, *Houses of Glass. A nineteenth-century building type* (English paperback edn), Cambridge, Mass. and London: MIT Press, 1990

### Chapter 13: Fireplaces and chimneys
Solid Fuel Association, *The Guide to Curing Chimney Problems* (brochure), Alfreton: SFA

Solid Fuel Association, *The Guide to Opening up Your Fireplace* (brochure), Alfreton: SFA

Solid Fuel Association, *The Guide to Solid Fuels* (brochure), Alfreton: SFA

Lucy Crane, *Art, and the Formation of Taste*, London: Macmillan & Co, 1882

David J. Eveleigh, *Firegrates and Kitchen Ranges*, Princes Risborough: Shire, 1983

Christopher Gilbert and Anthony Wells-Cole, *The Fashionable Fireplace 1660–1840*, Leeds: Leeds City Art Galleries, 1985

Nicholas Hills, *The English Fireplace. Its architecture and the working fire*, London: Quiller, 1983

Alison Kelly, *The Book of English Fireplaces*, London: Country Life, 1968

L.A. Shuffrey, *The English Fireplace and its Accessories*, London: Batsford, 1968

Peter Quennell (ed.), *Mayhew's London*, London: Spring Books

### Chapter 14: Lighting
David J. Eveleigh, *Candle Lighting*, Princes Risborough: Shire, 1985

David Gledhill, *Gas Lighting*, Princes Risborough: Shire, 1981

Leeds City Art Galleries, *Country House Lighting 1660–1890*, Leeds: Leeds City Art Galleries, n.d.

Roger W. Moss, *Lighting for Historic Buildings*, Washington, DC: Preservation Press, 1988

Thomas Webster and Frances B. (Mrs William) Parkes, *An Encyclopaedia of Domestic Economy*, London: 1844

### Chapter 15: Kitchens
Isabella Beeton, *The Book of Household Management* (reprint of 1861 edn), London: Cassell & Co., 2000

Isabella Beeton, *Every-day Cookery and Housekeeping Book* (reprint of 1865 edn), New York: Gallery Books, 1984

*Mrs Beeton's Cookery Book and Household Guide*, London: Ward, Lock & Co., 1897

Jennifer Davies, *The Victorian Kitchen*, London: BBC Books, 1989

D. Eveleigh, *Firegrates & Kitchen Ranges*, Princes Risborough: Shire, 1983

Mary Jewry (ed.), *Warne's Model Cookery and Housekeeping Book*, London: Frederick Warne & Co., 1868

Mary Jewry (ed.), *Warne's Every-day Cookery*, London: Frederick Warne & Co., 1887

A Lady, *The New London Cookery and Complete Domestic Guide*, London: George Virtue, 1827

Jane Loudon, *The Lady's Country Companion, or, How to Enjoy a Country Life Rationally*, London: 1845

Mrs Henry Mackarness, *The Young Lady's Book*, London: George Routledge & Sons, 1876

### Chapter 16: Bathrooms
Adam Hart-Davis, *Thunder, Flush and Thomas Crapper*, London: Micheal O'Mara Books, 1997

Kit Wedd, *The Victorian Bathroom Catalogue*, London: Studio Editions, 1996

L. Wright, *Clean and Decent*, London: Routledge & Paul, 1960

# Part 4: The interior
### Interior decoration: general
Joanna Banham, Sally Macdonald, Julia Porter, *Victorian Interior Design*, London: Cassell, 1991

Helena Barrett and John Phillips, *Suburban Style: The British Home 1840–1960*, London and Sydney: Macdonald Orbis, 1987

Dorothy Bosomworth, *The Victorian Catalogue of Household Goods* (reprint of Silber & Flemming catalogue, c.1883), London: Studio Editions, 1991

Asa Briggs, *Victorian Things*, London: Penguin, 1990

Jeremy Cooper, *Victorian and Edwardian Furniture and Interiors*, London: Thames & Hudson, 1998

Caroline Davidson, *The World of Mary Ellen Best*, London: Chatto & Windus, 1985

Charlotte Gere, *Nineteenth-century Decoration. The art of the interior*, London: Weidenfeld & Nicolson, 1989

Charlotte Gere, *Nineteenth Century Decoration*, London: Weidenfeld & Nicolson, 1984

Charlotte Gere and Lesley Hoskins, *The House Beautiful. Oscar Wilde and the aesthetic interior*, Aldershot: Lund Humphries, 2000

Lionel Lambourne, *The Aesthetic Movement*, London: Phaidon, 1996

Susan Lasdun, *Victorians at Home*, London: Weidenfeld & Nicolson, 1981

Shirley Nicholson, *A Victorian Household*, London: Barrie & Jenkins, 1988

Hermione Sandwith and Sheila Stainton, *The National Trust Manual of Housekeeping*, 2nd edn, London: National Trust, 1990

Peter Thornton, *Authentic Decor: The Domestic Interior 1620–1920*, London: Weidenfeld & Nicolson, 1984

Mark Turner and Lesley Hoskins, *Silver Studio of Design*, Exeter: Webb & Bower/Michael Joseph, 1988

### Nineteenth-century manuals
H.W. and A. Arrowsmith, *The Paper Hanger's and Upholsterer's Guide*, 1854

Mrs Florence Caddy, *Household Organisation*, London: Chapman & Hall, 1877

Christopher Dresser, *Studies in Design* (reprint of 1st edn, 1876), London: Studio Editions, 1988

Charles Locke Eastlake, *Hints on Household Taste* (reprint of 4th edn, 1878), New York: Dover Publications, 1969

R.W. Edis, *Decoration and Furniture of Town Houses*, London: Kegan Paul & Co., 1881

R.W. Edis, *Healthy Furniture* and Decoration, London: Handbook to International Health Exhibition, 1884

Mary Eliza Haweis, *The Art of Decoration*, London: Chatto & Windus, 1881

Owen Jones, *Plans, Elevations, Sections and Details of the Alhambra*, London: Vizetelly Bros & Co., 1842–5

Owen Jones, *The Grammar of Ornament* (reprint of 1856 edn), London: Studio Editions, 1986

Gleeson White (ed.), *Practical Designing. A handbook on the preparation of working drawings*, 3rd edn, London: George Bell & Sons, 1898

### Chapter 17: Plain and decorative plaster

John and Nicola Ashurst, *Practical Building Conservation: Volume 3: Plaster, Mortars and Renders*, Aldershot: English Heritage/Gower Technical Press, 1988

William Millar, *Plaster Plain and Decorative*, (reprint of 1897 edn), Shaftesbury: Donhead, 1998

W.D. Stagg and R. Masters, *Decorative Plasterwork: Its Repair and Restoration*, Eastbourne: Orion Books, 1993

### Chapter 18: Decorative tiles

Julian Barnard, *Victorian Ceramic Tiles*, London: Studio Vista, 1972

Jon Catleugh, *William de Morgan Tiles*, Shepton Beauchamp: Richard Dennis, 1991

William James Furnival, *Leadless Decorative Tiles, Faience and Mosaic*, Stone: W.J. Furnivall, 1904

Tony Herbert and Kathryn Huggins, *The Decorative Tile*, London: Phaidon, 1995

Hans van Lemmen, *Tiles: A Collector's Guide*, London: Souvenir Press, 1978

John Malam and Hans van Lemmen (eds), *Fired Earth. 1000 years of tiles in Europe*, Shepton Beauchamp: Richard Dennis, 1991

Terence A. Lockett, *Collecting Victorian Tiles*, Woodbridge: Antique Collectors' Club, 1979

D.S. Skineer and Hans van Lemmen (eds), *Minton Tiles 1835–1935*, (exh. cat.), Stoke-on-Trent: City Museum and Art Gallery, 1984

### Chapter 19: Paint colour and finishes

E. Barber, *The Painter's Grainer's and Writer's Assistant*, 1852

Ian C. Bristow, *Interior House-Painting Colours and Technology 1615–1840*, New Haven and London: Yale University Press, 1996

Ian C. Bristow, *Architectural Colour in British Interiors 1615–1840*, New Haven and London: Yale University Press, 1976

Ellis A. Davidson, *A Practical Manual of House-painting, Graining and Marbling and Sign-writing*, 1875

John Elliott, *Practical House Painting, Decorating, Sign Writing, Gilding, &c.*, Glasgow: The Incorporated Institute of British Decorators, Scottish Branch, 1910

David R. Hay, *The Laws of Harmonious Colouring adapted to Interior Decorations, Manufactures and other Useful Purposes* (1828), 5th edn, London: W.S. Orr & Co., 1844

David R. Hay, *The Laws of Harmonious Colouring adapted to Interior Decorations, with observations on the practice of house painting*, 6th edn, Edinburgh and London: William Blackwood, 1847

David R. Hay, *A Nomenclature of Colours Applicable to the Arts and Natural Sciences, to Manufactures, and other Purposes of General Utility*, Edinburgh and London: William Blackwood & Sons, 1845

David R. Hay, *The Principles of Beauty in Colouring Systematized*, Edinburgh, 1845

S. Jennings, *Paint and Colour Mixing*, 1902

W. Mullinger Higgins, *The House Painter*, 1841

### Chapter 20: Wallcoverings

Joanna Banham, *A Decorative Art: Nineteenth-century wallpapers in the Whitworth Art Gallery* (exh. cat.), Manchester: Whitworth Art Gallery, 1985

Eric Entwhistle, *Wallpapers of the Victorian Era*, Leigh-on-Sea: Frank Lewis, 1964

Lesley Hoskins (ed.), *The Papered Wall. History, pattern, technique*, London: Thames & Hudson, 1994

Richard Nylander, *Wallpapers for Historic Buildings*, 2nd edn, Washington, DC: The Preservation Press, 1992

Charles Oman and Jean Hamilton, *Wallpaper. A history and illustrated catalogue of the collection of the Victoria and Albert Museum*, London: Sothebys, 1982

Treve Rosoman, *London Wallpapers. Their manufacture and use 1690–1840*, London: English Heritage, 1992

Pamela H. Simpson, 'Cheap, Quick and Easy: Embossed Wallcoverings at the Turn of the Century', *Wallpaper History Review*, 1996–97, pp.22–26

V. Sugden and E.L. Edmondson, *A History of English Wallpaper 1509–1914*, London: Batsford, 1925

Clare Taylor, *Wallpaper*, Princes Risborough: Shire, 1991

Anthony Wells-Cole, *Historic Paper Hangings from Temple Newsam and other English Houses*, Leeds: Leeds City Art Galleries, 1983

### Chapter 21: Curtains and blinds

Pamela Clabburn, *The National Trust Book of Furnishing Textiles*, London: Penguin, 1989

Clare Jameson (ed.), *A Pictorial Treasury of Curtain and Drapery Designs 1750–1850*, Sessay: Potterton, 1987

A Lady, *The Workwoman's Guide* (reprint of 2nd edn, 1840), Doncaster: Bloomfield, 1975

Florence M. Montgomery, *Printed Textiles. English and American Cottons and Linens 1700–1850*, London: Thames & Hudson, 1970

Jane C. Nylander, *Fabrics for Historic Buildings. A guide to selecting reproduction fabrics*, 4th edn, Washington, DC: The Preservation Press, 1990

Mary Schoeser and Celia Rufey, *English and American Textiles. From 1790 to the present*, London: Thames and Hudson, 1989

**Chapter 22: Floorcoverings**

Art Journal, *The Crystal Palace Exhibition Illustrated Catalogue* (reprint of 1851 edn), New York: Dover Publications, 1970

Jane Fawcett, *Historic Floors*, Oxford: Butterworth/Heinemann, 2001

Christopher Gilbert, James Lomax and Anthony Wells-Cole, *Country House Floors 1660–1850*, Leeds: Leeds City Art Galleries, 1987

Bertram Jacobs, *The History of British Carpets*, Carpet Review, 1968

Mrs Merrifield, 'Essay on the Harmony of Colours, as Exemplified in the Exhibition', *The Crystal Palace Exhibition Illustrated Exhibition* (reprint of *Art-Journal* catalogue, 1851), New York: Dover, 1970

Mrs Henry Owen, *The Illuminated Book of Needlework*, London: Henry G. Bohn, 1847

George Robinson, *Carpets*, Textile Book Service, 1972

Helene von Rosenstiel and Gail Casey Winkler, *Floor Coverings for Historic Buildings. A guide to selecting reproductions*, Washington, DC: The Preservation Press, 1988

Sarah B. Sherrill, *Carpets and Rugs of Europe and America*, New York, London & Paris: Abbeville Press, 1996, esp. ch.5, 'Great Britain'

Pamela H. Simpson, 'Linoleum and Lincrusta: Democratic Coverings for Floors and Walls', *Exploring Everyday Landscapes, Perspectives in Vernacular Architecture VII*, Annmarie Adams and Sally McMurry (eds), Knoxville: University of Tennessee Press, 1997, pp.281–92

# Picture Credits

# Places to Visit

*Listed below are some sites and collections of interest, including one or two buildings that predate the nineteenth century but have Victorian interiors. Information about all National Trust properties is available from www.national-trust.org.uk. Information about all English Heritage properties is available from www.english-heritage.org.uk.*

**Audley End**
Audley End
Nr Saffron Walden, Essex CB11 4JF
Tel: 01799 522399 (information line)
Website: www.audley-end.co.uk
English Heritage. Jacobean mansion with Victorian interior decoration.

**Brighton Museum & Art Gallery**
Church Street
Brighton, East Sussex BN1 1UE
Tel: 01273 290900
Email: info@brighton-hove.gov.uk
Website: www.museums.brighton-hove.gov.uk
Good collection of nineteenth-century decorative arts.

**The Brooking Collection**
School of Architecture and Construction
University of Greenwich
Avery Hill Campus, Mansion Site,
Bexley Road, London SE9 2PQ
Tel: 020 8331 9312
Email: j.lynch@gre.ac.uk
Website: www.dartfordarchive.org.uk/
    technology/art.brooking.shtml
Large collection of building elements, from escutcheons to doorcases and complete sash windows. Visits by appointment.

**Cardiff Castle**
Castle Street, Cardiff CF10 2RB
Tel: 02920 878100
Email: cardiffcastle@cardiff.gov.uk
Website: www.cardiff.gov.uk
Designed by William Burges for the Marquess of Bute. Magnificent interiors of medieval and Oriental inspiration.

**Carlyle's House**
24 Cheyne Row
Chelsea, London SW3 5HL
Tel: 0207 352 7087

Infoline: 01494 755559
National Trust. Queen Anne house, decorated and furnished as it was when Thomas and Jane Carlyle lived there.

**Charlecote Park**
Warwick, Warwickshire CV35 9ER
Tel: 01789 470277
National Trust. Elizabethan mansion redecorated in nineteenth century and with large Victorian kitchen complex.

**Cheltenham Art Gallery & Museum**
Clarence Street
Cheltenham, Glos GL50 3JT
Tel: 01242 237431
Email: ArtGallery@cheltenham.gov.uk
Website: ww.cheltenham-museum.org.uk
Large collection of Arts and Crafts furniture, textiles, pottery and metalwork.

**Cragside**
Rothbury, Morpeth
Northumberland NE65 7PX
Tel: 01669 620333/620150
National Trust. House designed by Richard Norman Shaw for Lord Armstrong; the first in the world to be lit by electricity.

**Down House**
Luxted Road
Downe, Orpington
Kent BR6 7JT
Tel: 01689 859119
English Heritage. Home of Charles and Emma Darwin from 1842, with rooms furnished by EH based on contemporary descriptions and inventories.

**Geffrye Museum**
Kingsland Road
London E2 8EA
Tel: 020 7739 9893
Website: www.geffrye-museum.org.uk
Museum of domestic interiors. Roomsets and temporary exhibitions.

**Gladstone Pottery Museum**
Uttoxeter Road
Longton, Stoke-on-Trent ST3 1PQ
Tel: 01782 237777
Email: gladstone@stoke.gov.uk
Website: www.stoke.gov.uk
Large collection of tiles and sanitaryware.

**Gunnersbury Park**
Popes Lane
Acton, London W3 8LQ
Tel: 0208 992 1612
Georgian mansion with impressive late nineteenth-century kitchen.

**Hardy's Cottage**
Higher Bockhampton
Nr Dorchester, Dorset DT2 8QJ
Tel: 01305 262366
National Trust. A traditional cob and thatch cottage, birthplace of Thomas Hardy, with rooms furnished by the Trust in the style of the 1840s.

**Hill Top**
Sawrey,
Ambleside LA22 0LF
Tel: 015394 36269
National Trust. Seventeenth-century farmhouse; home of Beatrix Potter, with interiors preserved as she left them.

**Horniman Museum**
100 London Road, London SE23 3PQ
Tel: 0208 699 1872
Email: enquiry@horniman.ac.uk
Website: www.horniman.demon.co.uk
Gardens contain the magnificent 1894 conservatory from the family home of the tea importer Frederick Horniman.

**Hughenden Manor**
High Wycombe
Buckinghamshire HP14 4LA
Tel: 01494 532580
Infoline: 01494 755565
National Trust. Home of Disraeli from 1848 to 1881.

**The Ironbridge Gorge Museums Trust**
Ironbridge
Telford, Shropshire TF8 7AW
Tel: 01952 884391
Email: info@ironbridge.co.uk
Website: www.ironbridge.org.uk
Various sites relating to the industrial revolution and Victorian life, including Coalbrookdale Museum of Iron and Darby houses, Blists Hill Victorian town, Coalport China Museum and Tar tunnel, and Jackfield Tile Museum.

**Kelmscott Manor**
Kelmscott
Lechlade, Glos, GL7 3HJ
Tel: 01367 252486
Email: admin@kelmscottmanor.co.uk
Website: www.kelmscottmanor.co.uk
Country house furnished and decorated
by William Morris and his circle.

**Knightshayes Court**
Bolham, Tiverton
Devon EX16 7RQ
Tel: 01884 254665
National Trust. Designed by William
Burges and begun in 1869; lavish
decoration.

**Leighton House Museum and
Art Gallery**
12 Holland Park Road
London W14 8LZ
Tel: 020 7602 3316
Email: museums@rbkc.gov.uk
Website:
www.rbkc.gov.uk/leightonhousemuseum
Home of the painter Frederic Leighton.
Contains an Arab Hall, created in 1877 to
accommodate Lord Leighton's collection
of Islamic tiles, and including decoration
and fittings by Walter Crane, William de
Morgan, W.A.S. Benson and others.

**Linley Sambourne House**
18 Stafford Terrace, London W8 7BH
Tel: 020 7602 3316
Email: museums@rbkc.gov.uk
Website:
www.rbkc.gov.uk/linleysambournehouse
Home of the cartoonist and illustrator
Edward Linley Sambourne. Perfectly-
preserved late Victorian interiors.

**Museum of Domestic Architecture
and Design (MoDA)**
Middlesex University
Cat Hill, Barnet,
Hertfordshire EN4 8HT
Tel: 020 8411 5244
Email: moda@midx.ac.uk
Website: www.moda.midx.ac.uk
Contains the company archive of the
Silver Studio, which produced wallpaper
and textile designs between 1880 and 1963.

**Osborne**
East Cowes,
Isle of Wight PO32 6JY
Tel: 01983 200022
English Heritage. Victoria and Albert's
country house by the sea. Swiss
Cottage in grounds.

**Standen**
West Hoathly Road
East Grinstead, West Sussex RH19 4NE
Tel: 01342 323029
National Trust. Arts and Crafts house by
Philip Webb decorated by Morris & Co.

**The Potteries Museum & Art Gallery**
Bethesda Street
Hanley, Stoke-on-Trent ST1 3DW
Tel: 01782 232323
Email: museums@stoke.gov.uk
Website: www.stoke.gov.uk
Large collection of tiles and related items.

**Sunnycroft**
200 Holyhead Road
Wellington
Telford, Shropshire TF1 2DR
Infoline: 0870 6081259
National Trust. Late Victorian
gentleman's suburban villa and
surrounding 'mini-estate'.

**Victoria and Albert Museum**
Cromwell Road
South Kensington, London SW7 2RL
Tel: 020 7942 2000
Recorded Information: 0870 442 0808
E-mail: vanda@vam.ac.uk
Website: www.vam.ac.uk
Decorative arts of all kinds; grill room
lined with Minton tiles designed by Sir
Edward Poynter in 1869–70. Dining
room decorated by Morris and Co.

**Waddesdon Manor**
Waddesdon, Nr Aylesbury,
Bucks HP18 0JH
Infoline: 01296 651211
National Trust. French Renaissance-
style chateau, built by Baron
Ferdinand de Rothschild in the 1870s.
Large collection of French eighteenth-
century decorative arts.

**Weald and Downland
Open Air Museum**
Singleton
Nr Chichester,
Sussex PO18 0EU
Tel: 01243 811 1363
Email: office@wealddown.co.uk
Website: www.wealddown.co.uk
Collection of vernacular buildings.

**Museum of Welsh Life**
St Fagans,
Cardiff CF5 6XB
Tel: 02920 573500
Email: post@nmgw.ac.uk
Website: www.nmgw.ac.uk/mwl

**Whitworth Art Gallery**
University of Manchester
Oxford Road
Manchester M15 6ER
Tel: 0161 275 7450
Recorded information: 0161 275 7452
Email: whitworth@manchester.ac.uk
Website: www.whitworth.man.ac.uk
Collection of wallpapers and other
decorative arts of the nineteenth
century.

**Wightwick Manor**
Wightwick Bank
Wolverhampton
WV6 8EE
Tel: 01902 761400
National Trust. Home of the Mander
family, with interior decoration by
Morris & Co.

**William Morris Gallery**
Water House
Lloyd Park
Forest Road
Walthamstow
London E17 4PP
Tel: 020 8527 3782
E-mail: wmg.enquiries@lbwf.gov.uk
Website: www.walthamforest.gov.uk
Collection of decorative arts by
William Morris, William de Morgan
and others.

# Useful Addresses

## Conservation officers

Conservation officers work for local authorities, usually in the planning department. If your local district or city council has not yet appointed a conservation officer, try the county council.

## Crime prevention officers

Crime prevention officers can be contacted through your local police station.

## Professional institutions and research bodies

### Building Research Establishment (BRE)

Bucknalls Lane
Garston, Watford WD25 9XX
Tel: 01923 664000
Website: www.bre.org.uk
E-mail: enquiries@bre.co.uk
Titles include the 4-volume series Good Repair Guides and Defect Action Sheets listed above.

### Health and Safety Executive

HSE Infoline: 0845 345 0055, open 8.30 a.m. to 5.00 p.m. Monday to Friday
Website: www.hse.gov.uk
Various titles on safe use of gas and electricity, removal of lead paint, etc. HSE publications are available from: HSE Books,
Website: www.hsebooks.co.uk

### Institute of Structural Engineers

11 Upper Belgrave Street
London SW1X 8BH
Tel: 020 7235 4535
E-mail: mail@istructe.org.uk
Website: www.istructe.org.uk

### The Register of Architects Accredited in Building Conservation (AABC)

11 Oakfield Road, Poynton,
Cheshire SK12 1AR
Tel: 01625 871458
E-mail: info@aabc-register.co.uk
Website: www.aabc-register.co.uk

### The Royal Institute of British Architects (RIBA)

Clients Advisory Service
66 Portland Place, London W1B 1AD
Tel: 020 7580 5533
E-mail: info@inst.riba.org
Web: www.riba.org

### The Royal Institution of Chartered Surveyors (RICS)

RICS Contact Centre
Surveyor Court
Westwood Way
Coventry
West Midlands CV4 8JE
Tel: 0870 333 1600
Website: www.rics.org
E-mail: contactrics@rics.org

### The Institute for Conservation (ICON)

3rd Floor, Downstream Building,
1 London Bridge, London SE1 9BG
Tel: 020 7785 3807
Website: www.icon.org.uk
ICON maintains The Conservation Register, a list of accredited conservators
www.conservationregister.com

## Trade associations

### British Artist Blacksmiths Association

Ratho Byers Forge
Freelands Road
Ratho, Midlothian EH28 8NW
Tel: 0131 333 1300
Website: www.baba.org.uk

### British Coatings Federation Ltd

James House, Bridge Street
Leatherhead, Surrey KT22 7EP
Tel: 01372 360660
E-mail: enquiry@bcf.co.uk
Website: www.coatings.org.uk
Free information about lead test kits, the safe preparation or stripping of surfaces painted with lead-based paints, and specialist equipment hire.

### Federation of Master Builders

Gordon Fisher House
14-15 Great James Street
London WC1N 3DP
Tel: 020 7242 7583
E-mail: central@fmb.org.uk
Website: www.fmb.org.uk

### British Wood Preserving and Damp Proofing Association

1 Gleneagles House
Vernon Gate, South Street
Derby DE1 1UP
Tel: 01332 225100
E-mail: info@bwpda.co.uk
Website: www.bwpda.co.uk

### British Woodworking Federation

55 Tufton Street, London SW1P 3QL
Tel: 0870 458 6949
Fax: 020 7608 5051
E-mail: bwf@bwf.org.uk
Website: www.bwf.org.uk

### The Building Centre

26 Store Street, London WC1E 7BT
Tel: 020 7692 4000
E-mail: chenderson@buildingcentre.co.uk
Website: www.buildingcentre.co.uk
Samples of building materials and products, technical literature, bookshop.

### Draught Proofing Advisory Association (DPAA)

PO Box 12, Haslemere
Surrey GU27 3AH
Tel: 01428 654011
E-mail: dpaassociation.org.uk
Website: dpaassociation.org.uk

### Electrical Contractors Association

ECSA House
34 Palace Court, London W2 4HY
Tel: 020 7313 4800
E-mail: info@eca.co.uk
Website: www.eca.co.uk

### Glass and Glazing Federation

44–48 Borough High Street
London SE1 1XB
Tel: 0870 042 4255
E-mail: info@ggf.org.uk
Website: www.ggf.org.uk

### Lead Sheet Association

Hawkwell Business Centre
Maidstone Road, Pembury
Tunbridge Wells, Kent TN2 4AH
Tel: 01892 822773
E-mail: info@leadsheetassocation.org.uk
Website: www.leadsheetassocation.org.uk
The LSA publishes technical manuals and pocket guides, and organizes training courses for people working with lead in the building industry.

**Lead Contractors Association**
Centurion House, 38 London Road
East Grimstead,
West Sussex RH19 1AB
Tel: 01342 317888
Website: www.lca.gb.com

**Federation of Plastering and Dry Wall Contractors**
1st Floor, 8/9 Ludgate Square,
London EC4M 7AS
Tel: 020 7634 9480
E-mail: enquiries@fpdc.org
Website: www.fpdc.org

**National Association of Chimneysweeps**
Unit 15 Emerald Way
Stone Business Park
Stone, Staffordshire ST15 0SR
Tel: 01785 811732
E-mail: nacs@chimneyworks.co.uk
Website: www.chimneyworks.co.uk
Lists of local sweeps for all parts of the country.

**National Federation of Roofing Contractors**
24 Weymouth Street, London W1N 3FA
Tel: 0207 436 0387
E-mail: info@nfrc.co.uk
Website: www.nfrc.co.uk

**The Solid Fuel Association**
7 Swanwick Court
Alfreton, Derbyshire DE55 7AS
Tel: 0845 601 4406
E-mail: sfa@solidfuel.co.uk
Website: www.solidfuel.co.uk
(Information on fireplace installation and maintenance, and solid fuel.)

**Steel Window Association**
The Building Centre
26 Store Street, London WC1E 7BT
Tel: 020 7637 3571
E-mail: info@steel-window-association.co.uk
Website: www.steel-window-association.co.uk

## Conservation organizations and amenity societies

**English Heritage**
PO Box 569, Swindon SN2 2YP
Tel: 0870 333 1181
E-mail: customers@english-heritage.org.uk
Website: www.english-heritage.org.uk

Regional Offices:
London: 020 7973 3000
South East (Guildford): 01483 252000
South West (Bristol): 0117 975 0700
East of England (Cambridge):
    01223 582700
East Midlands (Northampton):
    01604 735400
West Midlands (Birmingham):
    0121 625 6820
North West (Manchester): 0161 242 1400
Yorkshire (York): 01904 601 901
North (Newcastle): 0191 261 1585

**The National Trust**
PO Box 39, Warrington,
Cheshire WA5 7WD
Tel: 0870 458 4000
E-mail: enquiries@thenationaltrust.org.uk
Website: www.nationaltrust.org.uk

**Society for the Protection of Ancient Buildings (SPAB)**
37 Spital Square, London E1 6DY
Tel: 020 7377 1644
E-mail: info@spab.org.uk
Website: www.spab.org.uk
Wide range of technical advice notes and booklets on all aspects of historic building repair. The SPAB can also recommend suitably experienced surveyors, architects and craftspeople to work on historic buildings.

**The Victorian Society**
1 Priory Gardens
Bedford Park, London W4 1TT
Tel: 020 8944 1019
E-mail: admin@victorian-society.org.uk
Website: www.victorian-society.org.uk

Membership open to anyone with an interest in architecture and design of the period 1837–1914. Lectures, walks and visits are arranged for members, who also receive regular newsletters.

## Special interest groups

(The special interest groups listed here can put you in touch with suppliers and contractors who work in their particular area.)

**Men of the Stones**
Membership Secretary
The Men of Stones, The Rosery,
Ryhall, Stamford, Lincolnshire PE9 4HE
Tel (Home): 01952 850269
E-mail: michaeltebbutt@lineone.net

**The Lime Centre**
Long Barn, Morestead, Winchester
Hampshire SO21 1LZ
Tel: 01962 713636
E-mail: info@thelimecentre.co.uk
Website: www.thelimecentre.co.uk

**Tiles and Architectural Ceramics Society**
Oakhurst, Cocknage Road, Rough Close,
Stoke-on-Trent, Staffordshire ST3 7NN
Website: www.tilesoc.org.uk
Membership open to anyone interested in tiles and other kinds of architectural ceramics, including faience and terracotta.

**Wallpaper History Society**
c/o Duncan Barton
49 Glenpark Drive
Southport, Merseyside PR9 9FA
Tel: 01704 225492
Membership open to anyone interested in wallpaper. The Society organizes events at which its members can meet other enthusiasts, see collections that are not usually open to the public, and have the opportunity to talk to experts and designers.

# Glossary

**Airbrick:** Perforated terracotta block or cast iron grill built into a wall to ventilate an interior void such as an underfloor space.

**Arris:** The sharp edge where two faces of a brick or masonry block meet.

**Ashlar:** Building stone cut into regular blocks and dressed to a fine surface finish; facing blocks of dressed stone used as an outer layer on brick walls to give the appearance of stone masonry.

**Baluster:** Stick- or urn-shaped post used to support a handrail or coping.

**Balustrade:** Row of balusters supporting a handrail or coping.

**Bargeboard:** Timber plank used under the roof covering at the eaves to protect the exposed ends of the rafters; joined in pairs in an inverted V-shape, bargeboards can be decoratively carved, and were a feature of Gothic Revival houses.

**Bay window:** Window with canted or right-angled sides that projects forward from the front of the building, and is built up from ground level.

**Bow window:** Window that projects forward from the front of the building and is curved in plan.

**Carton-pierre:** Patented papier-mâché used for applied ornaments in architectural mouldings.

**Casement:** Window frame that opens on hinges; usually side-hung (like doors).

**Ceiling band:** Shallow-relief mouldings applied to the edges of a ceiling to continue the decoration of the cornice onto the ceiling plane.

**Compo:** Mixture of whiting and glue size used as a substitute plaster or wood to make mouldings, commonly for picture frames but also in the architectural decoration of interiors.

**Coping:** Projecting top layer of brick, stone or iron on a wall, designed to throw off rainwater.

**Cornice:** In classical architecture, the top projecting section of the entablature, above the cornice and the frieze; in interior decoration, the moulding at the top of the wall, where it joins the ceiling.

**Cresting:** Row of pierced or moulded decoration, usually made of terracotta or cast iron, used to decorate a roof ridge.

**Crowsteps:** Manner of making a gable or coping ascends in a series of right-angled steps.

**Dado:** In classical architecture, the flat face of the middle section of a pedestal supporting the base of a column; in interior decoration, the part of the wall between the skirting boards and the chair or dado rail.

**Distemper:** Water-soluble, matt-finish paint made by mixing whiting (powdered chalk) with water and size and adding pigment as required.

**Door hood:** Doorframe that projects at the top, forming a small roof to protect the door from rain.

**Dormer window:** Window in the roof that projects forward of the roofline.

**Double ceiling:** A suspended ceiling.

**Drip mould:** Stone or terracotta moulding projecting from the masonry above a door or window frame; much used in Gothic Revival houses.

**Duckboard:** Slatted wooden board laid on stone floors to keep feet warm and dry.

**Eaves:** The line where the edge of the roof meets the top of the wall.

**Encaustic tiles:** Clay tiles decorated with contrasting-coloured clay stamped or poured into the body of the tile before firing.

**Filling:** The part of the wall above the dado and below the frieze, its bottom edge defined by the dado rail and its top edge by the picture rail.

**Finial:** Decorative tip to finish off a vertical post or spike.

**Flashing:** Strip of lead, zinc or other malleable, waterproof material used to cover the join between vertical masonry and a roof slope (e.g. between a chimney stack and the roof, or a lean-to roof and supporting wall).

**Flue:** Internal passage or tunnel to carry smoke, hot air or combustion gases from a fireplace to a chimney or vent.

**Frieze:** Upper part of the wall surface, between the picture rail and the cornice.

**Header:** The short (end) face of a brick.

**Jamb:** Vertical supporting member, e.g. the sides of a doorframe or fireplace surround.

**Joist:** Beam anchored into the walls and running across a room at right angles to the floorboards, which it supports.

**Laths:** Short lengths of riven (i.e. split, not sawn), rough timber, nailed to the undersides of joists or between wall studs, to provide a surface for plastering.

**Lintels:** Horizontal supporting member (e.g. the top of a door or window frame).

**Lugs:** Projections through which nails, screws or bolts can be passed to fix an item to a supporting surface.

**Modillion:** Decorative bracket.

**Mortice:** Slot cut in timber or stone to receive a connecting piece or a bolt.

**Mortice and tenon joint:** Method of joining two pieces of timber, usually at right angles, by inserting a projecting connection (tenon) into a slot (mortice) and pinning or gluing the two together.

**Mullion:** Vertical subdivision of a light in a window or doorframe.

**Ogee:** A line consisting of two curves, one convex and one concave; a moulding with an ogee profile; paired ogees are used to form a pointed and 'shouldered' arch, much used in Gothic Revival houses for door and window openings.

**Ormolu:** Gilded metal, usually bronze, used for mounts and mouldings.

**Parapet gutters:** Gutter running behind and hidden by a parapet, a feature used to preserve the regularity and proportions of a classical façade.

**Pedestal:** The base of a column.

**Pediment:** Triangle or segment framed by a moulding, formed by the eaves in a gable wall or used above a portico or a door or window opening.

**Picture rail:** Horizontal moulding, usually of timber, applied to a wall below the frieze and dividing the frieze from the filling.

**Pier:** Vertical post or column used to support a gate.

**Pier cap:** The decorative and protective top of a pier, often in the shape of a pineapple, urn, sphere or pyramidal coping.

**Pilaster:** Rectangular column attached to, and projecting only slightly from, a wall.

**Pointing:** Raking out the mortar forming the joints between bricks or masonry blocks and replacing it with fresh mortar to make a neat finished face.

**Portière:** Curtain hung over a door.

**Quoins:** Brick or masonry blocks used to accentuate the corners of a building.

**Render:** Mortar or plaster applied to the external face of a building to give a neat and weatherproof finish.

**Roughcast:** Form of render created by throwing gravel or other aggregate against wet plaster.

**Roundel:** A patera: a small, flat, round ornament consisting of a circle of moulding or a rosette.

**Rustication:** Stone masonry with deeply-incised joints that emphasize the separateness of the individual blocks, which may also be given a rough or vermiculated (wormlike) surface finish; usually restricted to the basement or ground floor. Rusticated finishes are often imitated in stucco.

**Soaker:** A small flashing cut to fit and interlock with slates or tiles, used in roofs to improve watertightness at hips, valleys and joins.

**Soffit:** The underside of a beam, arch, opening or staircase.

**Spandrel:** The triangular space formed at the top of an arch by the curve of the arch as it springs away from the vertical, the continuation of the vertical, and a horizontal line drawn across the apex of the arch; the space between two arches in an arcade or between two ribs in a vault.

**Stretcher:** The long (side) face of a brick.

**Stucco:** Hard plaster used as an external render.

**Studs:** Vertical timber members used at intervals between load-bearing columns, piers or posts to form partitions. Studwork supports lath and plaster, board, clapboard or wainscot.

**Tile-hanging:** Exterior cladding formed by nailing tiles to battens.

**Tracery:** In Gothic architecture the decorative interlacing of stone or timber mouldings at the top of a window.

**Tuck pointing:** Decorative pointing achieved by inserting a thin line of lime putty along the centre of a joint, which contrasts with, and stands slightly proud of, the surrounding mortar.

**Vermiculation:** Surface finish resembling writhing worms, given to stone or stucco.

**Voussoir:** Tapering brick or masonry block used to make up an arch.

**Wainscot:** Timber panelling.

**Weatherstruck pointing:** A modern style of pointing in which the mortar is smoothed off at angle designed to throw off rainwater.

# Index